The Origin of Modern Humans and the Impact of Chronometric Dating

The Origin of Modern Humans and the Impact of Chronometric Dating

A DISCUSSION ORGANIZED AND EDITED
BY M. J. AITKEN, C. B. STRINGER AND
P. A. MELLARS

PRINCETON UNIVERSITY PRESS

PRINCETON, NEW JERSEY

Copyright © 1993 by Princeton University Press
Published by Princeton University Press, 41 William Street,
Princeton, New Jersey 08540
In the United Kingdom: Princeton University Press, Chichester,
West Sussex

This book was originally published in journal form as *Philosophical Transactions: Biological Sciences*, vol. 337, no. 1280 of *Philosophical Transactions of the Royal Society*, series B
Copyright © 1992 by the Royal Society

Library of Congress Cataloging-in-Publication Data

The Origin of modern humans and the impact of chronometric dating : a
  discussion / organized and edited by M. J. Aiken, C. B. Stringer, and
  P. A. Mellars.
        p.   cm.
    Originally published: London : Royal Society, 1992.
    Discussion held Feb. 26–27, 1992.
    Includes bibliographical references.
    ISBN 0-691-03242-4
    1. Human evolution—Congresses.   2. Archaeological dating—
  Congresses.   I. Aitken, M. J. (Martin Jim)   II. Stringer, Chris,
  1947–   .   III. Mellars, Paul.
  GN286.075   1993
  573.2—dc20   92-38969
                                                                    CIP

This book has been composed in Baskerville no. 2 type.

Princeton University Press books are printed on acid-free paper
and meet the guidelines for permanence and durability of the
Committee on Production Guidelines for Book Longevity of the
Council on Library Resources

Printed in the United States of America

10 9 8 7 6 5 4 3 2 1

The origin of modern humans and the impact of chronometric dating

A DISCUSSION ORGANIZED AND EDITED BY
M. J. AITKEN, C. B. STRINGER AND P. A. MELLARS

(*Discussion held 26 and 27 February 1992*)

Contents

The Origin of Modern Humans and the Impact of Chronometric Dating

Outlining the Problem

P. A. Mellars,[1] *M. J. Aitken*[2] *and C. B. Stringer*[3]

SUMMARY

Few topics have generated more debate and controversy in the scientific literature over the past few years than the biological and behavioural origins of anatomically 'modern' human populations: i.e. populations belonging to our own form of *Homo sapiens sapiens*. What is common ground in all these debates is that populations that were fundamentally 'modern' in both a basic anatomical sense, and in at least the majority of cultural and behavioural senses, were effectively established throughout all the major regions of the Old World (i.e. Africa, Asia, Europe and parts of Australasia) by at least 30–35 ka ago (1 ka = 1000 years). The current controversy hinges essentially on what happened before this time—above all during the crucial formative phases of modern human development between *ca.* 200 and 30 ka ago. It is this period which forms the major battle ground of current debate over the evolutionary origins and mutual relationships of modern world populations, and which provides the central focus of the present symposium.

Throughout the greater part of the present century—effectively since the discovery of the 'classic' Neanderthal skeleton at La Chapelle-aux-Saints in 1908—the issue of the biological and demographic origin of modern human populations has been seen very largely as a dichotomy between two sharply opposed schools of thought. One view—frequently referred to in the more popular scientific literature as the 'Garden of Eden' or 'Noah's Ark' hypothesis—asserts that biologically and genetically modern human populations evolved initially in one fairly limited and closely prescribed region of the world and subsequently dispersed—at varying times—to all other regions, either with or without significant degrees of genetic intermixture and interbreeding with the pre-existing populations within the same regions. At various points throughout the present century, and with varying degrees of emphasis, this view has been maintained by (among others) Marcellin Boule, William Howells and F. Clark Howell. More recently, workers such as Günter Bräuer, as well as one of the present authors (e.g. Stringer &

---

[1] Department of Archaeology, University of Cambridge, Downing Street, Cambridge CB2 3DZ, U.K.

[2] Research Laboratory for Archaeology, Oxford University, 6 Keble Road, Oxford OX1 3QJ, U.K.

[3] Human Origins Group, Department of Palaeontology, Natural History Museum, London SW7 5BD, U.K.

Andrews 1988), have focused attention on Africa as the particular continent of origin: the so-called 'Out of Africa' model.

The principal alternative scenario—now generally referred to as the 'multiregional evolution' hypothesis—asserts that there was no such simple or discrete origin for the morphological and genetic characteristics of modern humans, and that human populations in all of the major regions of the Old World (i.e. Africa, Asia and Europe) have pursued an essentially parallel pattern of evolution over at least the greater part of the past million years or so. Central to the latter model, of course, is the assumption that there was a sufficient degree of interbreeding and resulting gene flow between these geographically dispersed populations to maintain a broadly similar pattern of evolutionary development within the different regions throughout the whole of this time range. The principal proponents of this hypothesis have been Ales Hrdlička, Franz Weidenreich, Carleton Coon, Loring Brace and (more recently) Milford Wolpoff and Alan Thorne (e.g. Wolpoff 1989; Thorne & Wolpoff 1992). Potentially one of the most significant points of conflict between these two models relates to the character and timing of the divergence of the modern patterns of regional ('racial') variation among present-day populations. Whereas the population-dispersal hypothesis asserts that all of these divergences are the result of relatively short-term evolutionary processes operating purely over the past 100 ka or so, the multiregional evolution viewpoint would trace these regional divergences back through a much longer timescale of at least several hundred thousand to one million years.

It is hardly possible here to review the ebb and flow of debate between these two conflicting hypotheses over the past 80 years or so. Reviews of the earlier years of this debate have been provided by Frank Spencer (1984), and more recently by Smith *et al.* (1989). What can be said is that over the course of the past 10–15 years, a number of significant developments emerged which appeared to shift the balance of the evidence fairly strongly in favour of the former (population dispersal) scenario. One of these developments was the application of new dating methods. The use of the newly developed dating methods of thermoluminescence (TL) to burnt flint and electron spin resonance (ESR) to tooth enamel associated with the large samples of skeletal remains recovered from the two sites of Mugharet es Skhul and Jebel Qafzeh in northern Israel revealed that these fossils—which had previously been generally assumed to be around 40–50 ka in age—in reality dated to around 100 ka (Grün & Stringer 1991; Aitken & Valladas, this symposium; Schwarcz & Grün, this symposium). Because these fossils had generally been accepted and described in the literature as showing modern features, this appeared to demonstrate that such forms had appeared in at least one region of the world at a much earlier date than suspected hitherto, and demonstrably at a time when much more 'archaic' forms (such as the Neanderthals) were still living in closely adjacent— or even overlapping—areas of Eurasia. Further discoveries seemed to reinforce the same pattern. Thus a number of other finds of essentially 'modern' skeletal remains at sites in southern and eastern Africa (such as Border Cave and Klasies River Mouth in South Africa, and Omo in Ethiopia) appeared to date from around 80–100 ka ago (Rightmire 1989), whereas, by contrast, a typically Neanderthal skeleton from the site of Saint-Césaire in western France was found to date from as recently as *ca.* 35 ka ago (Lévêque & Vandermeersch 1980; Mercier *et al.* 1991). All of these discoveries appeared, on the face of it, to conform much better with the predictions of the population dispersal scenario of modern human origins, than with the alternative hypothesis of essentially parallel, multiregional evolution within the different regions of the world.

The final, and perhaps most significant discovery which was claimed to argue specifically in favour of the population dispersal hypothesis emerged from the detailed work carried out on the patterns of mitochrondrial DNA variation in modern human populations in different regions of the world, undertaken by the late Allan C. Wilson and his colleagues at the University of California at Berkeley (e.g. Cann *et al.* 1987; Stoneking & Cann 1989; Wilson & Cann 1992). Basically, Wilson and his co-workers argued that modern human populations were far too similar in terms of their mitochondrial DNA makeup to be the products of largely independent evolution over a span of a million years or so, and must be the products of divergence from a single common ancestor at a much more recent period. Arguing that variations in mtDNA were most probably neutral in an adaptive sense and that the rate of mutation of mtDNA can be estimated from studies in other animal groups, they postulated that a common female ancestor had probably lived in the region of 200 ka ago (more broadly between *ca.* 50 and 350 ka), and that the descendants of this initial population had probably expanded to most other regions of the world by around 30–100 ka ago. Finally, they suggested that the geographical source of this common ancestor was most probably located somewhere in Africa. The latter conclusion was based partly on the demonstrably wider range of genetic variability apparent in modern African populations than among those in other parts of the world (suggesting a longer period of evolution of modern humans in this region than elsewhere) and partly on the construction of hypothetical trees of genetic descent by means of 'maximum parsimony' methods, all of which seemed to point to an African origin. At about the same time, similar claims for an apparently African origin were made by a number of workers based on analogous studies of the patterns of variation in 'classical' genetic markers, such as blood groups and proteins (e.g. Cavalli-Sforza *et al.* 1988), and by other workers based on variations in nuclear DNA in modern populations (e.g. Wainscoat *et al.* 1989; Lucotte 1989; Cavalli-Sforza 1991; Mountain *et al.*, this symposium). One of the most critical and controversial conclusions of the mtDNA studies was that the process of hypothetical population dispersal from the presumed African homeland appeared to have been achieved with no detectable interbreeding with the earlier, biologically 'archaic' populations within the different regions of Eurasia, and that these populations may therefore have become extinct without contributing any significant genetic legacy to the subsequent populations in the same regions (Stoneking & Cann 1989; Wilson & Cann 1992).

Reactions to these claims by proponents of the multiregional evolution school were swift, pointed, and forcefully argued (e.g. Wolpoff 1989; Thorne & Wolpoff 1992). Several workers pointed to the severe problems of estimating the rates of genetic divergence of mtDNA, and argued that by adopting rather different mutation rates (based, for example, on the assumption of an earlier date of divergence between the chimpanzee and human lineages, or earlier dates for the human colonization of the Americas and Australasia) one could recalibrate the date of the inferred common ancestor of all modern populations closer to one million years: that is, near the generally accepted date for the initial colonization of northern latitudes and eastern Asia by *Homo erectus* populations in the early Pleistocene. Further debate has centred on the methods of constructing the hypothetical genetic trees—particularly those involving the assumptions and methodology of 'maximum parsimony' approaches—a debate which flared up once again in the literature in the immediate run-up to the present symposium (e.g. Maddison 1991; Templeton 1992; Stoneking *et al.*, this symposium). If these objections are valid, then the presumed common ancestor of modern populations could potentially be located in almost any part of the Old World, rather than just Africa. Similarly, the implications of the skeletal remains themselves have become a topic of lively debate. Wolpoff, Thorne and others have argued that many of the current interpretations of individual skeletal remains (such as the recently discovered Neanderthal from Saint-Césaire) fail to make sufficient allowance for the probable degree of intrapopulation variability in Pleistocene hominids. More specifically, they have argued that the morphology of some of the relatively recent hominid remains from areas such as southeast Asia, Australasia and Central Europe, point strongly to a substantial element of morphological and genetic continuity between the 'archaic' and 'anatomically modern' populations in these regions (e.g. Wolpoff 1989; Thorne & Wolpoff 1992).

The spate of debate currently surrounding all of these issues in the origins and evolution of modern human populations served as a primary catalyst for the organization of the present meeting. The aim, essentially, has been to bring together a range of specialists in relevant scientific disciplines (i.e.

evolutionary anatomy, molecular biology, archaeology, dating methods, etc.) to review the most recent discoveries and changing theoretical perspectives in these wide-ranging debates. The central theme of the meeting of course was to assess the specific bearing of recent advances in various scientific dating methods on the interpretation of these crucial formative phases in modern human evolution. It is this field of research which has made some of the most striking advances over the past decade, and which—as indicated in the preceding discussion—is now proving to be critical in the systematic testing of the various alternative models for the emergence of modern human populations.

The chronometric techniques primarily relevant to the topic of this volume (i.e. uranium-series, luminescence, electron spin resonance and amino acid racemization) provide dates for such materials as stalagmitic calcite, burnt flint, sediment, tooth enamel, and ostrich eggshells. Most of these techniques have reached the stage of application to the Palaeolithic comparatively recently, and the results so far achieved are only a foretaste of the full realization of their potential. The longer-established radiocarbon method unfortunately has an effective limit of around 40 ka (except in special circumstances) and hence only reaches into the later phases of modern human development, for which its datings of bone, teeth and charcoal are indeed of critical importance. At the other end of the timescale, in the dating of early hominids, the potassium-argon and fission-track techniques have been of even greater importance. Although the time range of the former now extends into the Holocene, this method has not yet had significant impact on the issues under discussion here. This is because it is limited to circumstances in which there is chance association of human occupation with volcanic products (e.g. lava flows, air-fall deposits). Fuller discussion of these and other chronometric techniques will be found elsewhere (e.g. Aitken 1990).

Another important aspect of Palaeolithic chronology is the climatic framework within which sites are placed. Sites can be attributed to such climatic frameworks on several bases: (i) on their fossil flora, fauna and geological features; (ii) the characteristics of the associated archaeological assemblages; or, more recently, (iii) by direct chronometric dating. Initially, the climatic framework was in terms of the four major glaciations (Günz, Mindel, Riss and Würm) that had been recognized on the basis of geological evidence in the Alps; more complex regional frameworks were later evolved—for example, inclusion of warmish interstadials within the long glacial periods—with a correspondingly complex nomenclature. Fortunately a worldwide framework is now available. This is the oxygen-isotope stratigraphy, based on the climatic dependence of the ratio $^{18}O/^{16}O$ in marine fossil microfauna, studied in long cores obtained from the ocean floor; this ratio is used to define a succession of alternating cool and warm

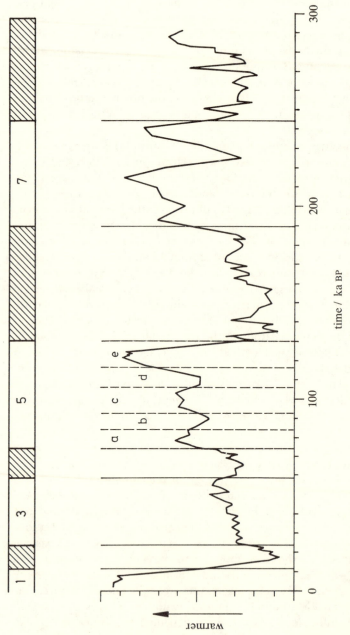

Figure 1. Oxygen-isotope variation for the past 300 ka with astronomically based timescale (redrawn, with additions, from Martinson *et al.* (1987)). The vertical axis represents changes in the averaged $^{18}O/^{16}O$ ratio found in benthic (bottom-living) foraminifera from five locations in the oceans of the world; five divisions equal a change of one part per thousand. Along the top the numbers allocated to warm stages are given, with intervening (even-numbered) cold stages being shown shaded. The letters (a, c, e) refer to warm substages of stage 5; there are intervening cool troughs, b and d.

stages. The remanent magnetization of the terrigeneous component of the sediment cores allowed correlation of one stage with the most recent major geomagnetic polarity reversal observed in volcanic rocks, for which absolute dating has been provided by the potassium-argon technique; other stages were dated by assuming a constant rate of sedimentation, with further control provided by radiocarbon and uranium-series datings.

Latterly it has been established that there is good correlation between the pattern of climatic variation so revealed and the Milankovitch astronomical predictions based on changes in the earth's orbital motion (eccentricity of the orbit around the sun; obliquity of the ecliptic; precession of the equinoxes); the changes result from gravitational perturbations due to the changing configuration of the planets. With this correlation established, the oxygen-isotope stages became datable with the same high accuracy as is possible for the orbital changes. In the context of the present symposium, the chronostratigraphy developed for the past 300 ka by Martinson et al. (1987) is of particular relevance. According to this (see figure 1) the penultimate major glaciation (stage 6) ended about 130 ka ago and the succeeding interglacial complex (stage 5) lasted until around 74 ka ago. The degree to which there is exact land–ocean synchroneity for all the detail revealed in the ocean sediments is the subject of continuing research, but the main features seem to be well reproduced on the continental land masses, thus giving a general chronological framework that is well dated in absolute terms. The isotope stages are now the fundamental time divisions of the Quaternary epoch.

Finally, it needs to be realized that although the new chronometric techniques mentioned earlier may be having a strong impact, there can be site-to-site variability in the reliability of results, and also that some sample types are not as satisfactory as others. Also, as some dating applications are made with the objective of exploring the performance of a technique in particular circumstances, it is important for a consumer to be aware of the pedigree of a date and to use restraint, if appropriate, in its utilization. For such discretion to be exercised it is necessary that the date should have been presented for publication in sufficient detail for assessment of its reliability to be made, at any rate by a specialist colleague; dates not so presented should be treated with caution, or ignored. Obviously it is advantageous if the consumer has familiarity with the dating method concerned, and one objective of the meeting on which this symposium is based was to encourage dialogue between consumer and dating specialist; hence the dating contributions which follow are addressed primarily to the non-specialist.

Note on dating terminology
The letters BP signify 'before present'. They have the strict connotation that the age quoted is given in radiocarbon years rather than calendar years;

radiocarbon ages that have been converted into calendar years by calibration are given as cal BP. Most other techniques yield ages directly in calendar (i.e. 'sidereal') years and the letters BP are then inappropriate; in the case of amino acid dates based on calibration against radiocarbon, BP should be retained.

REFERENCES

Aitken, M.J. 1990 *Science-based dating in archaeology.* London & New York: Longman.

Cann, R.L., Stoneking, M. & Wilson, A.C. 1987 Mitochondrial DNA and human evolution. *Nature, Lond.* **325**, 31–36.

Cavalli-Sforza, L.L. 1991 Genes, peoples and languages. *Scient. Am.* **265**(11) (November 1991), 72–78.

Cavalli-Sforza, L.L., Piazza, A., Menozzi, P. & Mountain, J. 1988 Reconstruction of human evolution: bringing together genetic, archeological and linguistic data. *Proc. natn. Acad. Sci. U.S.A.* **85**, 8002–8006.

Grün, R. & Stringer, C.B. 1991 Electron spin resonance dating and the evolution of modern humans. *Archaeometry* **33**, 153–199.

Lévêque, F. & Vandermeersch, B. 1980 Découverte des restes humains dans un niveau castelperronien a Saint-Césaire (Charente Maritime). *C. r. Acad. Sci., Paris* (Series II) **291**, 187–189.

Lucotte, G. 1989 Evidence for the paternal ancestry of modern humans: evidence from a Y-chromosome specific sequence polymorphic DNA probe. In Mellars & Stringer (1989), 39–46.

Maddison, D.R. 1991 African origin of human mitochondrial DNA reexamined. *Syst. Zool.* **40**, 355–363.

Martinson, D.G., Pisias, N.G., Hays, J.D., Imbrie, J., Moore, T.C. & Shackleton, N.J. 1987 Age dating and the orbital theory of the ice ages: development of a high resolution 0 to 300,000-year chronostratigraphy. *Quat. Res.* **27**, 1–29.

Mellars, P. & Stringer, C. (eds) 1989 *The human revolution; behavioural and biological perspectives on the origins of modern humans.* Edinburgh University Press.

Mercier, N., Valladas, H., Joron, J.L., Reyss, J.L., Lévêque, F. & Vandermeersch, B. 1991 Thermoluminescence dating of the late Neanderthal remains from Saint-Césaire. *Nature, Lond.* **351**, 737–739.

Rightmire, G.P. 1989 Middle Stone Age humans from eastern and southern Africa. In Mellars & Stringer (1989), 109–122.

Smith, F.H., Falsetti, A.B. & Donnelly, S. 1989 Modern human origins. *Yb. phys. Anthrop.* **32**, 35–68.

Spencer, F. 1984 The Neanderthals and their evolutionary significance: a brief historical survey. In *The origins of modern humans: a world survey of the fossil evidence* (ed. F. H. Smith & F. Spencer), pp. 1–49. New York: Alan R. Liss.

Stoneking, M. & Cann, R.L. 1989 African origin of human mitochondrial DNA. In Mellars & Stringer (1989), 17–30.

Stringer, C.B. & Andrews, P. 1988 Genetic and fossil evidence for the origin of modern humans. *Science, Wash.* **239**, 1263–1268.

Thorne, A.G. & Wolpoff, M.H. 1992 The multiregional evolution of humans. *Scient. Am.* **266**(4) (April 1992), 28–33.

Wainscoat, J.S., Hill, A.V.S., Thein, S.L., Flint, J., Chapman, J.C., Weatherall, D.J., Clegg, J.B. & Higgs, D.R. 1989 Geographic distribution of alpha- and beta-globin gene cluster polymorphisms. In Mellars & Stringer (1989), 39–46.

Wilson, A.C. & Cann, R.L. 1992 The recent African genesis of humans. *Scient. Am.* **266**(4) (April 1992), 22–27.

Wolpoff, M.H. 1989 Multiregional evolution: the fossil alternative to Eden. In Mellars & Stringer (1989), 62–108.

Uranium-Series Dating and the Origin of Modern Man

Henry P. Schwarcz[1]

SUMMARY

Uranium-series dating is based on measurement of the radioactivity of short-lived daughter isotopes of uranium formed in samples which initially contained only the parent uranium. Materials suitable for U-series dating are found in many prehistoric archaeological sites, and include stalagmitic layers (flowstones), and spring-deposited travertines. Some marls and calcretes are also datable using isochron methods, whereas dates on molluscan shells, bones and teeth are less reliable. Ages obtained using alpha counting to determine isotope ratios have errors greater than 5%, and can range from 1 to 350 ka. Mass spectrometric methods slightly increase the range (0.1–500 ka) but greatly decrease the error to less than 1%, making this the optimal method for high-precision dating of the origin of modern man.

1. REQUIREMENTS OF A DATING METHOD

Modern humans of the species *Homo sapiens sapiens* are now believed to have evolved from an ancestral species over the past few hundred thousands of years. Our ability to define this transition is critically dependent on the availability of chronometers with which to date the stages in this evolutionary process. Any such 'timepiece' must satisfy the following three requirements.

1. Range. All dating methods have a specific time range over which they are applicable; the upper and lower limits of this range must be appropriate to the interval of interest.
2. Applicability (datable materials). The method must be applicable to materials likely to be found at hominid sites. These must be materials which were either formed at the time of occupation of the site (e.g. faunal remains, stalagmitic deposits); or which were altered in some way at that time (e.g. burnt flint).
3. Precision and accuracy. The dating method must be precise enough to resolve

[1] Subdepartment of Quaternary Research, University of Cambridge, Cambridge CB2 3RS, U.K. Permanent address: Department of Geology, McMaster University, Hamilton, Ontario, L8S 4M1, Canada.

discrete evolutionary stages; although a low-precision method such as electron spin resonance (ESR) or thermoluminescence (TL) may be sufficient to define broad intervals, it is also desirable to have methods of high precision and accuracy with which to seriate hominids and artefact sequences from diverse loci.

Considering the time interval in which we are interested here, greater than 40 ka before present (BP), these criteria are satisfied by a variety of dating methods, including TL, optically stimulated luminescence (OSL), ESR, and uranium-series dating. Potassium–argon (K/Ar or ^{40}Ar/^{39}Ar) dating is applicable to the rare sites in volcanic areas such as Italy where *Homo sapiens* is found. However, of these various methods only one, uranium-series dating of calcite, can provide high precision dates on materials found at a wide variety of hominid sites. The precision of dates obtainable by the other methods listed is significantly less, even when the most advanced techniques are used for each method. The additional advantage of uranium-series dating is that it does not rely on knowledge of the environmental conditions at a site through the time elapsed since its formation. By contrast, environmental radiation dose rates are needed for OSL, TL and ESR dating while for methods which are based on the rate of chemical reactions such as amino acid racemization (AAR), it is necessary to know the thermal history at the site.

2. URANIUM-SERIES DATING

Uranium (U) is present as a trace element in all natural materials. The two primordial isotopes of this element, ^{238}U and ^{235}U, each undergo radioactive decay to form a series of short-lived daughter radioisotopes (figure 1). In any U-bearing material which has lain undisturbed for millions of years, the activities of the isotopes within one decay series will all be equal to one another and to their respective parent (^{238}U or ^{235}U). Here we speak of activities as measured in numbers of disintegrations per minute per gram of the material. This state of 'secular equilibrium' can be disturbed by chemical or physical processes; then the activity of some of these isotopes can be greater or less than the equilibrium level. Uranium-series dating refers to methods in which the time of this disturbance is estimated from the degree of departure from equilibrium. U-series dating is possible as long as the time elapsed is comparable to the half-life of the isotope being measured. Daughter isotopes of U have half-lives ranging from a fraction of second to 250 ka. Of these, three in particular have promise for dating of hominid evolution: ^{234}U, ^{230}Th, and ^{231}Pa. The last is a daughter of ^{235}U, which is an isotope of very low natural abundance (less than 1% of natural uranium), and is therefore less useful except where the U concentration is very high in the sample to be dated.

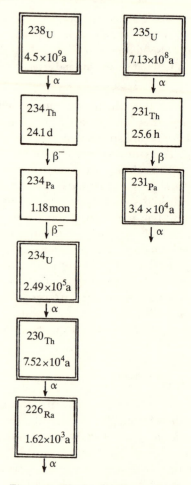

Figure 1. The beginning parts of the radioactive decay series that are produced by each of the primordial isotopes of uranium: [238]U and [235]U. The heavy boxes outline those longer-lived isotopes that are of use in dating prehistoric sites.

Most geological materials at hominid sites (sand, silt, rock fragments, etc.) are 'recycled' ancient materials and therefore are close to secular equilibrium. However, some materials are found which were formed *de novo*, such as stalagmites, travertines, bones, teeth or shells. Typically, all these materials are formed totally out of secular equilibrium. A typical example is

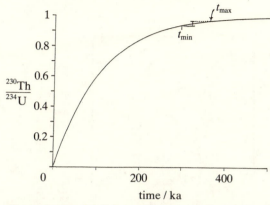

Figure 2. Graph of the ratio of the radioactivity of ^{230}Th to that of its parent isotope ^{234}U as a function of time. In a sample whose initial ^{230}Th/^{234}U ratio was zero (such as an uncontaminated stalagmite), the age can be determined by reading off on the horizontal axis the age corresponding to the sample's present-day ^{230}Th/^{234}U ratio. The error in age is determined by the error in measurement of the isotope ratio. For older samples, these errors are highly asymmetric as shown. The error bars shown are typical for alpha spectrometry; corresponding errors in thermal ionization mass spectrometry (TIMS) are about a tenth as large.

a stalagmitic layer in a cave, formed by precipitation of calcite from lime-rich waters dripping from the roof of the cave. U is quite soluble in water, whereas thorium (including the daughter isotope ^{230}Th) is not. Therefore, at the time of its formation the calcite contains some ^{234}U and ^{238}U but virtually no ^{230}Th. The latter isotope begins to grow by decay of its parent ^{234}U, and the ratio of the activities of these two isotopes rises as shown in figure 2. The age of the stalagmite can then be estimated from this ratio; for example, if this ratio of activities is today observed to be equal to 0.50, we infer that the stalagmite is 75 ka old. This inference requires that two assumptions be true, one of which can be easily tested: (i) at the time of deposition, the ^{230}Th/^{234}U ratio of the stalagmite was zero; (ii) the only changes in this ratio through time have been due to radioactive decay. To test the first assumption, we look for the presence of primary, 'common' thorium, which is recognizable because it consists partly of the long-lived isotope ^{232}Th. The presence of this isotope in the sample tells us that there was probably also present, at the time of deposition, a matching amount of

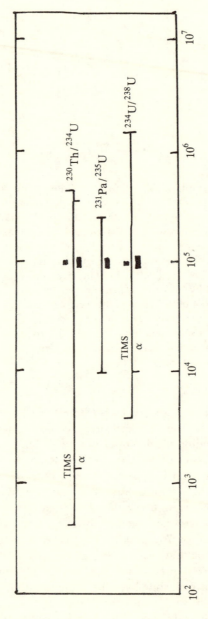

Figure 3. Range (lines) and precision (bars) of the U-series methods of dating. As explained in the text, the $^{234}U/^{238}U$ method is applicable only under special circumstances.

^{230}Th, in a known proportion that can be roughly corrected for. It is much more difficult to test the second assumption, that is, to prove or disprove that the sample has been disturbed by recrystallization or diagenesis.

Although the ratio ^{230}Th/^{234}U is the most widely used in dating, two other ratios, ^{231}Pa/^{235}U, and ^{234}U/^{238}U are also employed. The ranges of applicability of each ratio are shown in figure 3, together with estimates of the precision of each method. The first two, ^{230}Th/^{234}U and ^{231}Pa/^{235}U, require only the two assumptions cited above; ^{234}U/^{238}U ratios can be used for dating only where we also know the initial ratio at the time of deposition of the material. This is rarely true in archaeological sites except where the material (e.g. travertine) has been deposited from a source of water whose U isotope ratio has been stable for hundreds of millenia, such as seawater or spring water emerging from a large aquifer.

The measurement of the isotopes of U, Th and Pa can be done by two means. The more traditional approach is to prepare very thin layers of these isotopes (one atom thick) and to count their radioactivity. This can be done using an alpha-particle spectrometer (for U and Th) or a beta detector for Pa (which can also be determined indirectly by alpha counting). Alpha particles emitted from each isotope have characteristic energies which can be sorted electronically, permitting us to determine the ratio of the activities directly; it is the approach of these ratios to equilibrium that is our measure of age. The telltale ^{232}Th isotope, indicative of contamination, is also detectible by alpha spectrometry.

Recently we have begun to use thermal ionization mass spectrometry (TIMS) which is a more complex but also more sensitive technique, similar in concept to the accelerator mass spectrometry (AMS) method now used in ^{14}C dating in that we count atoms of the isotopes rather than wait for them to decay. The precision of TIMS is as much as ten times better than alpha counting, although the accuracy may not be improved by this factor, due to the limitations of the materials analysed.

3. DATABLE MATERIALS

Materials datable by U-series are widely available at archaeological sites, but the quality of these materials varies greatly. The best materials, from the standpoint of satisfying the criteria (i) and (ii) above, are deposits of calcite (calcium carbonate, $CaCO^3$) formed from dripping or running water: stalagmites, flowstones (*planchers stalagmitique*), and spring-deposited travertines. The first two of these materials are generally formed of densely packed crystals of calcite which can be quite pure (i.e. free of common thorium). Travertine, however, can be quite porous and subject to changes after deposition, as the pores gradually fill in with newly deposited calcite. The best travertine layers, however, resemble stalagmites and are usable for dating. Some sites are found enclosed in or associated with layers of freshwater limestone (marl) that may also be datable, as long as they are not too contaminated or altered.

Besides calcite deposits, other less satisfactory materials which are found in archaeological contexts include mammalian teeth and bones, ostrich egg shells, and the shells of molluscs. All of these biogenic materials contain very little U when they are formed. When they are analysed many thousands of years later, we observe them to contain substantial amounts of U which has been absorbed sometime during the period of burial in the site. If we can assume a history of U uptake for these materials then we can use this information together with the ratios of their radioisotopes to determine their ages. For ostrich shells (Wendorf *et al.* 1991) and the outermost layers of some bones (Rae & Ivanovich 1986) and teeth (McKinney 1991), it appears that the U is taken up very early, and we can treat them like stalagmites or travertines. Most bone material and mollusc shells do not behave as simply and have not proven to be satisfactory for U-series dating. Mollusc shells, in particular, tend to give anomalously low ages (Kaufmann *et al.* 1977).

In summary, the best materials for U-series dating appear to be calcitic flowstones and stalagmites which entrapped their present-day complement of uranium at the time they were formed. Although many such deposits are quite pure, some are found to contain substantial amounts of common thorium as a result of transport of detritus into the deposits by wind water, or on the feet of the occupants of the site. This imparts to the samples an anomalously high ^{230}Th content and hence an anomalously high ^{230}Th/^{234}U ratio. We have learned how to correct for this contamination, however, by analysing several portions of the sample with varying amounts of contaminant and observing how the isotope ratios change as a function of the amount of contaminant (Schwarcz & Latham 1990). Alternately, we can analyse the sample in two parts: the calcite component which is soluble in dilute acid; and the acid-insoluble residue (particles of sand and dust) which must be dissolved in stronger acids and which contains a purer fraction of the contaminant (Luo & Ku 1991; Bischoff & Fitzpatrick 1991). Using either method, we obtain the ^{230}Th/^{234}U ratio of the pure calcite component from the slope of a line called an isochron, on a graph of isotope ratios (figure 4). To be datable by the isochron method, the samples must consist of mixtures of a pure calcite and a single, homogeneous 'dirt' component (Ku & Liang 1987; Schwarcz & Latham 1990).

4. Range, Precision and Accuracy

The third requirement for a chronometer to be useful in calibrating the emergence of modern man is that the method should be able to produce dates of adequate precision and accuracy over the range of interest. Figure 2

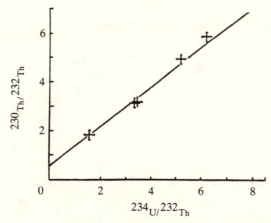

Figure 4. Isochron diagram: a plot of ^{230}Th/^{232}Th versus ^{234}U/^{232}Th, for contaminated carbonate samples: if a series of cogenetic samples forms a linear array, the slope of the line gives the ^{230}Th/^{234}U ratio of the chemically precipitated carbonate component, and thus the age of the deposit.

demonstrates the range of the ^{230}Th/^{234}U method. After that isotope ratio has reached its limiting value of 1.00, corresponding to secular equilibrium, no further changes occur, and the age of a sample with this ratio is indeterminate. This limit is reached at approximately 350 ka when using alpha spectrometry or about 500 ka with TIMS. The method of ^{231}Pa/^{235}U dating has a slightly shorter range (about 250 ka). In principle, the ^{234}U/^{238}U method has the largest range, greater than 1 million years. In practice, however, it is questionable whether any springs or other water sources had the same ^{234}U/^{238}U ratio when the sample formed as is observed in the spring water today.

The precision of ^{230}Th/^{234}U dates obtained by alpha counting is generally no better than ±5% of the date, and is limited by the number of counts obtained. This, in turn, requires that the samples be either rich in uranium (greater than 1 part per million) or that relatively large samples must be analysed. The TIMS method, on the other hand, requires smaller samples, and also provides higher precision. The best samples give dates with a reproducibility of better than 1% (e.g. less than 1000 years for a 100 000-year-old sample). This is comparable to the precision of ^{14}C or ^{40}Ar/^{39}Ar dating. If the isochron method is used, then the precision of the dates is constrained by the scatter of points around the isochron, which is mainly determined by how well the samples obey the assumptions of the isochron method.

The accuracy of ^{230}Th/^{234}U dates is believed to be comparable to the precision, as the only parameters affecting the accuracy are the half-lives of the relevant isotopes. No systematic intercomparisons of U-series and other dating methods have been made for samples of more than 50 ka. On the other hand, such is the confidence in the accuracy of U-series dates on corals, that they have been used to calibrate the ^{14}C Chronometer in the period 10 to 30 ka (Bard *et al.* 1990). Coral is one of the best materials for U-series dating but it is seldom found in an archaeological context.

5. APPLICATIONS OF U-SERIES DATING TO HOMINID EVOLUTION

This method is, in principle, the ideal method with which to obtain highly precise dates beyond the range of ^{14}C, and also by which to obtain highly accurate dates beyond the range of dendrochronological calibration of ^{14}C. For the study of early modern hominids, it would be especially useful to have datable samples from the sites where critical skeletal material has been recovered. Unfortunately, we are somewhat in the position of the drunken man who lost his keys on a dark stretch of road but who is searching for them a few yards away, under a lamp-post, because the light is better there! Thus, we must sometimes content ourselves with dating sites or strata in sites which are far removed from critical hominid loci, but which are better suited for dating and can, hopefully, be correlated with the hominid sites. At the present time only a single site has been dated using TIMS; all other U-series dates on hominid sites have been by the less precise method of alpha spectrometry, in some cases coupled with isochron analyses of the data.

During the past 200 ka, hominids have occupied two habitats which are particularly amenable to U-series dating: caves and warm springs (where travertine mounds have been deposited). Speleothems (stalagmites, flow-stones, etc.) are found in many of the caves which have also yielded hominids or Palaeolithic artefacts. It is not always possible to relate the timing of speleothem growth to the occupation of the site, however. Dates obtained on speleothems which are entirely out of a stratigraphic context are of no use to anthropologists. Unfortunately, the growth rate of speleothems is controlled by climate, and slows or ceases altogether during glacial stages (Gascoyne *et al.* 1983; Gordon *et al.* 1989). As a result it is more difficult (but not impossible) to find speleothems for U-series dating of those periods (e.g. 70 to 12 ka) in regions which experienced periglacial climate.

6. EUROPE

The last comprehensive summary of U-series dates from hominid sites was that of Cook *et al.* (1982), which surveyed and compared results from various other dating methods, as well, for hominid sites in Europe. Since then, U-series dates have been obtained on other Neanderthal sites in Europe including Grotte du Prince (Shen, 1986), Monte Circeo (Schwarcz *et al.* 1990), and Banyolas (Julia & Bischoff 1991). In addition, refinements of dates presented in Cook *et al.* (1982) have been published for some of these sites including Bilzingsleben (Schwarcz *et al.* 1988), La Chaise de Vouthon (Blackwell *et al.* 1983) and Petralona (Latham & Schwarcz 1992).

Examples from two of these sites should suffice to indicate the nature of the evidence that U-series dates provide. At the site of La Chaise-de-Vouthon, in the Charente district of France, two adjacent caves contain detrital sedimentary sequences which have yielded numerous hominid remains. Several layers of calcitic flowstone are interstratified with the sediments. Blackwell *et al.* (1983) obtained alpha-spectrometric dates on these flowstones, which serve as convenient datable horizons within the sequence. The calcite is relatively free of detrital contamination as was shown by the small activity of ^{232}Th in the alpha spectra. The ages of the flowstones range from $245 \pm _{28}^{45}$ ka to 97 ± 6 ka; the ages agree with the stratigraphic order of the flowstones. Hominid remains, consisting principally of teeth, are found in layers older than 101 ka.

The site of Banyolas in Spain exemplifies the application of U-series dating to a hominid site associated with a travertine deposit. The mandible of a hominid was discovered in 1887 in a travertine quarry, which has been subsequently filled in. Julia & Bischoff (1991) have, however, succeeded in discovering the probable location of the site and associating it with exposures of travertine in other open quarries nearby; they were also able to analyse travertine that was still attached to the mandible. The travertines were significantly contaminated with detritus but they obtained isochron dates on both the travertine deposits as well as the travertine coating of the mandible. The latter gave an isochron age of 45 ± 4 ka, which was in agreement with the uppermost layers of one of the travertine deposits. This date is, however, surprising, in view of the previous assignment of this fossil to an early stage of hominid evolution, prior to appearance of the Neanderthals (Roth 1989). A similar conflict between the evidence of U-series dating and inferences from anatomical as well as other site characteristics was encountered by Schwarcz & Latham (1984, 1990) in their study of travertines at the site of Vértesszöllös.

7. ASIA AND AFRICA

In recent years, the focus of interest in the study of late hominid evolution has shifted to inlude western Asia and Africa. Thanks to the application of TL and ESR dates to sites in these areas (Grün & Stringer 1991), we now recognize that the transition to *Homo sapiens sapiens* must have occurred long before the arrival of this species in Europe. The TL and ESR dates from these sites, while clearly pushing back the timing of the appearance of *H.s.s.* have large uncertainties associated with them, and it would be desirable to refine these results using high-precision U-series dates. Unfortunately, materials datable by U-series are not commonly found at these sites, and we must resort to dates at nearby sites which can be related to the hominid sites through archaeological or faunal correlations.

One example of this is the region of Nahal Zin, in the northern Negev Desert of Israel, where several Middle and Upper Palaeolithic sites were studied by A. Marks and colleagues in the 1970s and 1980s (Marks 1976). The site of Nahal Avdat consists of a travertine deposit in which are found embedded lithic artefacts correlatable with the earliest phase of the Upper Palaeolithic. The transition was better preserved at the nearby site of Boqer Tachtit which, however, contained no U-series datable materials. Samples of travertine from Nahal Avdat gave a date 47 ± 3 ka. The site of Ein Aqev a few km away contains Middle Palaeolithic (Levalloiseo–Mousterian) artefacts that were dated to 80 ± 10 ka.

These results are especially interesting in the light of the TL and ESR dates that have now been obtained for *H.s.s.* at sites in Galilee and Mount Carmel, of approximately 100 ka. The lithic artefacts associated with the hominids at these sites are of Middle Palaeolithic character. Therefore the transition from Middle to Upper Palaeolithic that we have dated at Nahal Zin may not represent the transition from Neanderthal to Modern humans, as is commonly assumed for this transition in Europe. Neanderthals were, however, present in Israel later than 100 ka (Schwarcz *et al.* 1989), and sites such as Nahal Zin may be critical in sorting out the relation between the cultural and biological transitions that have occurred over the past 100 ka.

Elsewhere in Israel, we have attempted to apply U-series dating to cave-deposited carbonates, with varying degrees of success (Schwarcz *et al.* 1979). These speleothems tend to be highly contaminated with detritus including a component of windblown limestone dust, that is particularly difficult to correct for. Therefore, it will be important to restudy these sites using TIMS-based U-series dating on subsamples of higher purity. Caves containing archaeological deposits occur elsewhere in this region, especially in the coastal caves of Lebanon. At the site of Nahr Ibrahim, for example we have analysed a flowstone capping a Mousterian sequence, and obtained a date of 100 ka. Spring deposited travertines from the Syrian desert are also potentially able to yield U-series over the last glacial cycle (Hennig & Hours 1982) but these deposits are also heavily contaminated with limestone particles that tend to increase the apparent ages.

In North Africa, critical archaeological sites are seldom found associated with U-series datable materials, with the possible exception of spring deposits of marls of spring-fed lakes. The area of Bir Tarfawi and Bir Sahara in southwestern Egypt is now a hyperarid desert. Sometime around 140 ka this area was occupied by a flourishing swampy, spring-fed lake which was visited by hominids using a Middle Paleolithic industry similar to that found in southwest Asia (Wendorf *et al.* 1992). Alpha-spectrometric U-series analyses were done on marls deposited in those lakes. The individual deposits give stratigraphically discordant results (age inversions), but when plotted on isochron diagrams they yield consistent ages of between 140 and 105 ka.

This site has also yielded the first TIMS U-series dates on archaeological material, namely ostrich egg-shell fragments from within one of the sites associated with lake filling. Three samples gave dates of 136 ± 3, 137 ± 3 and 126 ± 8 ka. The dates are consistent with the isochron dates for the associated marls, and imply that ostrich shells take up uranium soon after deposition and remain closed systems thereafter. A fourth sample from the same layer gave a date of 179 ± 19 ka; this shell fragment was contaminated with detritus. These data show the potential of high precision U-series for the fine temporal resolution of past hominid activities.

South of the Sahara, the possibilities of applying U-series methods to dating of the transition to *H.s.s.* are limited by the scarcity of carbonate deposits, with the exception of those in South Africa, where the sites of Boomplaas and Klasies River Mouth contain stalagmites whose U-series dates are under study by J. Vogel.

8. Conclusions: Potential for Further Studies

It should be clear that TIMS U-series dating can provide a high-resolution chronology for the later stages of hominid evolution, including the contentious transition from early modern *Homo sapiens sapiens* to the present species, and the disappearance of *Homo sapiens neandertalensis*. The application of this technique is, however, limited by the need to have suitable material for dating, preferably chemically precipitated calcite. Although this material is widely encountered in archaeological settings, it is necessary to use great care to select the correct material for analysis, especially so that the material satisfies two criteria: (i) purity; and (ii) chrono-stratigraphic relevance to the hominid remains or archaeological deposit. Both of these aspects have been discussed here and in earlier papers (e.g. Blackwell & Schwarcz 1992).

Potential areas where further advances may be made include the following.

1. Coatings on bone. Where fossil material, including hominid skeletal fragments, has been collected from sites in lime-rich terrains, a coating of calcium carbonate is commonly found adhering to the exterior of the bones, or as a

partial filling of cavities in the bone. This is particularly true in sub-arid regions. By dating this material we obtain an *ante quem* date for the individual. The amounts of carbonate encountered are usually so small that TIMS would be required for their analysis.

2. Stalactite 'rain'. In some caves, calcite deposition is intermittently active and results in the formation of fine tubular stalactites on the roof of the cave, which can then fall to the floor and make up several percent of the coarse fraction of the sediment in the cave. The lifetime of these stalactites on the roof of the cave is quite short (much less than 1000 years), and their age can be used as an estimate of the date for the layer in which they are found.

In addition, the more typical examples of stalagmitic layers, travertine deposits, etc., continue to provide targets for higher-resolution dating in the time range up to 400 ka. Further resolution and improvement of precision is attainable by coupling the TIMS method to the isochron technique. However, there is a purely analytical problem that must be considerd here as well: samples contaminated with common thorium have high ^{232}Th abundances and low ^{230}Th/^{232}Th ratios. In TIMS, this means that the isotopic (not activity) ^{232}Th/^{230}Th ratio is high, typically greater than 100 000, which introduces the problem of the contribution of the 'tail' of the very high ^{232}Th peak under the very small ^{230}Th peak only two mass units away. The use of two-stage mass spectrometers can provide adequate abundance sensitivity to eliminate the tail contribution. Clearly, however, such equipment is too expensive to be widely available, and it is expected that future advances in this field will require collaborative efforts comparable to those that have been seen in ^{14}C dating by AMS.

ACKNOWLEDGMENTS

Much of the research referred to here was carried out in collaboration with my colleagues including Bonnie Blackwell and Alf Latham. I also thank numerous archaeological and anthropological colleagues in Europe and Israel who, through the years, have presented me with challenging problems in dating. Valuable critical comments were made by Martin Aitken. This research was supported by grants from the Social Sciences and Humanities Research Council (Canada).

REFERENCES

Bischoff, J.L. & Fitzpatrick, J.A. 1990 U-series dating of impure carbonates: an isochron technique using total sample dissolution. *Geochim. cosmochim. Acta* **55**, 543–554.

Blackwell, B., Schwarcz, H.P. & Debenath, A. 1983 Absolute dating of hominids and Paleolithic artifacts of the cave of La Chaise-de-Vouthon (Charente), France. *J. archaeol. Sci.* **10**, 493–513.

Blackwell, B. & Schwarcz, H.P. 1986 Absolute age of the Lower Travertine at Ehringsdorf DDR. *Quat. Res.* **25**, 215–222.

Blackwell, B. & Schwarcz, H.P. 1992 Archaeometry. In *uranium series disequilibrium: application to environment problems in the earth sciences*, 2nd edn (ed. M. Ivanovich & R. S. Harmon). Oxford University Press. (In the press.)

Cook, J., Stringer, C.B., Currant, A., Schwarcz, H.P. & Wintle, A.G. 1982 A review of the chronology of the European middle Pleistocene Record. *Yb. phys. Anthrop.* **25**, 19–65.

Gordon, D., Smart, P.L., Ford, D.C., Andrews, J.N., Atkinson, T.C., Rowe, P.J. & Christopher, N.S.J. 1989 Dating of late Pleistocene interglacial and interstadial periods in the United Kingdom from speleothem growth frequency. *Quat. Res.* **31**, 14–26.

Hennig, G. & Hours, F. 1982 Dates pour le passage entre l'Acheuleen et le Paleolithique Moyen à El Kwom (Syrie). *Paleorient* **8**, 81–83.

Julia, R. & Bischoff, J.L. 1991 Radiometric dating of Quaternary deposits and the hominid mandible of Lake Banyolas, Spain. *J. archaeol. Sci.* **18**, 707–722.

Kaufman, A., Broecker, W.S., Ku, T.L. & Thurber, D.L. 1971 The status of U-series methods of mollusk dating. *Geochim. cosmochim. Acta* **35**, 1155–1189.

Ku, T.L. & Liang, Z.C. 1984 The dating of impure carbonates with decay-series isotopes. *Nucl. Instrum. Meth. Phys. Res.* **223**, 563–571.

Latham, A. & Schwarcz, H.P. 1992 The Petralona hominid site: uranium-series re-analysis of 'Layer 10' calcite and associated paleomagnetic analyses. *Archaeometry* **34**, 135–140.

Luo, S. & Ku, T.-L. 1990 U-series isochron dating: a generalized method employing total-sample dissolution. *Geochim. cosmochim. Acta* **55**, 555–564.

Marks, A.E. (ed.) 1976 *Prehistory and Paleoenvironments of the Central Negev, Israel*, vol. I (*The Avdat/Aqev Area*), part 1. Dallas: Southern Methodist University Press.

McKinney, C.R. 1991 The determination of the reliability of uranium series dating of enamel, dentine and bone. Ph.D. thesis, Southern Methodist University, Dallas.

Rae, A. & Ivanovich, M. 1986 Successful application of uranium series dating of fossil bone. *Appl. Geochem.* **1**, 419–426.

Schwarcz, H.P., Buhay, W.M., Grün, R., Valladas, H., Tchernov, E., Bar-Yosef, O. & Vandermeersch, B. 1989 ESR dates for the Neanderthal site of Kebara, Israel. *J. archaeol. Sci.* **16**, 653–661.

Schwarcz, H.P., Bietti, A., Buhay, W.M., Stiner, M., Grün, R. & Segré, E. 1991 U-series and ESR age data for the Neanderthal site of Monte Circeo, Italy. *Curr. Anthrop.* **32**, 313–316.

Schwarcz, H.P., Grün, R., Mania, D., Brunnacker, K. & Latham, A.G. 1988 New evidence for the age of the Bilzingsleben archaeological site. *Archaeometry*, **30**, 5–17.

Schwarcz, H.P. & Latham, A.F. 1984 Uranium series age determinations of travertines from the site of Vértesszöllös, Hungary. *J. archaeol. Sci.* **11**, 327–336.

Schwarcz, H.P. & Latham, A.G. 1989 Dirty Calcites, 1. Uranium series dating of contaminated calcites using leachates alone. *Isotope Geosci.* **80**, 35–43.

Schwarcz, H.P., Goldberg, P. & Blackwell, B. 1979 Uranium series dating of archaeological sites in Israel. *Israel J. Earth Sci.* **29**, 157–165.

Shen, G. 1986 U-series dating from the Prince Cave, northern Italy. *Archaeometry* **28**, 179–184.

Wendorf, F., Schild, R., Close, A., Schwarcz, H.P., Miller, G.H., Grün, R., Bluszcz, A., Stokes, S., Morawska, L., Huxtable, J. & McKinney, C. 1992 A chronology for the Middle and Late Pleistocene wet episodes in the eastern Sahara. (Submitted.)

Luminescence Dating Relevant to Human Origins

M. J. Aitken[1] and H. Valladas[2]

SUMMARY

Luminescence dating provided the first direct and independent evidence that anatomically modern humans had a presence in western Asia earlier than is consistent with the 'regional continuity' model. The reliability of the result concerned, 92 (± 5) ka for burnt flints from Qafzeh Cave, is excellent and consistent with isochron analysis of the data. Flint dating has also confirmed palaeoenvironmental indications that the Mousterian industry in Europe was present somewhat earlier than the 100 ka limit previously accepted. Burnt quartz and unburnt sediment have also been important in Palaeolithic dating and the latter has a particularly high potential.

1. INTRODUCTION

(a) Basis

The two commonly used techniques of luminescence dating are thermoluminescence (TL) and optically stimulated luminescence (OSL), the latter being called optical dating by its originators (Huntley *et al.* 1985). For TL the dating signal is stimulated by heat whereas for OSL it is stimulated by light. With both, the signal is a measure of the population of electrons trapped at defects in the crystal lattice of the mineral being utilized (e.g. quartz, flint, feldspars); the build-up of this population is the result of continued exposure to the weak flux of nuclear radiation emitted by radioactive impurities in the sample and in the immediately surrounding sediment, together with a minor contribution from cosmic rays. The relevant radioactive impurities are ^{232}Th, ^{235}U and ^{238}U together with their associated radioactive decay products, plus ^{40}K and ^{87}Rb, although the latter is of almost negligible importance. The relevant nuclear radiation consists effectively of α and β particles from within the sample, γ radiation from the burial surroundings (up to a distance of about 0.3 m) and cosmic ray mesons.

For the trapped electron population to be a useful measure of age it is essential that it was zero at some event in antiquity; it is that event which is dated. This 'zeroing' or 'resetting' can be by heating to upwards of around

[1] Research Laboratory for Archaeology, University of Oxford, 6 Keble Road, Oxford OX1 3QJ, U.K.

[2] Centre des Faibles Radioactivités, Laboratoire mixte CNRS-CEA, Avenue de la Terrasse, 91198 Gif sur Yvette Cedex, France

400°C or by sufficient exposure to daylight. If pottery is under study then the event will have been its firing in the potter's kiln. In the case of burnt flint it will have been accidental falling into the fire or deliberate heat treatment. For aeolian deposits such as wind-blown sand and loess the resetting event will have been exposure to light during transportation or while lying exposed on the surface before being covered by further deposition. Waterborne deposits will also have been reset, though not so effectively; the OSL technique is particularly advantageous for such sediment because with this technique the dating signal is stimulated only from highly light-sensitive traps whereas the TL signal comes from other traps too, some of which require hours of short wavelength 'bleaching' for their effective emptying; also there are some traps which are virtually immune to light exposure. This is in contrast to the 'brute force' zeroing that results from heating. Trapped electron populations of zero are also the case for newly-formed crystals e.g. stalagmitic calcite.

To translate the dating signal into calendar years two further quantities are required. First, for each sample studied it is necessary to measure the sensitivity, i.e. the signal resulting from a given dose of nuclear radiation; this is done by exposure to artificial radiation of known intensity. In this way the palaeodose, P, can be evaluated; this is the laboratory estimate of the dose that the sample must have received during antiquity for its dating signal to be equal to the observed value. Secondly, it is necessary to determine the dose-rate, D; this is the dose per year that the sample has been receiving during its period of burial. One approach is to determine the concentrations of radioactive elements present in sample and soil by means of neutron activation analysis. Alternatively, direct measurement of the natural radioactivity is used, both within the laboratory and on-site. The cosmic ray contribution is obtained by calculation, having regard to thickness of overburden, altitude and latitude. In principle the age, A, is then obtained from the equation.

$$A = P/D. \tag{1}$$

The unit of dose is the gray (Gy). The age so obtained is directly in calendar years and it is independent of any other chronological technique.

In practice, equation (1) is deceptively simple and even with automation the derivation of a reliable result is complex and labour intensive; a dozen or so parameters need to be measured to make allowance for various subtle effects: accounts of these have been given elsewhere (Aitken 1985, 1990). It should be noted that in contrast to the radiocarbon and uranium-series techniques the radioisotopes involved have very long half-lifes—in excess of 10^9 years; hence the dose-rate is basically constant (there may be small variations due to varying environmental conditions).

A measure of the trapped electron population can also be obtained by electron spin resonance (ESR) as discussed elsewhere in this volume. The three techniques are often collectively described as trapped electron dating. Recent reviews of luminescence techniques and applications have been given by Berger (1988), Wintle (1990), Zöller & Wagner (1990), Aitken (1989, 1992) and Valladas (1992); the solid-state mechanisms involved have been discussed, among others, by McKeever (1985).

2. RELEVANCE TO HUMAN ORIGINS

(a) Burnt Flint; Burnt Quartz

Flint is a form of chalcedony, another being chert; in the context of dating the two are not usually distinguished, both being called flint. Its dating came into prominence with the publication by Valladas *et al.* (1987, 1988) of results for two caves in Israel: Kebara and Qafzeh. The result for the latter gave the first hard evidence that anatomically modern humans were present in that region some 90 ka ago, thus firmly rebutting any notion of evolution from Neanderthals; the cave at Kebara had contained a Neanderthal skeleton and the TL dates for the relevant levels indicated an age of close to 60 ka. These were subsequently supported by ESR. Recently another TL age indicating early arrival of modern humans in that region has been obtained at the cave of es-Skhul (Mercier *et al.* 1992). The reliability of the Qafzeh date is examined in § 3*d*.

Another contribution, recently reviewed by Valladas (1992), has been confirmation of palaeoenvironmental indications that the Mousterian industry in Europe was present somewhat earlier than the 100 ka limit generally accepted. Thus at Biache-Saint-Vaast in northern France, TL dating of six burnt flints gave an age of 175 (±13) ka for the level in which two pre-Neanderthal skulls had been found; floral and faunal evidence indicated occupation during an interstadial of isotope Stage 6 (Huxtable & Aitken 1988*a*). Another site for which TL gave an earlier than expected age for a Mousterian (IV) level was at Abri Vaufrey in the Dordogne valley of France; four flints gave an average age of 120 (±13) ka (Huxtable & Aitken 1988*b*); a similar age had previously been obtained for a stalactite fragment found in the same level (Aitken & Bussell 1982). The oldest site for which flint dates have so far been published is the Acheulian site of Maastricht-Belvédère in eastern Holland, the age obtained for the earliest occupation layer being 263 (±22) ka (Huxtable & Aitken 1985).

Another silica mineral utilized is quartz and grains extracted from the clay of Palaeolithic fireplaces have been used for dating: ages of 31–36 ka have been obtained for the Lake Mungo fireplaces in Australia (Huxtable & Aitken 1977; Bell 1991). These are in satisfactory agreement with radiocarbon if allowance is made for that technique's probable underestimation by several thousand years (Mazaud *et al.* 1991).

(b) Unburnt Sediment

Although burnt flint is an excellent material for TL dating, a severe problem on many sites is the scarcity of flints which are both well enough burnt and large enough for satisfactory processing. Hence the feasibility of dating the time of deposition of unburnt sediment vastly extends the scope of luminescence dating on Palaeolithic sites. An early study of sediments from Garrod's Tabun Cave was made by Bowman (1985). Although this was on polymineral samples there was indication that TL from quartz was dominating the signal, the problem of feldspar fading hence being alleviated. Bowman (1985) was reluctant to quote a date on account of dose-rate uncertainties associated with observed escape of radon from samples in the laboratory. Nevertheless it is interesting to note that using the data reported, the ages obtained (making approximation about radon loss; S. G. E. Bowman, personal communication) for two samples from Garrod's level D (the level below the female Neanderthal skeleton) were both about 160 ka, close to the linear uptake (LU) age of 166 ($\pm$20) obtained for tooth enamel from that level by ESR (Grün *et al.* 1991). On the other hand TL dating (Mercier 1992) of 11 burnt flints from level D has given a preliminary average age of 250 ka. Of course in dating sediments in dark caves it is essential that the grains were carried in by wind (or water) rather than derived from the walls.

Another relevant study is that of Roberts *et al.* (1990), made as the first in a series concerning the time of initial human arrival on the Australian continent. Quartz grains extracted from sand on sites located on sand aprons at the foot of the Arnhem Land plateau were used and some dozen dates obtained at various depths in the profiles. There was satisfactory agreement with radiocarbon ages obtained for the upper layers of both sites, and at one of them three TL ages were associated with the lowest occupation level yielding stone artifacts; the authors suggest that human arrival in northern Australia occurred between 50 and 60 ka ago, somewhat earlier than previous indications obtained using the radiocarbon technique (which is of course at its limit around 40 ka).

In using TL for unburnt sediment the need to assess the effectiveness of resetting at deposition adds substantially to the work. The OSL technique avoids this and highly encouraging results have been obtained in test programmes (e.g. Smith *et al.* 1990; Stokes 1992). An age of around 130 ka has been obtained (Stokes 1993) for quartz grains extracted from sediment of the lowest lake at Bir Tafawi (Egypt) in agreement with uranium-series and amino acid dating of ostrich eggshells.

(c) Stalagmitic Calcite

Although TL can be used for dating this type of material in caves occupied by hominids back to 300 ka (e.g. at Caune de l'Arago, France, by Debenham & Aitken (1984)), in most contexts the heterogeneity of the calcite itself and of the surroundings means that reliable assessment of the external dose-rate is difficult. The uranium-series method does not have this drawback and hence is usually the preferred technique. The calcite date mentioned above for Abri Vaufrey was obtained for a small piece of stalactite which had fallen from the cave roof and become buried in sediment to a sufficient depth (0.3 m) for the external dose-rate to be reliably evaluated.

3. RELIABILITY

(a) *General*

In addition to the concordances with other techniques noted above, accumulated evidence from a wide variety of samples and sites has established the general validity of the technique (see Ancient TL date lists, Bailiff, n.d.). Nevertheless, with a particular sample-type or a particular site there may be special sources of inaccuracy. Hence, however thorough the demonstration that a particular mineral, say quartz, gives accurate results on a 'good' site, it does not prove it will do so on a site where interfering factors, e.g. radioactive disequilibrium, are present; conversely failure in one particular site or with one particular mineral does not prove the whole technique to be invalid.

The dates mentioned in § 2 are mainly based on flint, which has the advantage of being a geochemically stable mineral. In addition to the results obtained by one of us (H.V.), there has been extensive flint dating by J. Huxtable at Oxford (see Ancient TL date lists); all these indicate burnt flint to be an excellent dating material. Additional comparisons with other techniques have been summarized by Valladas (1992). The oldest was for La Vigne Brun (France), yielding a flint date of 27 ka; this was in excellent agreement with the age obtained using burnt quartz and also with the average radiocarbon date for four charcoal fragments after making allowance for the probable 3 ka underestimation by the latter technique at the time period concerned (Bard *et al.* 1990).

Some additional general aspects are considered in the next two subsections and then there is specific discussion of the critical date for Qafzeh.

(b) *The Plateau Test; Residual Signals*

An advantage with the luminescence techniques is that the dating signal is more than a quantity, it has a characteristic shape too, and irregularities in this are indicative that all is not well. In the case of TL dating the signal is in the form of a glow-curve and comparison of the glow-curve shape observed for portions of an ancient sample 'as found' (the natural TL) with that for portions that have received laboratory irradiation allow the all-important plateau test to be made (see figure 1). Failure to pass this test can be for a

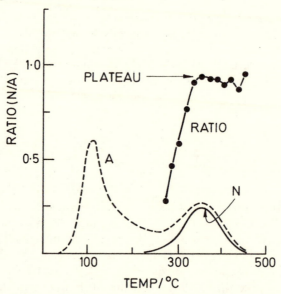

Figure 1. The plateau test. Curve N is the TL glow-curve for a flint that was well-burnt in antiquity and curve A is the additional TL observed from another portion to which a laboratory dose has been administered. The ratio (N/A) reaches a plateau in the glow-curve temperature region where the storage lifetime of the trapped electrons responsible for the TL is much greater than the age of the sample; at lower temperatures the TL is associated with electrons ejected from traps for which the storage lifetime is much shorter. It is the plateau value that is used for dating and in this example the ratio value (of 0.95) corresponds to the palaeodose being 0.95 times the laboratory dose administered. In practice a range of laboratory doses is used, with several portions for each dose point.

variety of reasons: e.g. contamination, presence of 'spurious' TL (a parasitic signal indicative of poor measurement conditions), inadequate stability of the trapped electrons (i.e. their lifetime in the traps was not long enough to avoid leakage during the burial period). Failure can also be caused by insufficient heating at the resetting event in antiquity and given the difficulty mentioned earlier of finding enough well-burnt samples this is of particular relevance to flint dating (see figure 2). Because the plateau test is an intrinsic part of the measurement process there is no risk of dates being obtained from 'half-baked' flints. This eliminates the possibility of a flint

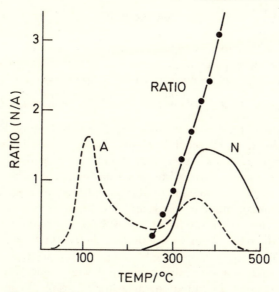

Figure 2. Failure to pass the plateau test. Curve N is the glow-curve from a flint that had not been burnt in antiquity; curve A represent the TL due to a laboratory dose administered after heating a sample of the flint to 500°C. Curve N has a different shape from that of figure 1 because in this unburnt case the trapped electrons have been accumulating during the very long time that has elapsed since the flint's formation. The data used are taken from Robins *et al* (1982).

For partially burnt flints the rise in the ratio is less steep but as is evident from the work of Melcher & Zimmerman (1977) there is no risk of even the semblance of a plateau with such flints, making calculation of a date impossible.

date being erroneously too old on account of the dating signal containing a contribution of residual 'geological' TL.

However, the question of residual signal is of more serious concern in the TL dating of unburnt sediment; as mentioned earlier, in such application the residual signal may be appreciable and needs to be subtracted. Here again the plateau test is employed, although usually substantial complication is involved (see Mejdahl 1988). There is great region-to-region variability in this respect dependent on mode of deposition and intensity of daylight; at the Arnhem Land site in Australia mentioned in § 2*b* the straightforward plateau was good, consistent with the observation that direct measurement of recently deposited sand at the site indicated a palaeodose of only one gray.

In the case of OSL the corresponding necessary condition for reliability is a satisfactory 'shine-plateau': i.e. there should be no change in the paleo-dose calculated for successive intervals of exposure to the stimulating light.

(c) Limitations on Age Range: Lifetime; Saturation; Anomalous Fading

Stable retention of trapped electrons over the burial period is obviously a basic requirement in respect of the traps providing the dating signal, and as mentioned above a satisfactory plateau indicates that this condition has been met. However, it is useful to have some estimate of trapped electron lifetimes since this is a possible limitation in the age range of application. Laboratory 'kinetic' measurements indicate the following rough values (see Aitken 1985): for quartz and burnt flint, 10^8 years; for calcite, 10^6 years; for K-feldspar, 10^7 years. Thus we see that for the 100 ka time span, which is this volume's focus of interest, the lifetimes are adequate.

However, there is another limitation on the age range. This is that with continued exposure to radiation all available traps become filled. For quartz and flint the radiation dose at which this occurs is of the order of several hundred grays, and depending on the level of radioactivity this corresponds to a limiting age of several hundred ka. Some types of these minerals saturate at lower doses and some at higher doses, so no strict limits can be laid down; it is a matter for investigation on each particular site. In general it seems that flint can reach further back than quartz.

For feldspars the saturation dose is much higher, a value of several thousand grays being applicable to K-feldspars for instance. However despite the adequate lifetime indicated by laboratory studies there is a tendency in some types for appreciable leakage of trapped electrons to occur. This is termed anomalous fading and whenever feldspars are used for dating special procedures and checks are necessary to exclude the possibility of interference by this malign phenomenon; this applies equally when a mixture of minerals is used: the luminescence from feldspars is usually dominant.

(d) Qafzeh

The date (Valladas et al. 1988) for this cave is based on 20 flints obtained from Mousterian layers within a 2.5 m section that had yielded anatomically modern humans ('Proto-Cro-Magnons'). According to the 'multi-regional model' these humans evolved from Neanderthals and the date (92 ka) should have been more recent than the 60 ka date for Kebara. Hence the question at issue with the Qafzeh date is whether there was some factor that caused it to be erroneously too old. The most easily dismissed is

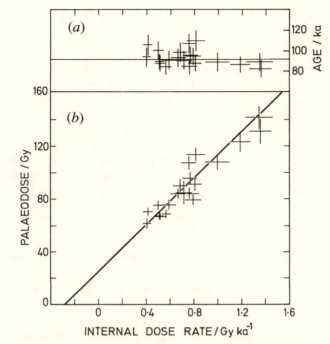

Figure 3. (*a*) (right-hand scale) TL ages for Qafzeh plotted against internal dose-rate values. The horizontal line represents the weighted average (as published by Valladas *et al.* (1988)). (*b*) (left-hand scale) Isochron plot of Qafzeh palaeodose values versus internal dose-rate values. The line is the least-squares fit, weighted for uncorrelated errors on both axes (York 1969); the slope indicates an age of 88 (±9) ka and the intercept on the horizontal axis indicates an external dose-rate of 0.28 (±0.09) Gy ka^{-1}.

the possibility that the flints were insufficently heated at time zero; besides this being ruled out by the considerations of § 3*b*, it is also ruled out by the tight clustering of the individual dates (see figure 3*a*): the degree of insufficiency would vary from flint to flint.

Given that the paleodose evaluation followed well-established practice other possible causes of overestimation have to be sought: could the dose-rate have been higher during the millennia of burial than indicated by measurements made today? The impervious nature of flint makes it highly unlikely that there would have been any leaching away of internal radio-isotopes (which contributed the dominant part of the total dose-rate) and even if it had occurred it would hardly have been the same from flint to flint.

Direct evidence against leaching is that in the five flints for which fission-track mapping of uranium was carried out there was practically uniform distribution.

Turning to external dose-rate, albeit of lesser importance for this site according to the measurements reported, there are possibilities that cannot be dismissed *a priori*. One is that there might have been progressive leaching away of radioisotopes in the burial sediment. Another is that the moisture content of the sediment might have been lower during antiquity than at present: the presence of moisture causes attenuation of the flux of γ radiation reaching the sample. A third is that there could have been a change in the cosmic ray flux (which on this site is estimated to provide approximately half the external dose-rate) due to a change in the degree of shielding by rock.

If leaching had occurred a progressive increase in external dose-rate with depth would be expected. Reference to Table 1 of Valladas *et al.* (1988) clearly shows this not to be the case; in fact the extreme values of 0.22 and 0.25 Gy ka^{-1} are easily contained within the quoted area limits (of ± 0.04 Gy ka^{-1}). Further, if leaching had occurred it would be expected that there would be disequilibrium in the uranium series; but measurements using α and γ spectrometry showed this not to be the case.

There is no direct evidence bearing on the other two possibilities but there is implicit indication in the reported data that any past variations in external dose-rate (and indeed in internal dose-rate too) have not been serious enough to distort the ages obtained. The internal dose-rates of the individual flints are widely spread: from 0.41 to 1.36 Gy ka^{-1}, unrelated to depth. Yet the ages obtained for flints of high internal dose-rate are not significantly different to those obtained for flints of low internal dose-rate (see figure 3*a*); if there was a significant systematic error in either dose-rate evaluation this would not be the case.

Similar evidence of reliability comes from isochron analysis, first used in TL dating by Mejdahl (1983) and demonstrated for ESR by Blackwell & Schwarcz (1992). This is possible because of the combined circumstances of a wide spread in the internal dose-rates, constancy of external dose-rate down the section, and the geological indications (see Valladas *et al.* 1988) that the sediment of the section accumulated rapidly. Isochron analysis allows evaluation of average age without insertion of any value for the external dose-rate; it is only required that this latter is the same for all samples. Figure 3*b* shows its application: the age so evaluated is 88 (± 9) ka; the published age (92± 5) is consistent with this.

ESR dates for tooth enamel from the burial levels have also been obtained (Schwarcz *et al.* 1988) giving an early uptake (EU) age of 96 (± 13) ka and a linear uptake age (LU) of 115 (± 15) ka, the latter being favoured. These dates utilized the external dose-rate that was evaluated for the TL but in the case of ESR this is the dominant contribution to the overall dose-rate. Hence the two techniques are not strongly interdependent as far as dose-rate is concerned, and given the different nature of the crystal structures in which the trapped electrons were accumulated the ESR result can be considered as independent confirmation of the site's great age. The fact that the favoured ESR age of 115 (±15) ka is somewhat greater than the TL age (92 ± 5 ka) may be due to underestimation of the external dose-rate. The isochron analysis of the TL dates (figure 3b) indicates an external dose-rate of 0.28 (±0.09) Gy ka^{-1} whereas the values used (for both TL and ESR) were in the range 0.22–0.25 Gy ka^{-1}. Because of the dominance of the external dose-rate in the case of ESR, use of the isochron value would tend to move the ESR result into agreement with the TL.

Finally, it is to be noted that the scatter in the twenty individual TL ages corresponds to a standard deviation of only 8%; this is very close to the predicted random ('statistical') error limits quoted for the individual dates. Hence these twenty ages form a remarkably coherent group, thus giving further strong support to the validity of the result. Such coherence is not always the case: for instance the six individual TL ages on which the average of 119 ka for es-Skhul (see § 2a) are based show a much wider scatter, the standard deviation being around 18%. This is indicative of less favourable circumstances, as was recognized by Mercier et al. (1992) who quoted predicted error limits of ±18 ka. Thus in making archaeological interpretation of these results for the presence in the region of anatomically modern humans, it is appropriate to put emphasis on the TL result for Qafzeh.

5. SUMMING UP

Luminescence techniques allow the independent dating, directly in calendar years, of burnt flint, burnt quartz and calcite, as well as unburnt wind- and water-borne sediment; for the latter it is advantageous to use the OSL technique. Consideration of the burnt flint TL data for Qafzeh underlines the reliability of that result, one of several which are critical for our understanding of the origin of modern humans.

ACKNOWLEDGMENTS

We are grateful to M. Whitehouse for carrying out the isochron plot and to S. G. E. Bowman, E. J. Rhodes, H. P. Schwarcz and S. Stokes for helpful comments.

REFERENCES

Aitken, M. J. 1985 *Thermoluminescence dating*. London: Academic Press.
Aitken, M. J. 1989 Luminescence dating: a guide for non-specialists. *Archaeometry* **31**, 147–159.

Aitken, M.J. 1990 *Science-based dating in archaeology.* London & New York; Longman.

Aitken, M.J. 1992 Optical Dating. *Quat. Sci. Rev.* **11**, 127–132.

Aitken, M.J. & Bussell, G.D. 1982 TL dating of fallen stalactites. *PACT* **6**, 550–554.

Bailiff, I.K. (ed.) *Ancient TL* Date Lists. Luminescence Dating Laboratory, University of Durham.

Bard, E., Hamelin, B., Fairbanks, R.G. & Zindler, A. 1990 Calibration of the C-14 timescale over the past 30,000 years using mass-spectrometric U-Th ages from Barbados corals. *Nature, Lond.* **345**, 405–410.

Bell, W.T. 1991 Thermoluminescence dates for the Lake Mungo Aboriginal fireplaces and the implications for radiocarbon dating. *Archaeometry* **33**, 43–50.

Berger, G.W. 1988 Dating Quaternary events by luminescence. *Geol. Soc. Am. spec. Pap.* **227**, 13–50.

Blackwell, B. & Schwarcz, H.P. 1992 Electron spin resonance isochron dating. *Appl. Rad. Isotopes* (In the press.)

Bowman, S.G.E. 1985 Thermoluminescence characteristics of sediments from the Tabun cave, Israel. *Nucl. Tracks Rad. Meas.* **10**, 731–736.

Debenham, N.C. & Aitken, M.J. 1984 Thermoluminescence dating of stalagmitic calcite. *Archaeometry* **26**, 155–170.

Grün, R., Stringer, C.J. & Schwarcz, H.P. 1991 ESR dating of teeth from Garrod's Tabun cave collection. *J. hum. Evol.* **20**, 231–248.

Huntley, D.J., Godfrey-Smith, D.I. & Thewalt, M.L.W. 1985 Optical dating of sediments. *Nature, Lond.* **313**, 105–107.

Huxtable, J. & Aitken, M.J. 1977 Thermoluminescence dating of Lake Mungo polarity excursion. *Nature, Lond.* **265**, 40–41.

Huxtable, J. & Aitken, M.J. 1985 Thermoluminescence dating results for the Palaeolithic site Mastricht-Belvédère. *Analecta Praehistorica Leidensia* **18**, 41–44.

Huxtable, J. & Aitken, M.J. 1988*a* Datation par thermoluminescence. In *Le gisement paléolithique moyen de Biache-Saint-Vaast (Pas de Calais): stratigraphie, environment, études archéologiques*, vol. 21 (ed. A. Tuffreau & J. Sommé), pp. 107–108. Mémoire de la société préhistorique français.

Huxtable, J. & Aitken, M.J. 1988*b* Datation par thermoluminescence de la grotte Vaufrey. In *La grotte Vaufrey à Cénac et Saint Julien (Dordogne): paléoenvironments, chronologie, et activités humaines*, vol. 19 (ed. J. P. Rigaud), pp. 359–364. Mémoire de la société préhistorique français.

Mazaud, A., Laj, C., Bard, E., Arnold, M. & Tric, E. 1991 Geomagnetic field control of C-14 production over the last 80 ky: implications for the radiocarbon timescale. *Geophys. Res. Lett.* **18**, 1885–1888.

McKeever, S.W.S. 1985 *Thermoluminescence of solids.* Cambridge University Press.

Mejdahl, V. 1983 Feldspar inclusion dating of ceramics and burnt stones. *PACT* **9**, 351–364.

Mejdahl, V. 1988 The plateau method for dating partially bleached sediments by thermoluminescence. *Quat. Sci. Rev.* **7**, 347–348.

Melcher, C.L. & Zimmerman, D.W. 1977 Thermoluminescent determination of prehistoric heat treatment of chert artefacts. *Science, Wash.* **197**, 1359–1360.

Mercier, N. 1992 Apport des méthodes radionucléaires de datation à l'étude du peuplement de l'Europe et du Proche-Orient du Pléistocène moyen et supérieur. Thèse présentée à l'Université de Bordeaux I, 139 pp.

Mercier, N., Valladas, H., Bar-Yosef, O., Vandermeersch, B., Stringer, C. & Joron, J-L. 1992 Thermoluminescence date for the Mousterian burial site of es-Skhul, Mt. Carmel. *J. archaeol. Sci.* (In the press.)

Roberts, R.G., Rhys Jones & Smith, M.A. 1990 Thermoluminescence dating of a 50,000-year-old human occupation site in northern Australia. *Nature, Lond.* **345**, 153–156.

Robins, G.V., Seeley, N.J., Symons, M.C.R. & Bowman, S.G.E. 1982 The Institute of Archaeology (London) ESR flint project. *PACT* **6**, 322–332.

Schwarcz, H.P., Grün, R., Vandermeersch, B., Bar-Yosef, O., Valladas, H. & Tchernov, E. 1988 ESR dates from the burial site of Qafzeh in Israel. *J. hum. Evol.* **17**, 733–737.

Smith, B.W., Rhodes, E.J., Stokes, S.J., Spooner, N.A. & Aitken, M.J. 1990 Optical dating of sediments: initial quartz results from Oxford. *Archaeometry* **32**, 19–31.

Stokes, S. & Gaylord, D.R. 1992 Geochronology of the Cleer Creek dune field: a test of optical dating. *Quat. Res.* (In the press.)

Stokes, S. 1993 Optical dating of sediment samples from Bir Tafawi and Bir Sahara: an initial report. In *The Middle Palaeolithic in the Egyptian Sahara during the last interglacial* (ed. F. Wendorf, A. E. Close & S. C. Schilde). Southern Methodist University Press. (In the press.)

Valladas, H. 1992 Thermoluminescence dating of flint. *Quat. Sci. Rev.* **11**, 1–5.

Valladas, H. Joron, J.L., Valladas, G., Arensburg, B., Bar-Yosef, O., Belfer-Cohen, A., Goldberg, P., Laville, H., Meignen, L., Rak, Y., Tchernov, E., Tiller, A.M. & Vandermeersch, B. 1987 Thermoluminescence dates for the Neanderthal burial site at Kebara in Israel. *Nature, Lond.* **330**, 159–160.

Valladas, H, Reyss, J.L., Joron, J.L., Valladas, G., Bar-Yosef, O. & Vandermeersch, B. 1988 Thermoluminescence dating of Mousterian 'Proto-Cro-Magnon' remains from Israel and the origin of modern man. *Nature, Lond.* **331**, 614–616.

Wintle, A.G. 1990 A review of current research on TL dating of loess. *Quat. Sci. Rev.* **9**, 385–397.

York, D. 1969 Least squares fitting with correlated errors. *Earth planet. Sci. Lett.* **5**, 320–324.

Zöller, L. & Wagner, G.A. 1990 Thermoluminescence dating of loess. *Quat. Int.* **7/8**, 119–128.

Electron Spin Resonance (ESR) Dating of the Origin of Modern Man

Henry P. Schwarcz[1] *and Rainer Grün*[2]

SUMMARY

Many materials found in archaeological sites are able to trap electronic charges as a result of bombardment by radioactive radiation from the surrounding sediment. The presence of these trapped charges can be detected by electron spin resonance (ESR) spectroscopy: the intensity of the ESR signal is a measure of the accumulated dose and thus of the age. Tooth enamel is ubiquitous at archaeological sites and is well suited for ESR dating, with a precision of about 10–20%. This method has now been used to date many sites critical to the biological and cultural evolution of modern man. Dates for sites in Israel and Africa have demonstrated the existence of anatomically modern humans more than 100 ka ago.

1. INTRODUCTION

Over the past few years attention of archaeologists and anthropologists has focused on the stages leading to the appearance of modern man, *Homo sapiens sapiens*, and the disappearance of archaic modern hominids including Neanderthal man. The timescale of this transition lies beyond the dating range of ^{14}C and therefore has necessitated the employment of a battery of new dating techniques. One such method which has been developed over the last decade is electron spin resonance (ESR) dating; this method is also sometimes referred to as electron paramagnetic resonance (EPR) dating. The method was invented by Zeller (1968) who did not, however, further develop it. This was left to M. Ikeya who, in a series of papers beginning in 1978, showed the utility of the technique in dating stalagmitic calcite, shells, animal bones, and teeth, all of which are found in archaeological sites. Reports on ESR dating of tooth enamel from archaeological sites began to appear in the 1980s. Grün (1989) has recently summarized the theory and applications of the ESR techniques.

[1] Subdepartment of Quaternary Research, University of Cambridge, Free School Lane, Cambridge CB2 3RS, U.K. Permanent address: Department of Geology, McMaster University, Hamilton, Ontario, L8S 4M1, Canada.

[2] Subdepartment of Quaternary Research, University of Cambridge, Free School Lane, Cambridge CB2 3RS, U.K. Permanent address: Research Laboratory for Radiocarbon Dating, Australian National University, G.P.O. Box 4, Canberra, ACT 2601, Australia.

2. THEORY OF ESR DATING

The principles of ESR dating are in part the same as those of luminescence dating as discussed elsewhere in this symposium by Aitken & Valladas; the main difference is in regard to the dating signal. In brief, electronic charges are trapped at defects in crystalline materials as a result of radioactive bombardment of the crystal. The age of the material can be obtained from the ratio of the amount of trapped energy to the rate of trapping. The number of trapped charges is determined from the intensity of a characteristic signal in an ESR spectrum; in luminescence dating, on the other hand, trapped charges are measured by the intensity of light emitted from the sample. The number of trapped charges is converted to a palaeodose, P, and the age, t, is then obtained from the relation

$$t = P/D, \tag{1}$$

where D = the average dose rate (in grays per year) and P is given in grays (Gy).

In principle, any crystalline, non-conducting material could be dated, but in practice we require that: (i) the material be free of all but traces of iron or manganese whose ESR signals interfere with those produced by radiation; (ii) that the lifetime of trapped electrons be much greater than the age to be determined, say greater than 10^8 years; (iii) that the material be widely encountered at archaeological sites; and (iv) that, at the time of occupation of the site, the material should either be formed *de novo* or that the pre-existing trapped charges have been zeroed by some process, such as heating in a fire. Thus the signal is assumed to start at zero at the time of burial of the sample, and to grow steadily thereafter as a result of natural irradiation. The radiation occurs in two forms: internal, which is due to traces of the radioactive elements uranium (U), thorium (Th) and potassium (K) which are present in the material; and external, from U, Th, and K in the surrounding sediment, plus cosmic rays.

The material which has proven to be most useful for ESR dating at archaeological sites is tooth enamel (Grün *et al.* 1987); currently burnt flint is being investigated (Porat & Schwarcz 1991). Stalagmitic calcite and molluscan aragonite show some promise but have not been widely applied (Grün 1989). Enamel displays a single, well-defined ESR signal with a *g*-value of 2.0018 (figure 1), whose intensity can be easily measured at room temperature. Bone, which displays the same ESR signal as enamel, is however not useful for dating (Grün & Schwarcz 1987). The applications of ESR to the evolution of modern hominids have all involved dating of tooth enamel, so we shall limit the discussion to this material.

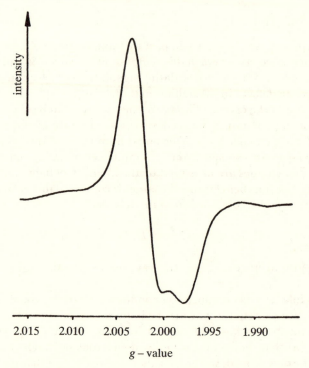

Figure 1. Typical ESR signal from tooth enamel. The signal is obtained by subjecting the sample to a beam of microwaves while it sits in a strong, varying magnetic field. The peak shown is characterized by a dimensionless parameter, g, which determines the value of the magnetic field at which the signal crosses the base line; for tooth enamel and bone, $g = 2.0018$.

3. ESR Dating of Tooth Enamel

Teeth of large mammals are commonly found at most archaeological sites, and provide an excellent material for ESR dating. Teeth are composed of two anatomical components: enamel which consists of relatively well-crystallized hydroxyapatite mineral, and less than 1% organic matter; and dentine + cementum, which contain much smaller apatite crystals and a much larger proportion of organic matter (more than 20% by weight). Like bone, dentine and cementum are not suitable for ESR dating. At the time of death of the animal, none of these materials contain any U, Th or K. Shortly after burial U alone begins to be absorbed by both materials, and old teeth are found to contain more than 100 p.p.m. (parts per million) of uranium in the dentine, and a few p.p.m. in the enamel.

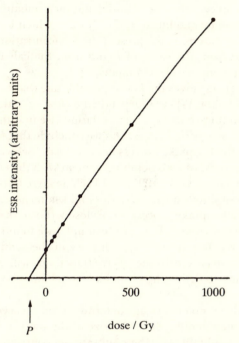

Figure 2. Growth curve for artifical irradiation of an archaeological sample of tooth
enamel. P = palaeodose, obtained by logarithmic extrapolation of data (modified
from Grün & Stringer (1991)).

The palaeodose of a sample of tooth enamel is obtained by measuring the
intensity (I) of the $g = 2.0018$ signal in unirradiated powdered enamel, as
well as in eight or more portions of enamel that have been given successively
larger doses of gamma radiation from a ^{60}Co source. A plot of I versus
added dose yields a curve which can be extrapolated back to $I = 0$ in order
to obtain P (figure 2). The external dose rate at the burial site can be
measured directly using gamma dosimeters; the internal dose rate is determined from the U content of the enamel and dentine. The age cannot be
obtained simply from equation (1), however, because the dose rate D has
changed (increased) through time for two reasons. First, because U has
been taken up by the tooth since it was buried; and second, because U in the
tooth has been increasing in effective radioactivity through time due to the
growth of U-series daughter isotopes (as discussed by Schwarcz, this symposium). The latter process can be modelled exactly from physical principles, as long as the process of U uptake is known as a function of time. We
generally consider two specific models of U uptake: early uptake (EU), in

which U is taken up very soon after burial and then remains at the concentration observed today; and linear uptake (LU), in which U is taken up at a constant rate, culminating in the present-day concentration. Then the age can be calculated from the value of P and from the calculated temporal history of D, based on the selected model.

In general the EU age gives the lowest possible age that can be computed from a given set of data. Where independent estimates of the age are available (e.g. from luminescence or U-series dating) we find that these generally agree most closely with LU ages, and we conclude that this model most closely describes the U uptake process in most cases (Schwarcz et al. 1988). However, at some sites, we find better agreement with the EU model (e.g. at Le Moustier (Mellars & Grün 1991) and Pech de l'Azé (Grün et al. 1991)). It is possible to use simultaneous U-series and ESR measurements of tooth enamel to define the uptake process more closely (Grün et al. 1988). When applied to the site of Hoxne, U.K., for example, we found that U uptake must have occurred late in the burial history of the sample. The use of thermal ionization mass spectrometry (TIMS) methods will make it easier to use U-series dating to define the U uptake model for enamel and dentine samples.

Typically, we do complete ESR age determinations on several portions of enamel from a single tooth, where the size of the tooth permits. Concordance between ages obtained on these subsamples contributes to our confidence in the result. Lately Blackwell & Schwarcz (1992) have also shown that subsamples can be used collectively to define an isochron whose slope gives the age of the tooth as a whole. When using this method, however, it is still necessary to make some assumption about the U uptake model.

4. APPLICATION OF ESR DATING TO THE ORIGIN OF MODERN HOMINIDS

ESR dating has been applied to a number of sites in Israel and Africa at which anatomically modern hominids had been discovered. The first such site was the cave of Qafzeh, Israel, at which the remains of at least 20 modern ('Cro Magnon') hominids had been found buried (Vandermeersch 1981). In 1988, Valladas et al. (1988) reported a date of 92 ± 5 ka for this site, based on thermoluminescence (TL) measurements of heated flint. Shortly afterwards, Schwarcz et al. (1988) reported ESR dates for this site; Grün & Stringer (1991) have slightly revised this result, obtaining ages of 100 ± 10 ka (EU) and 120 ± 8 ka (LU). The dose rates for flint (on which TL dates were based) were dominated by the internal dose rate, whereas the dose rate to the tooth enamel at this site was dominated by the external component. Therefore these two dates are effectively independent estimates of the age. Aitken & Valladas (this symposium) have suggested that the external dose rate at Qafzeh may have been underestimated, which would cause the ESR ages to be shifted slightly towards better agreement with the TL ages.

The site of Skhul in Mt Carmel also contained a number of burials of anatomically modern hominids. Stringer *et al.* (1989) obtained an ESR date on subsamples from two teeth taken from the collection in the Museum of Natural History, London. The external dose rates were estimated from chemical analyses of associated sediments. These samples gave ages of 81 ± 15 ka (EU) and 101 ± 12 ka (LU), consistent with the dates obtained at Qafzeh.

It is interesting to compare these dates with ESR ages obtained on Neanderthal hominids from the same region. At the nearby site of Tabun, a Neanderthal skeleton had been recovered by Garrod from her excavations in the 1930s. This hominid was believed to come either from layer C or the base of layer B in the stratigraphic sequence of the site. Linear uptake ESR dates on teeth from layer B average around 100 ka whereas those in layer C average around 120 ka. These dates are comparable to the age obtained at Skhul and Qafzeh and show that both Neanderthals and fully modern hominids may have been present in the same time interval (though they need not have coexisted, given the uncertainties in dating). At the nearby cave of Kebara, a Neanderthal skeleton was found, apparently a burial into layer XII of this site. ESR dates on teeth from the immediately overlying layer X gave ages of 60±6 ka (EU) and 64±6 ka (LU) (Schwarcz *et al.* 1989). Valladas *et al.* (1987) had obtained a TL date of 60±4 ka on burnt flint from layers XI and XII. Note that there is no significant difference between the LU and EU ages of the teeth from this site because of the low U content of the enamel from the site.

The dates obtained so far at sites from Israel have demonstrated the presence of modern hominids in western Asia long before they appeared in Europe. These results set the stage for a revolution in the chronology of the evolution of modern hominids, as discussed by Grün & Stringer (1991). These authors also noted preliminary estimates for the age of the Neanderthal from Wadi Amud, of around 50 ka.

Three important sites in Africa have also been dated. At Jebel Irhoud, mammal teeth associated with a modern hominid have yielded preliminary LU–ESR dates between 105 and 190 ka (Grün & Stringer 1991). In South Africa, two sites, Border Cave and Klasies River Mouth have been studied. At Border Cave, a long sequence of sediments contains teeth whose LU–ESR ages range from 31 ka (top) to 128 ka (bottom). The critical Howiesons Poort layer mid-way in the sequence gives ESR ages ranging from 45 ± 5 to 75 ± 5 ka (average = 62 ka) while amino-acid dates on this layer suggest an age of about 80 ka (Miller & Beaumont, this symposium). Skeletal remains of modern hominids were recovered from this site but most were found out of stratigraphic context. Specimen BC3, the buried partial skeleton of an infant, was apparently recovered from unit 4BS and would therefore have an age of about 70–80 ka (Grün *et al.* 1990*a*). Other specimens appear to correspond to younger layers.

At Klasies River Mouth, ESR ages were obtained on teeth from various strata. A modern hominid mandible had been recovered from the basal SAS layer. Subsamples of a mammalian tooth from this layer gave LU ages of 94 ± 10 and 88 ± 8 ka, consistent with U-series dates on a stalagmite that give an upper limit of 110 ka for the layer (Grün *et al.* 1990*b*). Younger ESR dates are found for the overlying layers at the site, ranging to about 40 ka.

In summary, these dates on modern hominids in African sites suggest that *Homo sapiens sapiens* was present on this continent early in the last glacial stage, and possibly during the last interglacial (stage 5). This is consistent with the dates obtained at sites in Israel and has contributed to a model of an African origin for this taxon.

5. Conclusions

The ESR method of dating as applied to tooth enamel has provided useful estimates for the ages of many of the critical anatomically modern hominid fossils in the time range from 50 to 150 ka. Thse dates have contributed to a new and longer chronology for the history of this taxon, and have helped to define the possible region of origin of our species. At the same time, ESR dates have confirmed the late Pleistocene chronology of Neanderthal hominids in western Europe (Grün & Stringer 1991; Schwarcz *et al.* 1991).

At present, the precision of the ESR ages ranges from 10 to 20% of the age, and is largely limited by uncertainties in the estimates of internal and external dose rates. Both of these are amenable of refinement, the former through U-series analyses, and the latter through the use of the isochron method.

Although all dates reported for hominid sites so far have been obtained on tooth enamel, we are now also able to obtain ESR dates on heated flint (Porat & Schwarcz 1991). Dates obtained from burned flints from the site of Kebara agree well with that obtained by TL on the same material at this site (Porat *et al.* 1992).

Acknowledgments

This research was partly funded by grants from the National Science Foundation, U.S.A. to the University of California (BNS 8801699, to F. C. Howell), and the Social Sciences and Humanities Research Council, Canada. We appreciate the encouragement of M. J. Aitken in the preparation of this manuscript, and his critical comments as well as those of C. B. Stringer.

REFERENCES

Blackwell, B. & Schwarcz, H.P. 1992 Electron spin resonance (ESR) isochron dating: solving the external gamma problem. *Appl. Rad. Isotopes* (In the press.)

Grün, R. 1989*a* Electron spin resonance (ESR) dating. Quat. Int. **1**, 65–109.

Grün, R., Beaumont, P. & Stringer, C.B. 1990*a* ESR dating evidence for early modern humans at Border Cave in South Africa. *Nature, Lond.* **344**, 537–539.

Grün, R., Shackleton, N.J. & Deacon, H. 1990*b* Electron spin resonance dating of tooth enamel from Klasies River Mouth Cave. *Curr. Anthropol.* **31**, 427–432.

Grün, R., Mellars, P. & Laville, H. 1991 ESR chronology of a 100,000 year archaeological sequence at Pech de l'Azé II, France. *Antiquity* **65**, 544–551.

Grün, R., Schwarcz, H.P. & Chadam, J. 1988 ESR dating of tooth enamel: Coupled correction for U-uptake and U-series disequilibrium. Nucl. Tracks Rad. Meas. **14**, 237–241.

Grün, R. & Schwarcz, H.P. 1987 Some remarks on 'ESR dating of bones'. *Ancient TL* **5**, 1–9.

Grün, R., Schwarcz, H.P. & Zymela, S. 1987 ESR dating of tooth enamel. *Can. J. Earth Sci.* **24**, 1022–1037.

Grün, R. & Stringer, C.B. 1991 Electron spin resonance dating and the evolution of modern humans. *Archaeometry* **33**, 153–199.

Ikeya, M. 1978 Electron spin resonance as a method of dating. *Archaeometry* **20**, 147–158.

Mellars, P. & Grün, R. 1991 A comparison of the electron spin resonance and thermoluminescence dating methods: the results of ESR dating at Le Moustier (France). *Cambr. Archaeol. J.* **1**, 269–276.

Porat, N., Schwarcz, H.P. & Bar-Yosef, O. 1992 ESR dating of burned flint from Kebara cave in the Carmel. *Ann. Mtg. Geol. Soc. Israel* (Abstract), pp. 114–115.

Porat, N. & Schwarz, H.P. 1991 ESR dating of chert. *Nucl. Tracks* **18**, 203–212.

Schwarcz, H.P., Bietti, A., Buhay, W.M., Stiner, M., Grün, R. & Segre, E. 1991 U-series and ESR age data for the Neanderthal site of Monte Circeo, Italy. *Curr. Anthropol.* **32**, 313–316.

Schwarcz, H.P., Buhay, W.M., Grün, R., Valladas, H., Tchernov, E., Bar-Yosef, O. & Vandermeersch, B. 1989 ESR dates for the Neanderthal site of Kebara, Israel. *J. archaeol. Sci.* **16**, 653–661.

Schwarcz, H.P., Grün, R., Vandermeersch, B., Bar-Yosef, O., Valladas, H. & Tchernov, E. 1988 ESR dates for the hominid burial site of Qafzeh in Israel. *J. hum. Evol.* **17**, 733–737.

Stringer, C.B., Grün, R., Schwarcz, H.P. & Goldberg, P. 1989 ESR dates for the hominid burial site of Es Skhul in Israel. *Nature, Lond.* **338**, 756–758.

Valladas, H., Joron, J.L., Valladas, G., Arensburg, B., Bar-Yosef, O., Belfer-Cohen, A., Goldberg, P., Laville, H., Meignen, L., Rak, Y., Tchernov, E., Tillier, A.M. & Vandermeersch, B. 1987 Thermoluminescence dates for the Neanderthal burial site at Kebara cave in Israel. *Nature, Lond.* **330**, 159–160.

Valladas, H., Reyss, J.L., Valladas, G., Bar-Yosef, O. & Vandermeersch, B. 1988

Thermoluminescence dates of Mousterian 'Proto-Cro-Magnon' remains from Israel and the origin of modern man. *Nature, Lond.* **331**, 614–616.

Vandermeersch, B. 1981 *Les hommes fossiles de Qafzeh, Israel.* Paris: CNRS.

Zeller, E.J. 1968 Use of electron spin resonance for measurement of natural radiation damage. In *Thermoluminescence of geological materials.* (ed. D.J. McDougall), pp. 271–279. London: Academic Press.

Pleistocene Geochronology and Palaeothermometry from Protein Diagenesis in Ostrich Eggshells: Implications for the Evolution of Modern Humans

Gifford H. Miller,[1,2] *Peter B. Beaumont,*[3] *A. J. T. Jull*[1,4] *and Beverly Johnson*[1,2]

Summary

Proteinaceous residues incorporated within the crystal structure of ostrich eggshells (OES) are retained without loss over geological time exceeding 10 million years. Degradation of the polypeptides, including hydrolysis to smaller peptide fragments and eventual release of free amino acids, decomposition, and racemization and epimerization occur at regular, predictable rates dependent on ambient temperature. The extent of isoleucine epimerization (aIle/Ile ratio) in OES follows linear first-order reversible kinetics in controlled-temperature laboratory simulations of time up to an aIle/Ile ratio in excess of 1.0. The hydrolysis of leucine also follows a predictable pattern, but deviates from first-order kinetics. A non-linear mathematical model has been developed that adequately describes the pattern of leucine hydrolysis through a wide temperature range. Arrhenius parameters were derived from laboratory experiments combined with rate constant values found for ^{14}C-dated OES from stratified caves in southern Africa. These parameters for isoleucine epimerization and leucine hydrolysis differ by *ca.* 10%, allowing the simultaneous solution of the two equations for temperature, independent of sample age. Although the uncertainty of the simultaneous temperature is relatively high (±10°C), it provides an effective means of identifying burned samples. If sample age is known, palaeotemperatures (the integrated thermal history experienced by an eggshell as opposed to an 'instantaneous' temperature) can be calculated with a precision of better than ±1°C.

The ages of levels at Border Cave, South Africa, from which anatomically modern human skeletal remains have been recovered, are dated by the extent of isoleucine epimerization in associated OES. The reaction is cali-

[1] Center for Geochronological Research, University of Colorado, Boulder, Colorado 80309-0450, U.S.A.

[2] Institute of Arctic and Alpine Research and Department of Geological Sciences, University of Colorado, Boulder, Colorado 80309-0450, U.S.A.

[3] McGregor Museum, P.O. Box 316, Kimberley 8300, South Africa

[4] NSF Regional Facility for Radioisotope Analysis, University of Arizona, Tucson, Arizona 85721, U.S.A.

brated in the upper levels by a series of concordant radiocarbon dates on charcoal at 38 ka before present (BP). The amino acid dates on deeper levels indicate that the Howiesons Poort stratum at Border Cave is more than 70 ka old, and that anatomically modern humans occupied the site as early as 100 ka ago.

1. INTRODUCTION

As the dates on the first appearance of anatomically modern humans have receded steadily backward in time to beyond the limits of the radiocarbon method, the need for additional techniques that can provide chronological information in the time range between about 30 ka and 200 ka has become increasingly apparent. Despite more than two decades of effort, and the rapid advances in conventional and accelerator mass spectrometry, no single technique has emerged that can reliably fill this temporal gap for most sites. For the foreseeable future, the best dating strategies are going to be those that combine a variety of independent methods, the results of which can be cross-checked at key stratigraphic horizons. The best results will be from those techniques that require sufficiently small samples that individual specimens can be dated.

One technique that has gained increasing attention in recent years is based on the epimerization of the protein amino acid isoleucine preserved within the calcite crystals of ostrich eggshells (OES). The integrity of the eggshell and the precision of the epimerization measurements have been addressed previously (Brooks *et al.* 1990). In this paper, we present new data that better define the temperature sensitivity of the epimerization reaction, derive the average temperature independent of sample age by simultaneous solution of the isoleucine epimerization and leucine hydrolysis reactions, and use this as an objective basis for identifying burnt eggshell. We conclude with a discussion of the implications of isoleucine epimerization ratios in OES recovered from archaeological excavations at Border Cave, South Africa.

2. MATERIALS AND METHODS

Ostrich eggshells were cleaned for amino acid analyses by physically removing the outer layers, followed by the removal of one-third of the sample with 2 N HCl. The naturally hydrolyzed fraction (free fraction) was prepared by digestion in 1 ml 7 N HCl per 50 mg of eggshell, followed by desiccation under vacuum and rehydration in weak HCl (pH 1.8). The total fraction (naturally occurring free amino acids plus those still peptide-bound) was prepared by digestion in 1 ml 7 N HCl per 50 mg of eggshell, followed by hydrolysis under N_2 at 110°C for 22 h in a forced-convection oven. After hydrolysis, excess HCl was removed under vacuum and the sample rehydrated with dilute (pH 1.8) HCl. In both free and total fractions the 7 N HCl was spiked with the non-protein amino acid norleucine (1.25 nmol mg^{-1} OES) to enable quantitative recovery of amino acids. Amino acid separation was by automated ion-exchange liquid chromatography followed by post-column derivitization with o-phthalaldehyde and fluorescence detection integrated electronically. Each analysis requires 0.2 mg of eggshell. All preparations were analysed at least twice, many were analysed three or more times. AIle/Ile ratios are based on the average ratio of peak heights as computed by the integrators. The aIle/Ile ratio for modern OES is 0.018. Leucine hydrolysis is based on peak areas normalized to the norleucine calibration spike. A standard amino acid protein hydrolysate, to which a known amount of D-alloisoleucine had been added, was included with each batch of 15 samples and used to judge instrumental errors. High-temperature simulations were carried out in forced-convection ovens continuously monitored by a precision thermometer.

Eggshell was prepared for radiocarbon dating by mechanical cleaning followed by removal of 50 to 90% of the remaining eggshell in 2 N HCl to minimize contamination by exchange with younger carbon. Cleaned OES were submitted to the Arizona facility where they were digested in phosphoric acid (85%); the released CO_2 was purified and then reduced to graphite. Details of the Arizona laboratory procedures are given by Linick $et\ al.$ (1986) and Donahue (1992).

3. Protein Diagenesis in Ostrich Eggshell

Dating methods must satisfy two broad prerequisites: a process is required that is dependent on time (radioactive decay, chemical reaction), and a medium must be available in which the initial conditions are known, and no subsequent uptake or loss of interfering molecules occurs. In this study we rely on two well documented reactions: (i) the racemization, or in the case of isoleucine, epimerization, reaction, by which the original protein L-amino acids invert to a mixture of D- and L-configurations; and (ii) the hydrolysis reaction, by which the bonds linking amino acids into peptide chains are cleaved, releasing free amino acids. The medium in this study is the ostrich eggshell, which satisfies the prerequisite for closed system behaviour with respect to peptides and amino acids to a degree not previously found in any other biomineralized remains (e.g. Brooks $et\ al.$ 1990).

(a) Isoleucine Epimerization

Although most amino acids can occur in two configurations, designated D- (right-handed) or L- (left-handed), only L-amino acids occur in most poly-

Table 1. *Calibration samples from which the Arrhenius parameters for isoleucine epimerization and initial leucine hydrolysis were derived*

(Ages of samples heated in the laboratory were directly measured; radiocarbon dates on all other samples were obtained by AMS ^{14}C dating of a fragment that was also analysed for the extent of protein diagenesis. Temperatures were monitored by precision thermometer for the heating experiments, and are based on the period of instrumentation for the nearest weather station for the archaeological sites unless otherwise indicated.)

site name	dated samples	Temp. (°C)	k_{Ile}	$\ln(k_{Ile})$ (avg)	$k_{Leu\ Hyd}$	$\ln(k_{Leu\ Hyd})$
lab. simulation	0.0006 to 0.007 years	161	2.11 e+2	5.35	1.112 e+2	4.71
lab. simulation	0.001 to 0.06 years	142.5	4.06 e+1	3.70	3.343 e+1	3.51
lab. simulation	0.02 to 0.8 years	110	2.05	0.718	2.363	0.86
Bir Tarfâwi[a]	7500 ± 80 years BP (AA-3292A)	29.5			7.667 e−5	−9.48
Heuningsneskrans	9675 ± 75 years BP (AA-6449)	21	1.25 e−5	−11.23	3.591 e−5	−10.23
	12 030 ± 139 years BP (AA-5829)	21	1.34 e−5			
	14 450 ± 105 years BP (AA-6450)	21	1.40 e−5			
Apollo 11 Cave	9290 ± 70 years BP (AA-6448)	20	1.35 e−5	−11.21	3.916 e−5	−10.15
	9150 ± 70 years BP (AA-5824)	20				
Elands Bay Cave	8110 ± 90 years BP (AA-5832)	18	6.83 e−6	−11.89	2.656 e−5	−10.50
	10 840 ± 70 years BP (AA-5833)	18				
	11 415 ± 80 years BP (AA-5834)	18				
Boomplass Cave	10 430 ± 80 years BP (AA-6958)	16.5	4.93 e−6	−12.22	no data	no data
Equus Cave[b]	11 870 ± 105 years BP (AA-5826)	16	5.34 e−6	−12.14	2.176 e−5	−10.74
	27 730 ± 340 years BP (AA-5827)					

[a] Owing to shallow depth of burial, this site has an effective temperature significantly higher than the current mean annual temperature (26.5°C). The effective temperature was calculated from the D/L ratio and radiocarbon age.

[b] The older sample has experienced glacial-age temperature reduction. However, the effective temperature, calculated from the D/L ratio and radiocarbon age, is not significantly different from the current site temperature.

peptides, including those within the OES. Isoleucine, a particularly stable protein amino acid, has two chiral carbon centres, and although racemization of L-isoleucine (L-Ile) could form the D-enantiomer (D-Ile), thermodynamics favours racemization about the alpha carbon only, creating D-alloisoleucine (D-aIle). The different physical and chemical properties of the diasteriomers allow rapid separation and precise quantification of the proportion of D-alloisoleucine to L-isoleucine (aIle/Ile) by high-pressure liquid chromatography; analytical uncertainty is generally better than ±1%. The aIle/Ile ratio increases from near zero in a modern eggshell to an equilibrium ratio of 1.30, by which time the inversion of L- to D-forms is balanced by the reverse reaction.

The extent of isoleucine epimerization in fossil eggshell is a function of sample age and the integrated thermal history experienced by the sample. Thus, although it is possible to use the aIle/Ile ratio directly as a measure of relative age for nearby sites for which the average temperatures are similar (less than 1°C difference), conversion of the epimerization ratio to absolute age requires an assessment of thermal history.

The dependency of the rate constant for isoleucine epimerization (k_{Ile}) on temperature is described by the Arrhenius equation:

$$k_{Ile} = A e^{(-E_a/RT)}, \tag{1}$$

where A is a constant, E_a is the energy of activation, R is the universal gas constant, and T is the effective temperature in Kelvin.

The Arrhenius parameters ($\ln(A)$ and E_a) can be derived empirically from high-temperature experiments where reaction rates in modern OES are monitored over specific time and temperature increments and from independently dated sites at ambient temperatures. In practice, laboratory simulations can be undertaken at temperatures between about 100 and 170°C, and natural samples no older than 12 ka are used to avoid uncertainties in the glacial–interglacial temperature change. We undertook laboratory simulations using modern OES at 110, 142.5 and 161°C, and have numerous radiocarbon-dated early Holocene samples with current mean annual temperatures ranging from 16 to 29°C (table 1).

Isoleucine epimerization obeys first-order reversible kinetics in modern OES heated at 142.5°C up to an aIle/Ile ratio close to 1.2 (figure 1), whereas it deviates from the linear kinetic model much earlier in similar experiments conducted on molluscan fossils (see, for example, Mitterer (1989), Kaufman (1992)). By plotting the rate constants derived from the high-temperature simulations and dated ambient temperature samples on an Arrhenius diagram (figure 2), the temperature sensitivity of the epimerization reaction is defined. From these parameters a single expression can be derived relating aIle/Ile (D/L) ratio to time (t) and temperature (T):

$$\ln\left(\frac{1 + D/L}{1 - 0.77\ D/L}\right) = 1.77\ t\left(e^{\left(40.23 - \frac{15152}{T}\right)}\right) + 0.032. \tag{2}$$

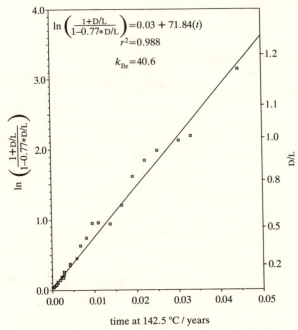

Figure 1. Measured aIle/Ile ratio in modern OES heated for specific time intervals at 142.5°C. Points are the mean of at least two different eggshell fragments at each temperature. Linear kinetics are approximated up to an aIle/Ile ratio of at least 1.2 (scale on right).

Arrhenius parameters have been reported previously for isoleucine epimerization in OES; Brooks *et al.* (1989) derived values of 30.01 kcal mol^{-1} (E_a) and 40.37 (ln(A)), whereas Miller (1992) reported values of 30.33 and 40.83, respectively. The current derivation (30.11, 40.23, respectively) incorporates the most complete set of dated control sites, and differs only slightly from the earlier determinations.

(b) Leucine Hydrolysis and Decomposition

Leucine, a protein amino acid only slightly less stable than isoleucine, hydrolyses more rapidly and thus offers better resolution in the early stages of diagenesis. The general pattern of leucine hydrolysis and decomposition in OES is shown in figure 3. Because the eggshell acts as a closed system, the decrease in total leucine over time is due strictly to decomposition, whereas the concentration of free leucine reflects the competition between the hydrolysis reaction, which releases free leucine from polypeptides, and the decomposition reaction. Initially, hydrolysis exceeds decomposition and

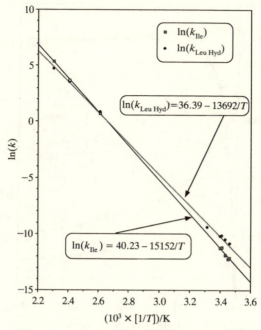

Figure 2. Arrhenius plot of isoleucine epimerization (k_{Ile}) and initial leucine hydrolysis ($k_{\mathrm{Leu\ Hyd}}$) based on high temperature simulations (e.g. figure 1) and radiocarbon-dated samples for which the current site temperature can be used as the long-term average (table 1). The difference in slope for the two reactions allows the simultaneous solution for temperature independent of time (figure 5).

the concentration of free leucine increases, but in the later stages of diagenesis (aIle/Ile>1.2), decomposition exceeds hydrolysis and the concentration of free leucine decreases steadily, although the proportion of free to total leucine continuously increases.

The rate of leucine hydrolysis initially follows linear irreversible first-order kinetics of this form:

$$\ln(\mathrm{Leu_B}/\mathrm{Leu_T}) = -k_{\mathrm{Leu}}t, \tag{3}$$

where $\mathrm{Leu_B}$ and $\mathrm{Leu_T}$ are the concentration of peptide-bound and total leucine respectively, k_{Leu} is the rate constant leucine hydrolysis and t is the time in years.

Based on the same series of experimental and natural samples as for epimerization (table 1), the Arrhenius parameters for the initial linear

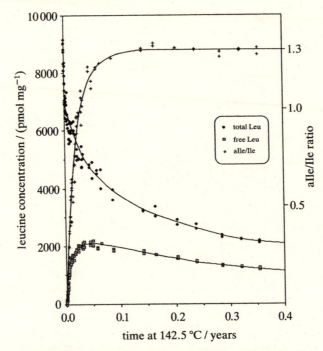

Figure 3. The observed decomposition (total Leu), leucine hydrolysis (expressed as the concentration of free leucine), and isoleucine epimerization (scale on right axis) in modern OES heated at 142.5°C. Each point represents a different eggshell fragment. The isoleucine epimerization reaction reaches equilibrium after about 0.15 years, whereas leucine hydrolysis continues, albeit at reduced rates, throughout the experiment.

portion of leucine hydrolysis (figure 2) are 27.21 kcal mol^{-1} (E_a) and 36.39 (ln(A)).

After the initial linear period the rate of leucine hydrolysis decreases. This deviation is due to the variable bonding strength between leucine and other amino acids in the original polypeptide chains. The observed hydrolysis rate (figure 4) is a composite of nearly 20 different rate constants, modulated by decomposition reactions. A nonlinear mathematical model (Appendix) defines an effective rate constant (k_{eff}) from which the observed nonlinear pattern of leucine hydrolysis for any temperature is given by:

$$\ln(\text{Leu}_B/\text{Leu}_T) = -k_{eff}t. \tag{4}$$

In figure 4, the predicted pattern of leucine hydrolysis (from equation (4)) is superimposed on observed leucine hydrolysis in modern OES heated for specific intervals at 142.5°C.

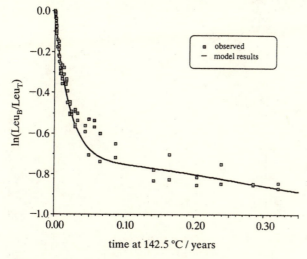

Figure 4. Leucine hydrolysis in modern OES heated at 142.5°C, expressed as the log of the peptide-bound leucine (Leu$_B$) divided by total leucine (Leu$_T$) plotted against heating time. The deviation from linear kinetics is due to the variable bonding strengths between leucine and adjacent amino acids in the peptide chain, modulated by decomposition reactions. The model results are based on equation (4).

(c) Simultaneous Temperatures

Because the activation energies for leucine hydrolysis (27.2 kcal mol^{-1} in both linear and extended models) and isoleucine epimerization (30.1 kcal mol^{-1}) differ by almost 10%, it is possible to solve the equations simultaneously and estimate the effective sample temperature directly from the extent of the two reactions, without knowledge of sample age (Appendix). To distinguish this temperature from that derived from the extent of epimerization or hydrolysis alone in a sample of known age, we define it as the simultaneous temperature. In figure 5, isotherms of simultaneous temperature are shown for a spectrum of possible aIle/Ile and ln(Leu$_B$/Leu$_T$) values.

Calculating the extent of leucine hydrolysis is inherently less precise than for isoleucine epimerization because it requires measuring naturally hydrolysed leucine (free fraction) in one portion of the eggshell, and the total amount of leucine in a different part of the same fragment. Reproducibility is ±7%, significantly less than for isoleucine epimerization (±1%). Consequently, the uncertainty in the simultaneous temperature solution has a coefficient of variation of about ±3% in the Kelvin temperature, or ±10°C for most sites. The simultaneous temperatures from OES in our high-

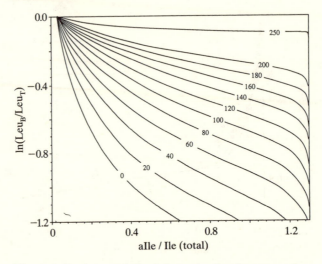

Figure 5. Isotherms derived from the simultaneous solution of the isoleucine epimerization and leucine hydrolysis reactions as described in the Appendix. Isotherms are labelled in °C.

temperature experiments and from OES in archaeological sites compare favorably to their known temperatures (table 2).

4. APPLICATIONS TO ARCHAEOLOGY

(a) *Resolving the Dilemma of Burnt Eggshell*

Ostrich eggshell is commonly associated with archaeological sites primarily because the egg was a food source, and to a lesser degree the eggshell was utilized for artistic and practical purposes. It is to be expected that the eggs were cooked, and after consumption of the egg, the eggshell may have been discarded near or into the hearth area. At many sites obvious examples of burnt OES occur, for which the temperatures were so high that polypeptides were reduced to elemental carbon. Because the rates of racemization, hydrolysis and decomposition are dependent on temperature, heating of the eggshell by humans will accelerate the extent of protein degradation, artificially 'ageing' the eggshell. In contrast, the act of cooking, even if the eggshell is placed directly in a fire, is not of sufficient duration or intensity to cause significant epimerization or hydrolysis (temperatures rarely exceed 100°C, and cooking time is less than one hour).

Although extreme heating is obvious from visual inspection, more subtly heated samples cannot be recognized by visible characteristics; the simultaneous temperature offers an objective criterion by which such samples

Table 2. *Comparison between simultaneous temperatures and known temperatures for high-temperature simulations and unburnt radiocarbon-dated late Quarternary ostrich eggshell*

site	experimental or site temperature (°C)	Ln(Leu$_B$/Leu$_T$)	aIle/Ile ratio(s)	number of samples	simultaneous temperature (°C)
lab. simulation	161	−0.075 to −0.547	0.11 to 1.09	20	149 ± 13
lab. simulation	142.5	−0.017 to −0.594	0.03 to 1.18	62	137 ± 8.5
lab. simulation	110	−0.014 to −0.782	0.04 to 1.14	32	98 ± 12
Apollo 11 Cave	20	−0.361 ± 0.026	0.144 ± 0.001	3	26 ± 5
Heuningsneskrans	21	−0.364 ± 0.003	0.141 ± 0.003	2	22 ± 1
	21	−0.427 ± 0.055	0.181 ± 0.003	2	28 ± 5
Elands Bay Cave	18	−0.233 ± 0.012	0.082 ± 0.009	3	17 ± 5
	18	−0.370 ± 0.001	0.115 ± 0.013	2	10 ± 7
Equus Cave	16	−0.292 ± 0.032	0.091 ± 0.005	4	11 ± 3

can be identified. From the isotherms in figure 5 it can be seen that the aIle/Ile ratio increases more rapidly relative to the extent of hydrolysis at higher temperatures than at lower temperatures. Consequently, epimerization should be more advanced than hydrolysis within eggshell discarded in a campfire and subjected to brief periods of relatively high temperature. Such fragments will have simultaneous temperatures well above the site temperature.

For example, four well-preserved eggshell fragments collected from each of two superimposed early Late Stone Age (ELSA) horizons (strata 2a and 3b) at Heuningsneskrans, South Africa, showed no visual indication of heating. The aIle/Ile ratios measured in two of the fragments from each level were in close agreement and an accelerator mass spectrometry (AMS) ^{14}C date on one of these fragments at each level (table 3) is consistent with the associated artifacts. In contrast, the other two fragments from each level gave inconsistent and much higher ratios; they may have been subtly heated or reworked from older levels. The simultaneous temperatures for each pair of fragments with low aIle/Ile ratios are similar to the site temperature, whereas the two other fragments have significantly higher simultaneous temperatures (table 3), implying that they experienced short-term heating. To test this conclusion, we subsequently submitted one of the 'heated' fragments from each level for AMS ^{14}C dating. The dates (table 3) confirm that the 'heated' samples are indeed of the same age as the OES with lower, concordant aIle/Ile ratios. A more subtle degree of heating is identifiable in stratum 3e within the same excavation where two eggshells had very different aIle/Ile ratios. The sample with lower aIle/Ile ratio has a simultaneous temperature similar to the current site temperature and an AMS ^{14}C of about 22 ka BP, whereas the sample with higher ratio has a simultaneous temperature more than 10°C higher, but a similar radiocarbon age (table 3). Apparently this sample has been slightly heated, causing the epimerization ratio to be more advanced than expected.

A different conclusion can be drawn from a series of OES excavated at the mouth of Apollo 11 Cave in Namibia (Wendt 1972, 1975a,b; figure 6), in which the different fragments from an ELSA level gave essentially identical aIle/Ile ratios, one of which has an AMS ^{14}C age of 9290 ± 70 years BP, but a fourth fragment had a much higher ratio (table 3). In this instance, all samples produced similar simultaneous temperatures, implying that the higher ratio cannot be explained by heating, and that it must have been reworked. Four OES from only slightly deeper in same excavation have aIle/Ile ratios and, with one exception, simultaneous temperatures similar to that of the outlier from the younger horizon; one fragment in this collection gave an AMS ^{14}C date of 41 200 ± 1650 years BP. To test whether the anomalously high aIle/Ile ratio in the ELSA horizon was reworked as indicated by its simultaneous temperature, rather than burnt, a piece of the

Table 3. *Isoleucine epimerization, leucine hydrolysis and derived simultaneous temperatures for* OES *from stratified sites in southern Africa, ordered by increasing simultaneous temperature within each stratum.* AMS ^{14}C *dates are on a portion of the same fragment for which amino acid analyses were completed*

T_{Simul} = site temperature (°C) as defined by the solution to the simultaneous temperature equation (see figure 5).
T_{Site} = current mean annual site temperature (°C) based on the arithmetic mean annual temperature extrapolated from the nearest weather station.

depth	stratum	laboratory identification	aIle/Ile	$\ln(\text{B/T})_{Leu}$	T_{Simul}	T_{Site}	AMS ^{14}C age BP
Heuningsneskrans (Honey Nest Cave), N.E. South Africa (P. B. Beaumont, unpublished data)							
69–122 cm	2a	AAL-6012C	0.144	−0.387	21	21	9675 ± 75 (AA-6649)
69–122 cm	2a	AAL-6012D	0.138	−0.362	23	21	
69–122 cm	2a	AAL-6012A	0.261	−0.428	52	21	9935 ± 75 (AA-8563)
69–122 cm	2a	AAL-6012B	0.567	−0.467	100	21	
221–259 cm	3b	AAL-6014A	0.184	−0.463	23	21	
221–259 cm	3b	AAL-6014C	0.178	−0.390	34	21	12 030 ± 130 (AA-5829)
221–259 cm	3b	AAL-6014D	0.851	−0.779	69	21	
221–259 cm	3b	AAL-6014B	0.529	−0.517	84	21	12 405 ± 90 (AA-8564)
373–434 cm	3e	AAL-6014B	0.254	−0.563	26	21	21 940 ± 230 (AA-6451)
373–434 cm	3e	AAL-6014C	0.388	−0.664	38	21	24 700 ± 250 (AA-8565)
Apollo 11 Cave, Namibia (Wendt 1972, 1975a,b)							
78–82 cm	D	AAL-5911C	0.145	−0.384	22	21	
78–82 cm	D	AAL-5911B	0.144	−0.367	25	21	
78–82 cm	D	AAL-5911A	0.144	−0.337	31	21	9290 ± 70 (AA-6448)
78–82 cm	D	AAL-5911D	0.365	−0.668	33	21	34 955 ± 775 (AA-8562)
87–93 cm	D	AAL-5912D	0.343	−0.660	30	21	
87–93 cm	D	AAL-5912A	0.346	−0.655	31	21	
87–93 cm	D	AAL-5912B	0.344	−0.590	41	21	41 200 ± 1650 (AA-5825)
87–93 cm	D	AAL-5912C	0.367	−0.576	47	21	

Lithostratigraphy			Industry	¹⁴C age	alle/Ile ratio	amino age
1	1BS	UP				
		LR.A				
		LR.B		38 ± 2	0.271 ± 0.018 (25)	*
		LR.C	ELSA			
	1WA			38–40	0.255 ± 0.022 (9)	*
2	2BS	UP	MSA 3b	>49	0.328 ± 0.022 (2)	47
		LR.A				
		LR.B				
		LR.C	MSA		0.388 ± 0.012 (18)	56
	2WA		3a		0.468 ± 0.018 (4)	69
3	3BS		MSA2 (H.P.)			
	3WA					
4	4BS/4WA				0.87 ± 0.11 (4)	145[1]
5	5BS		MSA1		0.87 ± 0.07 (7)	106[2]
	5WA					
6	6BS					

Figure 6. Summary of the stratigraphy at Border Cave, showing the mean aIle/Ile ratio in unburnt OES (number of analyses at each level given in parentheses), available radiocarbon dates, and the amino acid dates derived from the calibration in stratum 1. The two options for the age of stratum 4/5 is based on a maximum age model (1) and a minimum age model (2) as discussed in the text.

same fragment was subsequently dated by AMS ¹⁴C; its age, *ca.* 35 ka BP (table 3), confirms reworking. Note that the average simultaneous temperature for eggshell with aIle/Ile ratio at *ca.* 0.35 is 36 ± 7°C, suggesting that all five shells may have been slightly heated, possibly when more recent occupants built fires on top of the older deposits.

By deriving the simultaneous temperature from isoleucine epimerization and leucine hydrolysis it is possible to evaluate whether samples of mixed apparent age are caused by heating. As long as the heating was due to a brief interval of high temperature, the simultaneous temperature will be significantly above the mean annual site temperature.

(b) Geochronology

(I) CHRONOSTRATIGRAPHY

The extent of isoleucine epimerization can be used directly to provide a relative chronostratigraphic framework for a specific site, or for sites that are sufficiently close goegraphically that they can be considered to have experienced a similar thermal history (within 1°C). It is important to note in this regard, however, that depth of burial in open-air sites can influence the effective temperature of a sample. If the sample has been close to the surface, within the zone of high-amplitude annual temperature cycles (range greater than 12°C), there can be a significant acceleration of the diagenetic reactions (McCoy 1987; Miller 1992). Stratified cave sites, where seasonal and diurnal temperature fluctuations are highly attenuated, provide optimal samples for amino acid geochronology.

Isoleucine epimerization ratios in a series of OES from excavations at Border Cave, South Africa (figure 6) define a relative chronostratigraphy. Conclusions that can be drawn from these data, without evaluating temperature variations due to climate change, are (i) that there is no significant age difference between strata 1BS and 1WA, (ii) that stratum 2BS is significantly older than either 1BS or 1WA and (iii) that a long time interval separates stratum 4 from stratum 2, but that stratum 5 may not be much older than stratum 4.

(II) ABSOLUTE DATING

Converting the aIle/Ile ratios to absolute age requires a suitable calibration or evaluation of the thermal history. Unless there is a series of samples within the range of radiocarbon dating, from which the glacial/interglacial temperature changes can be assessed, it is preferable to use the calibration technique. The conversion of aIle/Ile ratios to age at Border Cave is described in § 5.

(c) Palaeothermometry

Although the simultaneous temperature provides an estimate of average site temperature, the lack of precision (± 10°C) limits its application beyond identification of heated eggshells. If the age of a sample is known, it is possible to compute the average, or effective temperature experienced by the sample with reasonable precision from the aIle/Ile ratio. This temperature differs from most other palaeotemperature estimates in that it is an integration of the entire thermal history since the egg was laid, as opposed to instantaneous temperatures derived from faunal or floral assemblages. Where several independently dated strata occur, it is possible to compute the average site temperature between dated horizons. If these temperatures are expressed as differences between intervals (ΔT), then a precision of $\pm 1°C$ is attainable, whereas the accuracy of absolute temperature estimate is somewhat less ($\pm 3°C$; McCoy 1987).

5. DATING THE EARLIEST OCCURRENCE OF MODERN HUMANS

Anatomically modern human skeletal material beyond the range of radiocarbon dating has been recovered in stratigraphic context from caves in southern Africa. The common association of OES with human occupation sites, and the potential of the isoleucine epimerization in OES to provide chronological information, offers the possibility of dating the first appearance of anatomically modern humans at these sites.

Excavations at Border Cave, South Africa, revealed alternating strata of powdery brown sandy silts (BS) and white-black ash (WA), with a cumulative thickness of about 4 m. Based on typological and morphometric studies three major phases of the Middle Stone Age (MSA 1, 2, 3) and a very early manifestation of the ELSA have been identified (Beaumont 1980). Partial human skeletons (individuals designated BC1–5) have been recovered during excavations at the cave. BC1, BC2, and various postcranial pieces were recovered out of stratigraphic context in 1940–1941 (Cooke *et al.* 1945), but matrix in the interstices of one skull (BC1) only matched the sediments at the base of stratum 4BS (Beaumont 1980). Subsequent excavation in 1941 produced a largely complete infant skeleton (BC3) associated with a perforated *Conus* shell, in a shallow grave cut from within the upper 4BS and certainly older than stratum 3 (Cooke *et al.* 1945; Beaumont 1973, 1980). BC5, a nearly complete adult mandible with four teeth, was found more recently at the base of stratum 3WA (Howiesons Poort level; Beaumont 1980; De Villiers 1976). Most researchers, but not all (e.g. van Vark *et al.* 1989), have attributed all of these remains to modern *Homo sapiens*, although the precise provenance of some bones remains contentious.

The aIle/Ile ratio was measured at least twice in 146 preparations of OES fragments excavated from Border Cave that did not appear to be burnt on visual inspection. Of these, 16 had been so severely heated that amino acids were absent, and a further eight had such low levels of amino acids that severe heating must have occurred. Simultaneous temperatures could be calculated for 51 fragments (only total amino acid analyses were completed for the remainder). Of these, 19 had simultaneous temperatures more than 15°C above the site temperature, and are consequently rejected as burnt. In all cases, these samples also contained aIle/Ile ratios higher than expected. The aIle/Ile ratios in unburnt, un-reworked OES show a clear increase with increasing stratigraphic age (figure 6). We were unable to locate any unburnt OES from stratum 3BS (MSA 2) containing hominid remains and lithic pieces of the Howiesons Poort industry. The underlying strata 4WA,

5BS and 5WA (MSA 1) contained occasional OES fragments, most of which were burnt. Insufficient unburnt fragments were available from the deeper strata (stratum 6 (MSA 1)) to provide chronological information.

Twelve new radiocarbon dates on wood charcoal from strata 1BS averaging 38 ± 2 ka BP (J. Vogel and P. Beaumont, unpublished data) calibrate the epimerization rate at Border Cave. The mean aIle/Ile based on 34 separate measurements of OES from these two units is 0.266 ± 0.020; the corresponding rate constant (k_{Ile}) is 6.438 × 10^{-6}. An AMS ^{14}C date on one of these eggshell fragments is 36.1 ± 0.9 ka BP (AA-4254), confirming that the eggshell is of the same age as the associated charcoal. Because this calibrated rate constant incorporates almost equal parts of the Holocene warm period (0 to 10 ka BP), the temperature depression of the last glacial maximum (*ca.* 13–25 ka BP) and intermediate temperatures of the intervening interstadials, we argue that it can be used to date samples between *ca.* 30 and 80 ka old, but for older levels the temperature may have deviated from the average of the last 40 ka, particularly for samples from the last interglacial. Using the calibrated rate constant and an uncertainty of ±10%, the age of stratum 2BS is 47 ± 7 ka BP at the top and 56 ± 6 ka BP at its base, and stratum 2WA is 69 ± 7 ka BP.

For samples older than 80 ka, the prolonged warmth of the last interglacial (*sensu lato*; 130 to 75 ka ago), may yield a higher effective temperature than for younger samples. To address this uncertainty we propose two models, a minimum age model that assumes the average temperature between about 80 and 130 ka (isotope stage 5) was continuously the same as the Holocene (19.5°C), and a maximum age model in which we assume that the average rate constant for the last 40 ka is valid for the entire Pleistocene. It is almost certain that the actual thermal history lies between these two extremes. Stratum 3 (Howiesons Poort) is bracketed between 69 ± 7 ka BP and 106 ± 11 ka BP, the minimum age of underlying stratum 4. The MSA 1 levels at Border Cave were deposited at least 100 ka ago (minimum age model), and possibly predate the last interglacial (linear extrapolation from the ELSA calibration).

6. DISCUSSION AND CONCLUSIONS

The integrity of the ostrich eggshell, retaining indigenous organic molecules and excluding the immigration of secondary amino acids, results in a predictable pattern of protein diagenesis in which the extent of the various reactions is dependent on the age of the sample and the effective diagenetic temperature. The extent of isoleucine epimerization in OES can be used directly as relative age indices, and with suitable calibration, can be converted to absolute age with an accuracy of *ca.* ±10% back to at least 80 ka, and with less precision to 500 ka. The simultaneous solution for temperature from the isoleucine epimerization and leucine hydrolysis reactions provides an effective means of differentiating subtly burned OES from those that have been reworked from deeper levels. Burnt eggshell occurs at most sites, often amounting to one-third to one-half of all samples, but reworked pieces, from both younger and older levels, are also common, indicating that despite meticulous sampling procedures, some faunal elements in any horizon may not be in place.

The significance of the four hominid specimens recovered from the MSA levels at Border Cave has been much debated, at least in part due to uncertainties in the dating of the stratigraphic sequence. Recent datings by electron spin resonance (ESR) using tooth enamel have been reported for Border Cave (Grün et al. 1989). The ESR dates for Border Cave are consistently younger than the amino acid dates (except for units 4WA and 5BS where the two methods agree); for stratum 1, the ESR dates are about 30% younger than the radiocarbon dates. Because we calibrate the isoleucine epimerization rate using the radiocarbon dates from stratum 1, we cannot independently evaluate the discrepancy between the ESR and amino acid dates. Although paired ^{14}C and U-series dates are not yet available prior to 30 ka (Bard et al. 1991), the magnitude of the carbon reservoir is so large that it is improbable that the ^{14}C production rate could change in such a way that a radiocarbon age of 38 ka BP could have a calendar age of 28 ka as predicted by the ESR dates; we suggest that the ESR dates have a systematic error that underestimates the accumulated dose and/or overestimates the annual dose rate.

Based on the calibrated amino acid dates (figure 6) Border Cave skeleton BC5 is older than 70 ka, whereas BC3 and BC1 (if its association with level 4BS.LR is correct) are presumably at least 100 ka old, and probably date from the early to middle period in the last interglacial. These conclusions support the contention of an African origin for *Homo sapiens*.

ACKNOWLEDGMENTS

Amino acid analyses were performed at the University of Colorado with financial support from the U.S. National Science Foundation (BNS-9010622) and the University of Colorado. We thank Brenden Roark, Leslie Bracewell and Richard Ernst for assistance with sample preparation and analyses. Excavations at Border Cave were supported by a grant from the Anglo-American and De Beers Chairman's Fund. Ostrich eggshell and supporting stratigraphic observations from Apollo 11 Cave were generously supplied by W. E. Wendt; additional OES used in the calibration of the reactions was supplied by John Parkington (Elands Bay Cave), Hilary Deacon (Boomplaas Cave) and Tim Dalby (modern OES from South Africa); other samples were collected by the authors. We extend our sincere thanks to these individuals for supplying the material upon which this work is based. We also thank P. E. Hare, D. S. Kaufman, and A. Brooks for helpful discussions, and RSES, Australian National University, for assistance in manuscript preparation.

REFERENCES

Bard, E., Hamlin, B., Fairbanks, R.G. & Zindler, A. 1990 Calibration of the ¹⁴C timescale over the past 30,000 years using mass spectrometric U-Th ages from Barbados corals. *Nature, Lond.* **345**, 405–410.

Beaumont, P.B. 1973 Border Cave, a progress report *S. Afr. J. Sci.* **69**, 41–46.

Beaumont, P.B. 1980 On the age of the Border Cave hominids 1–5. *Paleont. Afr.* **23**, 21–33.

Brooks, A.S., Hare, P.E., Kokis, J.E., Miller, G.H., Ernst, R.D. & Wendorf, F. 1990 Dating Pleistocene archeological sites by protein diagenesis in ostrich eggshell. *Science, Wash.* **248**, 60–64.

Cooke, H.B.S., Malan, B.D. & Welss, L.H. 1945 Fossil man in the Lebombo Mountains, South Africa: the "Border Cave", Ingwavuma district, Zululand. *Man* **45**, 6–13.

De Villiers, H. 1976 A second adult human mandible from Border Cave, Ingwavuma district, KwaZulu, South Africa. *S. Afr. J. Sci.* **72**, 212–215.

Donahue, D. 1992 Measurements of radiocarbon ages at the University of Arizona Accelerator Mass Spectrometer Facility. *Proc. Beijing Int. Conf. AMS, Beijing, 1990.* (In the press.)

Grün, R., Beaumont, P.B. & Stringer, C. 1990 ESR dating evidence for early modern humans at Border Cave in South Africa. *Nature, Lond.* **344**, 537–539.

Kaufman, D.K. 1992 Aminostratigraphy of Pliocene-Pleistocene high-sea-level deposits, Nome coastal plain and adjacent nearshore area, Alaska. *Geol. Soc. Am. Bull.* **104**, 40–52.

Linick, T.W., Jull, A.J.T., Toolin, L.J. & Donahue, D.J. 1986 Operation of the NSF-Arizona accelerator facility for radioisotope analysis and results from selected collaborative research projects. *Radiocarbon* **28**, 522–533.

McCoy, W.D. 1987 The precision of amino acid geochronology and paleothermometry. *Quat. Sci. Rev.* **6**, 43–54.

Miller, G.H. 1992 Chronology of hominid occupation at Bir Tarfawi and Bir Sahara East, based on the epimerization of isoleucine in ostrich eggshells. In *Archaeology of the Bir Tarfawi and Bir Sahara East depressions* (ed. A. E. Close & F. Wendorf). (In the press.)

Mitterer, R.M. & Kriausakul, N. 1989 Calculation of amino acid racemization ages based on apparent parabolic kinetics. *Quat. Sci. Rev.* **8**, 353–358.

van Vark, G.N., Bilsborough, A. & Kijkema, J. 1989 *Anthrop. Prèhist.* **100**, 43.

Wendt, W.E. 1972 Preliminary report on an archaeological research programme in South West Africa. *Cimbebasia* (B) **2**, 1–61.

Wendt, W.E. 1975a 'Art mobiler' aus der Apollo 11-Grotte in Südwest-Afrika: Die ältesten datierten Kunstwerke Afrikas. *Acta Praehist. Arch.* **5** (1974), 1–42.

Wendt, W.E. 1975b Die älteste datierten Kunstwerke Afrikas. *Bild Wiss.* **10**, 44–50.

APPENDIX: SIMULTANEOUS TEMPERATURE EQUATION

A mathematical expression defining the changing rate constant for leucine hydrolysis over time was derived empirically from the 142.5°C experiment (figure 4), then adjusted for temperature by comparing predicted and observed rates of leucine hydrolysis at other temperatures. The equation below defines an effective rate constant (k_{eff}) that is applicable to all temperatures between *ca.* 0 and 170°C.

$$k_{eff} = ac(0.685e^{(-1.9atb)} + 0.43e^{(-0.43atb)} + 0.145e^{(-0.06atb)}), \quad (A1)$$

where

$a = e^{(36.39-13692/T)}$, the rate of initial Leu hydrolysis from equation 3 and figure 2

$b = 2.29 + [(9.774 \times 10^{-4} \times T) - (9.74 \times 10^{-6} \times T^2)]$

$c = 1.34 - (8.16 \times 10^{-4} \times T)$

T = the effective diagenetic temperature (Kelvin)

t = time in years

and leucine hydrolysis is then defined by equation (4).

Equation 2 describes the relation between aIle/Ile ratio, time and temperature. Solving equation (2) for t yields:

$$t = \frac{\ln((1 + D/L)/(1 - 0.77 \times D/L) - 0.032}{1.77 \times e^{(40.23 - (15152/T))}}. \quad (A2)$$

Substituting equation (A2) into equation (4) and solving for T results in a single expression in which the only variables are aIle/Ile and (Leu_B/Leu_T), both of which may be measured, allowing a value for T to be determined (the simultaneous temperature) without knowledge of sample age.

Evolution of Modern Humans: Evidence From Nuclear DNA Polymorphisms

Joanna L. Mountain,[1] *Alice A. Lin,*[1] *Anne M. Bowcock*[2]
and L. Luca Cavalli-Sforza[1]

SUMMARY

Previously we have described studies of the evolution of modern humans based upon data for classical genetic markers and for nuclear DNA polymorphisms. Such polymorphisms provide a different point of view regarding human evolution than do mitochondrial DNA sequences. Here we compare revised dates for major migrations of anatomically modern humans, estimated from archaeological data, with separations suggested by a genetic tree constructed from classical marker allele frequencies. Analyses of DNA polymorphisms have now been extended and compared with those of classical markers; genetic trees continue to support the hypothesis of an initial African and non-African divergence for modern humans. We have also begun testing non-human primates for a set of human DNA polymorphisms. For most polymorphisms tested so far, humans share a single allele with other primates; such shared alleles are likely to be ancestral. Populations living in humid tropical environments have significantly higher frequencies of ancestral alleles than do other populations, supporting the hypothesis that natural selection acts to maintain high frequencies of particular alleles in some environments.

1. INTRODUCTION

Although genetic data have recently begun to play an important role in clarifying our understanding of the evolution of modern humans, results derived from currently available data are far from conclusive. While mitochondrial DNA (mtDNA) data are being generated at a rapid rate, the mitochrondrial genome represents only a small fraction of an individual's genetic material and may not be representative of the whole. Allele frequencies for 'classical' nuclear genetic markers (blood group, protein, and HLA polymorphisms) are available for thousands of human populations, but these markers are very few. Although nuclear DNA polymorphisms are much more numerous, they have been tested on a limited scale, for only a

[1] Department of Genetics, Stanford University, Stanford, California 94305, U.S.A.
[2] Department of Pediatrics, University of Texas Southwestern Medical Center, Dallas, Texas 75235, U.S.A.

69

few populations. For these reasons, among others, current genetic data sets often fail to provide answers to any but the most simple of hypotheses. Additional data, along with novel approaches to data analysis, are beginning to provide more robust conclusions, as well as insight into more complex issues.

One means of evaluating the robustness of results is to examine consistency among various data sets, both genetic and non-genetic (i.e. archaeological, paleoanthropological, linguistic, etc.). Consistency between data sets is examined here for two cases. First, separation points of a genetic tree are compared with dates of human migrations estimated from archaeological data. Second, genetic distances and tree topologies estimated from two independent genetic data sets are examined.

A new perspective on human DNA polymorphisms is provided by data on non-human primates. Testing of human DNA polymorphisms in primates reveals a high degree of sharing among the species and indicates that humans are more closely related to chimpanzees than they are to any other species. Frequencies of the alleles shared by humans and chimpanzees, assumed to be ancestral, provide insight into evolutionary rates within human populations. In addition, distributions of ancestral allele frequencies in different populations indicate that natural selection may have acted on some loci.

2. Classical Markers

(a) Tree of 42 Populations

Previously we published a tree relating forty-two aboriginal populations according to genetic differences (Cavalli-Sforza et al. 1988). These differences, called genetic distances, were estimated using population frequencies for 120 alleles associated with 44 polymorphisms. The data represent an abstraction of a large collection of classical marker allele frequencies (Cavalli-Sforza et al. 1993). A condensed version of the genetic tree is shown in figure 1. The first split in this tree separates Africans from non-Africans, lending support to the hypothesis that humans originated in Africa, and spread from there throughout the rest of the world. The second split separates southeast Asians and Pacific Islanders from northeast Asians, Caucasoids, and Amerindians, suggesting two main migrations into Asia. This tree was compared to a classification of languages; a test of significance demonstrated that there is a highly significant correlation between genetic and linguistic evolution (Cavalli-Sforza et al. 1992).

(b) Comparison With Archaeological Data

Major separations in this tree can be compared to dates of human migrations, estimated from archaeological data (see Cavilli-Sforza et al. (1988)

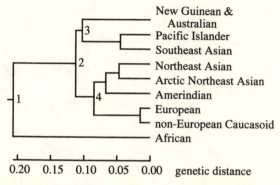

Figure 1. Condensed version of a genetic tree for 42 aboriginal populations (see Cavalli-Sforza *et al.* 1988). Each of the nine populations represents many samples. The tree was constructed according to the average linkage algorithm (Sokal *et al.* 1958) from F_{ST} genetic distances (Reynolds *et al.* 1983) based on frequencies of 120 alleles associated with 44 classical markers (blood group, HLA, and protein polymorphisms). Numbers indicate nodes comparable with those of figure 4*a*.

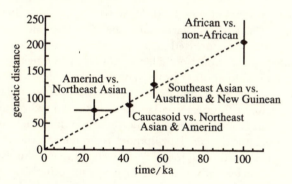

Figure 2. Graphical comparison of genetic distances and dates of early intercontinental migrations of anatomically modern humans, estimated from archaeological data. Genetic distances are those suggested by the tree of figure 1, $\times 10^3$. Standard errors for these distances were obtained from 100 bootstraps of the genetic distances (Efron 1982). Dates are given in ka. The date for migration to the Americas is given as a range (15–35 ka BP). The dashed line passes through both the origin and the weighted average of the three points other than that representing migration into America.

and figure 2). Anatomically modern humans are assumed to have migrated from Africa roughly 100 ka ago (Braüer 1989; Clark 1989; Stringer 1990). Expansion from southeast Asia to Australia and New Guinea is assumed to have taken place approximately 55 ka ago (Roberts *et al.* 1990), and migration of modern humans into Europe is assumed to have taken place about 43 ka ago (Straus 1989). The ratio of genetic distance (G) to time (T, in years) for these three events is roughly constant ($G/T = 2.07 \pm 0.15$). While no time scale is provided by the genetic tree, consistency between the archaeological and genetic data lends support to the hypothesis that the genetic tree corresponds roughly to the evolution of human populations over the last 100 ka.

The time of the first migration of modern humans to the Americas remains controversial; although estimates range from 15 ka to 35 ka before present (BP) (Fagan 1987), these genetic data support a date at the upper end of that range (figure 2). The more detailed set of nuclear genetic data agree with the three major migrations suggested by Greenberg (Cavalli-Sforza *et al.* 1993). MtDNA restriction site data have recently confirmed two of the major migrations leading to the peopling of the Americas (Torroni *et al.* 1992).

3. DNA Markers: Comparisons of Human Populations

Over the past ten years new methods for detecting genetic differences have been developed. These detect variation at the DNA sequence level, whether or not this variation is expressed at the peptide or protein level. One such method involves the comparison of lengths of DNA fragments; individuals may differ from one to another in the lengths of specific fragments. Thousands of these restriction fragment length polymorphisms (RFLPS) are currently available for testing. A second method involves a technique called the polymerase chain reaction (PCR). While sequence data such as those analysed for mitochondria can be obtained for nuclear genes, nuclear sequence data are more difficult to interpret at the intraspecific level because, unlike mtDNA, nuclear DNA undergoes frequent recombination. The resulting gene tree is therefore more complex, being reticulated (Hudson 1991). Instead, allele frequencies for DNA polymorphisms are usually employed to measure genetic variation across human populations.

(a) Data for Eight Populations

Previously we described a study of 100 DNA polymorphisms in five aboriginal populations (Bowcock *et al.* 1991*a*). Although based on a small number of population samples, the analysis improved on earlier studies of classical markers because a larger number of genetic markers were analysed: it has been shown that the number of independent markers is extremely important in obtaining accurate estimates of genetic distances and in tree reconstruction (Astolfi & Cavalli-Sforza 1981; Nei 1987). The populations considered were Pygmies of the Central African Republic (C.A.R.) and of Zaire, Melanesians of the Bougainville Islands, Chinese, and northern Europeans. This study is currently being extended to include additional populations. To date 80 of the 100 DNA polymorphisms mentioned above have been tested in the five populations, plus Japanese, Australians, and New Guineans. Allele frequency data for these three populations are to be published elsewhere.

(b) Comparison of Genetic Distances

Genetic distances, calculated using a standardised measure of the variance of gene frequencies, F_{ST} (Reynolds et al. 1983), were compared with distances between similar samples calculated from classical marker data (figure 3). While the points are expected to fall along a straight line, they deviate substantially: the Melanesians, Australians, and New Guineans are relatively more distant from Japanese and Chinese populations according

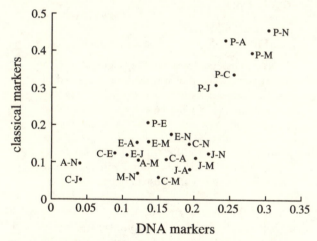

Figure 3. Comparison of two sets of genetic distances among seven populations. Classical marker distances were estimated from frequencies of 120 alleles associated with 44 blood group, protein, and HLA polymorphisms (Cavalli-Sforza et al. 1988). DNA distances were estimated from allele frequencies for 80 of the 100 nuclear DNA polymorphisms described by Bowcock et al. (1991a). A, Australians; C, Chinese; E, Europeans; J, Japanese; M, Melanesians; N, New Guineans; P, Zairean Pygmies.

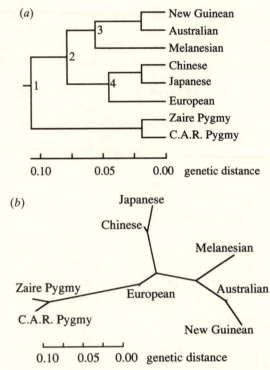

Figure 4. Genetic trees relating eight aboriginal populations. Each tree was constructed based on genetic distances estimated from allele frequencies for 80 nuclear DNA markers. Two methods of reconstruction were employed. (*a*) Average linkage, or UPGMA (Sokal *et al.* 1958); and (*b*) neighbour-joining (Saitou & Nei 1987). The former assumes a constant evolutionary rate. Numbers in (*a*) indicate nodes comparable with those in figure 1.

to the DNA data than they are according to the classical marker data. This may be due in part to differences in population samples. The Chinese population sample for the DNA study, for instance, includes both northern and southern Chinese, while the classical marker sample includes only southern Chinese.

The deviations may also be an indication that more markers are necessary to obtain valid estimates of genetic distance; 44 polymorphisms were considered for the classical marker study, while 80 were considered for the DNA marker study. Furthermore, sample sizes for classical markers are much larger than those for DNA polymorphisms. A larger number of markers plus increased sample sizes should lead to smaller standard errors for estimates of genetic distances, and consequently to greater consistency between independent studies.

(c) Tree of Eight Populations

An average linkage tree (Sokal & Michener 1958) relating the eight populations was constructed based on the genetic distances estimated from allele frequencies for 80 DNA polymorphisms. The tree (figure 4a) indicates an initial separation of Africans and non-Africans, followed by a separation of Melanesians, Australians and New Guineans from Japanese, Chinese, and Europeans. While the population samples tested for these 80 markers differ somewhat from those tested for classical markers, common components of the two trees can be compared (figures 1, 4a). Although branch lengths differ, all four possible divergences which can be compared occur in an identical order, indicating a high degree of consistency for the two data sets at this level of resolution. In particular, the greatest degree of divergence is between Africans and non-Africans. Thus, differences between genetic distance estimates are too small to translate into different tree topologies.

(d) European Admixture

These nuclear DNA data are inconsistent with the bifurcating, constant rate model of the evolution of human populations; Europeans are much closer genetically to the Africans than are any of the other non-African populations, whereas all non-African populations are expected to be equidistant from the Africans if the evolutionary history suggested by the tree of figure 4a is reasonably accurate. The discrepancy becomes apparent through construction of a tree using a method which does not assume a constant evolutionary rate (figure 4b). The method, called 'neighbour-joining', finds the shortest tree representing the genetic distances among the populations. The position of the European population in this tree differs from that in the average linkage tree (figure 4a) and the branch length leading to Europeans is extremely short. Such a short branch can arise when one population has been formed as an admixture of two or more others. The previous study of five populations indicated that Europeans arose as an admixture of ancestral Africans and ancestral Asians (Bowcock et al. 1991b). Other hypotheses may also be consistent with this tree structure; evidence against the hypothesis that the short branch length is due to a lower evolutionary rate among Europeans is presented below.

4. Comparison with Other Primates

In order to place the human gene frequencies into a broader context, we have begun testing other primate species (chimpanzee, gorilla, and orangutan) for the same set of DNA polymorphisms as has been tested in the human populations. Humans have been found to share a polymorphism (at least two shared alleles at a genetic locus) with one of these closely related species in only two cases; they share one polymorphism with chimpanzees and another with orangutans. For many other polymorphisms, however, humans share exactly one allele with other primates. These shared alleles indicate sequence similarity for a small stretch of DNA. Considering only those 71 polymorphisms for which all three of the non-human primate species have been tested, in 57 out of 71 cases chimpanzees and humans share a single allele, in 39 cases gorillas and humans share one allele, and in 41 out of 71 cases orangutans and humans share one allele.

(a) Tree of Primate Species

Although these polymorphisms were initially detected in humans, and are therefore a biased sample, the number of cases of shared alleles provides some insight into primate evolution. Given that chimpanzees and humans share more alleles, humans and chimpanzees are significantly more closely related to each other than humans and gorillas ($\chi^2 = 10.4$, 1 d.f., $p < 0.005$) or humans and orangutans ($\chi^2 = 8.4$, 1 d.f., $p < 0.005$). These data therefore represent some of the strongest evidence available in support of the hypothesis that humans and chimpanzees are more closely related to each other than either is to any other species (Goodman et al. 1989; Tajima 1992). Furthermore, given that gorillas and orangutans share similar numbers of alleles (although often different alleles) with humans, a tree placing these two species in separate clusters is most consistent with the data.

(b) Ancestral Alleles

We have reexamined the frequencies within the human populations for those alleles shared with chimpanzees. For 60 out of 80 polymorphisms studied for all eight human populations, chimpanzees share a single allele with humans. These 60 alleles are assumed to have existed from the time of the separation of ancestral humans and ancestral chimpanzees, and to represent the ancestral alleles at their respective genetic loci. Mean frequencies of these 60 ancestral alleles for each population were calculated (table 1). The standard error estimates are inappropriate for assessing the significance of differences between the populations: they encompass not only variation between populations but also variation between markers. A more appropriate approach to the question of whether mean frequencies differ significantly among populations is an analysis of variance. The results of this analysis (table 2) indicate that the frequencies of ancestral alleles differ very significantly from population to population ($p < 0.005$).

Table 1. *Mean frequencies, for each of eight populations, of 60 alleles present among both humans and chimpanzees*

(Shared alleles are assumed to be the ancestral at their respective loci. Populations are listed in decreasing order of mean frequency. See text for discussion of standard errors (s.e.).)

population	mean frequency ± s.e.
Zaire Pygmies	0.648 ± 0.038
C.A.R. Pygmies	0.618 ± 0.039
Melanesians	0.578 ± 0.046
New Guineans	0.564 ± 0.046
Europeans	0.563 ± 0.035
Australians	0.560 ± 0.042
Japanese	0.545 ± 0.042
Chinese	0.534 ± 0.039

This implies, at the very least, that the two Pygmy populations have significantly higher frequencies of ancestral alleles than do the two Asian populations.

(c) *Distributions of Ancestral Allele Frequencies*

To further explore the differences among human populations, histograms of the ancestral allele frequencies were plotted for each (figure 5). The variation among mean frequencies of ancestral alleles, as shown in table 1 and evaluated in table 2, is reflected in these histograms. Some populations have a very uneven distribution, with many ancestral alleles in the highest class (frequencies of 90–100%). Figure 5a,b represents histograms which deviate significantly from equality; a larger proportion of ancestral alleles have high

Table 2. *Comparison of means of 60 ancestral allele frequencies across eight populations.*

(Analysis of variance was carried out after angular transformation of the allele frequencies (Sokal & Rohlf 1969). Mean frequencies for each population are given in table 1.)

source	d.f.	mean square	F-test	P value
Among alleles	59	0.9688	17.653	< 0.0001
Among populations	7	0.1633	3.080	0.0036
residual	413	0.0530		
total	479			

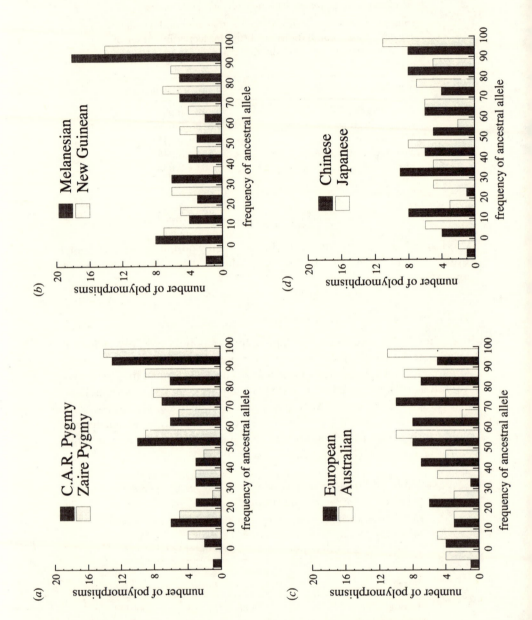

frequencies in these populations (C.A.R. Pygmies, Zaire Pygmies, Melanesians, and New Guineans) than in the remaining four populations (Australians, Europeans, Japanese, and Chinese, figure 5*c,d*).

5. DISCUSSION

(*a*) Dates for Origin of Modern Humans

DNA polymorphisms are currently being examined in a number of aboriginal human populations. Although genetic distances estimated from data for the eight populations discussed here differ from those estimated from classical marker data, the resulting genetic trees are similar. Both indicate an initial separation between Africans and non-Africans. The suggestion of an African origin for humans could reflect a migration out of Africa either 1–1.5 Ma ago, 100 ka ago, or both. Nuclear genetic data alone provide no timescale. Internal calibration can be carried out, however, through comparison with archaeological data. Classical polymorphisms indicate a correlation between genetic and archaeological data sets, lending support to the hypothesis that the migration out of Africa corresponds to the more recent date.

In this analysis Africans are represented by two African Pygmy populations. Two factors, however, suggest that the Pygmy populations are reasonably representative. First, one of these two Pygmy populations, that of the Central African Republic, is known to be highly mixed with non-Pygmy Africans. Despite this level of admixture, the two Pygmy populations cluster fairly closely in the inferred trees. Second, many more African populations have been studied for classical nuclear polymorphisms such as blood groups. These data indicate that while African Pygmies differ somewhat, genetically, from other sub-saharan African populations, they cluster with them in the inferred trees. Bushmen may be slightly more different from other sub-saharan African populations than Pygmies, but they still cluster with them (Cavalli-Sforza *et al.* 1988). In any case, additional African

◄

Figure 5. Histograms recording, for each of eight populations, the number of ancestral alleles with frequencies in each of 11 classes. Alleles shared with chimpanzees are considered ancestral. The first class includes only alleles with frequencies of 0%. All other classes represent alleles with frequencies in a 10% range (0–10%, 10–20%, etc.), excluding the lower value. Two populations are given per panel. (*a*, *b*) Distributions for these four populations (C.A.R. Pygmies, Zaire Pygmies, Melanesians, and New Guineans) differ significantly from equality; the populations tend to have high frequencies for more ancestral alleles than do the other four populations. (*c*, *d*) Distributions for these four populations (Australians, Caucasians, Japanese, and Chinese) do not differ significantly from equality.

populations are currently under study, and will eventually provide more complete representation.

Mitochondrial DNA data are also consistent with the date of 100 ka, suggesting a date of about 200 ka for the common ancestor of modern mtDNA types. Although estimates of dates based on mtDNA span a broad range, the upper values do not appear to extend far beyond 500 ka (Stoneking & Cann 1989; Stoneking *et al.*, this symposium). These dates, if accurate, provide upper limits to the date of migration from Africa, assuming that the genetic trees herein reflect evolutionary history. Gene trees (such as those relating mtDNA types) and trees representing population histories are unlikely to correspond; the divergences within gene trees necessarily predate those within corresponding population trees. Dates of 200 ka, or even of 500 ka, for the common ancestor are therefore consistent with the hypothesis that modern humans first began expanding and migrating throughout the world around 100 ka ago.

(b) Evolutionary Rates

The testing of non-human primate populations for human nuclear DNA polymorphisms has provided not only reinforcement for the hypothesis that humans and chimpanzees are closely related compared to other species, but also an indication of which alleles are ancestral. The variation in frequencies of ancestral alleles provides evidence against two hypotheses superficially suggested by some evolutionary trees. In both the classical marker and DNA marker trees the African populations are found at the end of a very long branch (figures 1 and 4). The length of this branch may indicate either a higher evolutionary rate within African populations, or an African origin for modern humans. The former would have occurred if African populations remained relatively small, or experienced bottlenecks, after separation from other populations. The African populations, however, have higher frequencies of ancestral alleles, indicating that these populations have experienced a relatively low rate of allele frequency change (tables 1 and 2).

Likewise, the short branch leading to Europeans (figure 4b) may indicate either that Europeans have evolved more slowly than other populations, due to a large population size, or that Europeans are an admixture of other populations. Europeans, however, have relatively intermediate frequencies of ancestral alleles, and therefore do not appear to have evolved at a particularly low rate. The hypothesis that Europeans arose as an admixture appears to be more consistent with the data.

(c) Natural Selection

Examination of the distributions of ancestral allele frequencies reveals variation among the eight populations. Four of them tend to have significantly uneven distributions, with high frequencies of many ancestral alleles (figure 5a,b). This variation among the populations may be due to differences in effective population sizes; if the African populations were larger, then gene frequencies would have changed at a slower rate in these populations than in other populations. This hypothesis is now being examined analytically.

Natural selection may also have acted on some of the polymorphisms, contributing to differences among populations in the frequencies of ancestral alleles. An earlier analysis indicated that up to one-third of the 100 DNA polymorphisms may be under the influence of either stabilizing or disruptive selection (Bowcock et al. 1991b). Given that the 60 putative ancestral alleles are associated with a subset of these 100 polymorphisms, at least a fraction are likely to be influenced by natural selection. Because the two African, the Melanesian, and the New Guinean populations each appear to have many ancestral alleles with high frequencies, the alleles in the top class (90–100%) were examined in these populations. For significantly many polymorphisms ($\chi^2 = 4.8313$, 1 d.f., $p < 0.05$) Africans (figure 5a) have high frquencies of the same alleles as do the Melanesians and New Guineans (figure 5b). The number of cases where Africans have high frequencies of the same alleles as do the Chinese and Japanese (figure 5d) is not significant ($\chi^2 = 0.891$, 1 d.f.). Thus, the equatorial populations tend to have very high frequencies for the same ancestral alleles. This finding indicates that natural selection may be influencing some allele frequencies, maintaining high frequencies of those alleles shared with chimpanzees. Because Pygmies, Melanesians, New Guineans tend to inhabit a rain forest environment similar to that of chimpanzees, natural selection may be acting on a few polymorphisms within these populations, maintaining high frequencies of ancestral alleles.

Currently there is an effort underway to collect samples for DNA analysis from vanishing peoples around the world (Cavalli-Sforza et al. 1991). If successful, this effort will lead to much larger databases for both mitochondrial and nuclear DNA variation. Each of these types of data will continue to make distinct contributions to our understanding of the evolution of modern humans. Any such findings can then be compared to those of other disciplines; additional data should enable us to detect further details and obtain more consistent results at each level of comparison. We may eventually clarify details of major migration events, population size changes, and the magnitude of selection effects.

ACKNOWLEDGMENTS

This investigation has been supported in part by National Institutes of Health grants GM20467 and EY07106. We thank the Royal Society for providing funding (to J.L.M.) for travel to attend this meeting, and the Lucille P. Markey Charitable Trust for providing funding (to L.C.S.) for travel to Africa to collect samples.

REFERENCES

Astolfi, P. & Cavalli-Sforza, L.L. 1981 A comparison of methods for reconstructing evolutionary trees. *Syst. Zool.* **30**, 156–169.

Bowcock, A.M., Hebert, J.M., Mountain, J.L., Kidd, J.R., Rogers, J., Kidd, K.K. & Cavalli-Sforza, L.L. 1991*a* Study of an additional 58 DNA markers in five human populations from four continents *Gene Geog.* **5**, 151–173.

Bowcock, A.M., Kidd, J.R., Mountain, J.L., Hebert, J.M., Carotenuto, L., Kidd, K.K. & Cavalli-Sforza, L.L. 1991*b* Drift, admixture, and selection in human evolution: A study with DNA polymorphisms. *Proc. natn. Acad. Sci. U.S.A.* **88**, 839–843.

Brauer, G. 1989 The evolution of modern humans: a comparison of the African and non-African evidence. In *The human revolution: behavioural and biological perspectives on the origins of modern humans* (ed. P. Mellars & C. Stringer), pp. 123–154. Princeton University Press.

Cavalli-Sforza, L.L., Minch, E. & Mountain, J.L. 1992 Coevolution of genes and languages revisited. *Proc. natn. Acad. Sci. U.S.A.* **89**, 5620–5624.

Cavalli-Sforza, L.L., Piazza, A. & Menozzi, P. 1993 *History and geography of human genes*. Princeton University Press. (In the press.)

Cavalli-Sforza, L.L., Piazza, A., Menozzi, P. & Mountain, J. 1988 Reconstruction of human evolution: Bringing together genetic, archaeological, and linguistic data. *Proc. natn. Acad. Sci.* **85**, 6002–6006.

Cavalli-Sforza, L.L., Wilson, A.C., Cantor, C.R., Cook-Deegan, R.M. & King, M.-C. 1991 Call for a worldwide survey of human genetic diversity: a vanishing opportunity for the Human Genome Project. *Genomics* **11**, 490–491.

Clark, J.D. 1989 The origin and spread of modern humans: a broad perspective on the African evidence. In *The human revolution: behavioural and biological perspectives on the origins of modern humans* (ed. P. Mellars & C. Stringer) pp. 565–588. Princeton University Press.

Efron, B. 1982 *The jackknife, bootstrap, and other resampling plans*. Philadelphia: Society for Industrial and Applied Mathematics.

Fagan, B.M. 1987 *The great journey: the peopling of ancient America*. London: Thames and Hudson.

Goodman, M., Koop, B.F., Czelusniak, J., Fitch, D.H.A., Tagle, D.A. & Slightom, J.L. 1989 Molecular phylogeny of the family of apes and humans. *Genome* **31**, 316–335.

Hudson, R.R. 1991 Gene genealogies and the coalescent process. *Oxf. Surv. Evol. Biol.* **7**, 1–44.

Nei, M. 1987 *Molecular evolutionary genetics*. New York: Columbia University Press.

Reynolds, J., Weir, B.S. & Cockerham, C.C. 1983 Estimation of the coancestry coefficient: basis for a short-term genetic distance. *Genetics* **105**, 767–779.

Roberts, R.G., Jones, R. & Smith, M.A. 1990 Thermoluminescence dating of a 50,000-year-old human occupation site in northern Australia. *Nature, Lond.* **345**, 153–156.

Saitou, N. & Nei, M. 1987 The neighbor-joining method: a new method for reconstructing phylogenetic trees. *Molec. Biol. Evol.* **4**, 406–425.

Sokal, R.R. & Michener, C.D. 1958 A statistical method for evaluating systematic relationships. *Univ. Kansas Sci. Bull.* **38**, 1409–1437.

Sokal, R.R. & Rohlf, F.J. 1969 *Biometry: The principles and practice of statistics in biological research*. San Francisco: W. H. Freeman.

Stoneking, M. & Cann, R.L. 1989 African Origin of Human Mitochondrial DNA. In, *The human revolution: behavioral and biological perspectives on the origins of modern humans* (ed. P. Mellars & C. Stringer), pp. 17–30. Princeton University Press.

Straus, L.G. 1989 Age of modern Europeans. *Nature, Lond.* **342**, 476–477.

Stringer, C.B. 1990 The emergence of modern humans. *Scient. Am.* **Dec.** 98–104.

Tajima, F. 1992 Statistical method for estimating the standard errors of branch lengths in a phylogenetic tree reconstructed without assuming equal rates of nucleotide substitution among different lineages. *Molec. Biol. Evol.* **9**, 168–181.

Torroni, A., Schurr, T.G., Yang, C.-C., Szathmary, E.J.E., Williams, R.C., Schanfield, M.S., Troup, G.A., Knowler, W.C., Lawrence, D.N., Weiss, K. & Wallace, D.C. 1992 Native American mitochondrial DNA analysis indicates that the Amerind and Nadene populations were founded by two independent migrations. *Genetics* **130**, 153–162.

New Approaches to Dating Suggest a Recent Age for the Human mtDNA Ancestor

Mark Stoneking, Stephen T. Sherry, Alan J. Redd and Linda Vigilant[1]

SUMMARY

The most critical and controversial feature of the African origin hypothesis of human mitochondrial DNA (mtDNA) evolution is the relatively recent age of about 200 ka inferred for the human mtDNA ancestor. If this age is wrong, and the actual age instead approaches 1 million years ago, then the controversy abates. Reliable estimates of the age of the human mtDNA ancestor and the associated standard error are therefore crucial. However, more recent estimates of the age of the human ancestor rely on comparisons between human and chimpanzee mtDNAs that may not be reliable and for which standard errors are difficult to calculate. We present here two approaches for deriving an intraspecific calibration of the rate of human mtDNA sequence evolution that allow standard errors to be readily calculated. The estimates resulting from these two approaches for the age of the human mtDNA ancestor (and approximate 95% confidence intervals) are 133 (63–356) and 137 (63–416) ka ago. These results provide the strongest evidence yet for a relatively recent origin of the human mtDNA ancestor.

1. INTRODUCTION

The idea that all mitochondrial DNA (mtDNA) variation in modern populations traces back to a single ancestor who lived in Africa some 200 ka ago (Cann *et al.* 1987) has stimulated much interest, research, and debate concerning the origins of modern humans. This African origin hypothesis was reinforced by a recent study (Vigilant *et al.* 1991) that addressed many of the perceived weaknesses of the original study by Cann *et al.* (1987)[†]. Controversy focuses not so much on the geographic origin of the human

---

[1] Department of Anthropology, Pennsylvania State University, University Park, Pennsylvania 16802, U.S.A.

[†] The statistical tests used by Vigilant *et al.* (1991) to buttress the support for an African origin of the human mtDNA ancestor have since been shown to be invalid, due to the inadequacy of parsimony analysis for these data (Hedges *et al.* 1992; Maddison *et al.* 1992; Templeton 1992). Nevertheless, although not statistically proven, an African origin remains as the best explanation for all of the human mtDNA data (Stoneking & Cann 1989; Horai & Hayasaka 1990; Hasegawa & Horai 1991; Kocher & Wilson 1991; Merriweather *et al.* 1991; Vigilant *et al.* 1991; Stoneking *et al.* 1992*a*).

mtDNA ancestor, but rather on when she lived: if the analyses suggesting a 200 ka date are correct, then the implication is that non-African populations older than 200 ka could not have contributed mtDNA types to modern populations. The non-African populations would have been replaced, without much (if any) interbreeding, by anatomically-modern populations spreading from Africa in the past 100 ka (Cann *et al.* 1987; Stoneking & Cann 1989).

If, however, the age of the human ancestor has been estimated incorrectly and is in fact nearer to 1 Ma ago, then the mtDNA results would instead be indicating the first spread of hominids (presumably *Homo erectus*) out of Africa some 1 Ma ago. The replacement controversy then disappears (for mtDNA), as few anthropologists disagree with the contention that these were in fact the first hominids to migrate from Africa, and that therefore there were no prior populations to replace.

The critical aspect of the African origin hypothesis is clearly the age of the human mtDNA ancestor, and most studies have produced estimates which centre around 200 ka ago (Cann *et al.* 1987; Stoneking & Cann 1989; Hasegawa & Horai 1991; Kocher & Wilson 1991; Vigilant *et al.* 1991). There are two parameters which need to be estimated to arrive at an age for the human mtDNA ancestor: (i) the amount of sequence evolution that has occurred since the ancestor lived; and (ii) the rate of human mtDNA sequence evolution. Unfortunately, variances of these parameters are usually unknown, making it difficult to ascertain the reliability of previous age estimates[‡].

In addition, the rate of human mtDNA sequence evolution is usually determined by comparing human mtDNA to chimpanzee mtDNA. For this interspecific comparison to be accurate, human and chimpanzee mtDNA must evolve at the same rate. However, patterns of nucleotide substitution appear to differ between human and chimpanzee mtDNA (Hasegawa & Horai 1991; Kocher & Wilson 1991), which implies that the rates of substitution might differ as well. Another complication is that for the most rapidly evolving regions of the mtDNA genome (the non-coding control region), so many multiple substitutions have occurred that it is difficult to obtain an accurate measure of the true amount of sequence evolution between human and chimpanzee mtDNAs (Hasegawa & Horai 1991; Vigilant *et al.* 1991). Finally, the time of separation of human and chimpanzee mtDNAs must be stipulated, possibly introducing a further source of error into the rate calibration.

We present here two approaches to an intraspecific calibration of the rate

---

[‡] Although estimates of the age of the human mtDNA ancestor are often expressed as ranges, these are not 95% confidence intervals, but rather reflect the range of possible values for the parameters used to determine the age.

of human mtDNA sequence evolution. Intraspecific calibration (i.e. relying solely on mtDNA sequence evolution within human populations) avoids the aforementioned shortcomings of chimpanzee–human comparisons, providing independent estimates of the age of the human mtDNA ancestor. The two approaches to intraspecific calibration also produce standard errors of the parameters, enabling construction of approximate 95% confidence intervals for the age estimates. The results from these two approaches are nearly identical, and provide some of the strongest evidence yet for a relatively recent age of human mtDNA ancestor.

2. Rationale

The rationale behind the intraspecific calibration of the rate of human mtDNA evolution was described in detail by Stoneking *et al.* (1986), and applied previously to restriction map variation (Stoneking *et al.* 1986; Stoneking & Cann 1989). In brief, the procedure relies on the identification of monophyletic clusters or 'groups' of mtDNA types specific to a defined geographic region of the world. Ideally, this region of the world should have been colonized once at a definite time that is firmly established from archaeological or biogeographical evidence, with little or no back-migration. Although no human population will exactly meet these criteria, the colonization of Papua New Guinea (PNG) comes reasonably close (Stoneking *et al.* 1986).

The first approach to an intraspecific calibration is that developed by Stoneking *et al.* (1986). This approach is based on the diversity within groups of PNG-specific mtDNA types, and hence is termed the 'within-group' approach. According to this model (figure 1), the deepest branch-point within each group of PNG mtDNA types represents an estimate of the amount of sequence evolution that has occurred exclusively within PNG, after colonization. If we know the colonization time for PNG, then the amount of sequence evolution to the origin of the PNG group, divided by the colonization time, provides an estimate of the rate of human mtDNA sequence evolution. Our modification of the previous development of this approach is to use a method of tree analysis that also produces standard errors of each branchpoint (Nei *et al.* 1985). This enables construction of 95% confidence intervals for the crucial parameters: namely, the rate of mtDNA sequence evolution, the amount of sequence evolution since the human mtDNA ancestor, and the age of the human mtDNA ancestor.

The second approach to an intraspecific calibration is also based on the amount of sequence evolution within each group of PNG mtDNA types, but in addition it utilizes the divergence between different groups. Hence, we call this the 'between-group' approach. Figure 2 illustrates the rationale behind the between-group approach for a hypothetical tree of two PNG

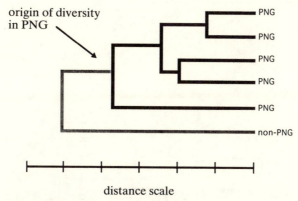

origin of diversity
in PNG

PNG

PNG

PNG

PNG

PNG

non-PNG

distance scale

Figure 1. Rationale for using the divergence within mono-phyletic groups of PNG mtDNA types to estimate the rate of CR sequence evolution. A hypothetical group of PNG types is shown (black lines) with a nearest neighbour that is not from PNG (shaded lines). The arrow points to the branchpoint at which this group began diversifying within PNG; the amount of sequence evolution from this point (determined from the distance scale) can, together with the colonization time, be used to estimate the rate of CR sequence evolution.

groups. These two PNG groups have a common mtDNA ancestor that lived at some unknown time prior to the colonization of PNG. At the colonization time, ancestors of these two groups migrated to PNG and the process of within-group divergence began. The observed mean intergroup divergence (d_{XY}) for these two groups is therefore the result of two processes: divergence prior to colonization, and divergence after colonization. The divergence that occurred after colonization (d_A) can be estimated by the following formula (Nei 1987, p. 276):

$$d_A = d_{XY} - (d_X + d_Y)/2 \qquad (1)$$

where d_X and d_Y are the observed mean sequence divergence within groups X and Y. If the rate of sequence evolution is constant, then d_A is equal to $2\lambda T$, where T is the time of divergence and λ is the rate of sequence evolution. Thus, by knowing the colonization time and the observed sequence divergence within and between each group, we can estimate the rate of mtDNA sequence evolution. Furthermore, standard errors of the mean divergence within and between groups can be obtained by the method of Nei & Jin (1989) and used to construct 95% confidence intervals.

These two approaches to an intraspecific calibration have several advantages over the more traditional rate estimates derived from interspecific

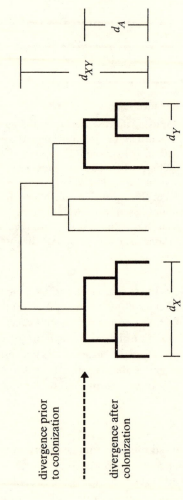

Figure 2. Hypothetical tree of two PNG groups of mtDNA types, illustrating how divergence since the colonization of PNG (d_A) can be determined from the observed mean within-group (d_X and d_Y) and between-group (d_{XY}) divergences.

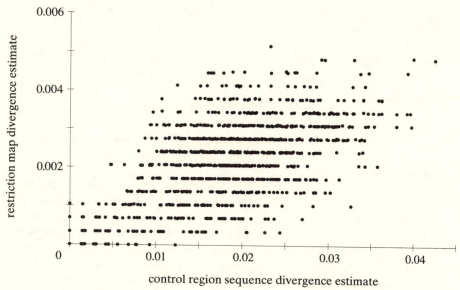

Figure 3. Relationship between the estimates of pairwise sequence divergence based on restriction maps and those based on CR sequences for the 50 PNG mtDNAs. Each point indicates the Jukes–Cantor divergence for one pair of individuals. The horizontal 'stripe' effect arises because the divergences based on restriction maps can only take on certain discrete values (i.e. one restriction site difference = 0.034% divergence, two site differences = 0.068% divergence, etc.).

comparisons: the rate of mtDNA evolution is not assumed to be constant across different species (but it is assumed to be constant across different human populations); species divergence times are not required (but colonization times must be known); and the period of evolutionary time is so short that the correction for multiple substitutions at the same nucleotide position is not important.

In this paper we detail the application of these two approaches to intraspecific calibration to an extensive dataset that includes many PNG mtDNA sequences. We derive estimates of the rate of mtDNA sequence evolution, the age of the human mtDNA ancestor, and associated 95% confidence intervals. After mentioning some caveats to this procedure, we compare our findings to previous estimates and discuss the resulting implications for the origin of modern humans.

3. MATERIALS AND METHODS

Sequences of the two hypervariable segments of the mtDNA control region (CR) were obtained for 30 individuals from PNG and 20 individuals from

Indonesia. Additional sequences (including 20 from PNG) were from Vigilant *et al.* (1991). The 50 PNG mtDNAs come from various highland and coastal localities and were pre-selected from 119 PNG mtDNAs to be representative of the mtDNA diversity in this sample that had previously been characterized by high-resolution mapping with restriction enzymes (Stoneking *et al.* 1990). The Indonesian samples come from the Moluccas and the Lesser Sunda islands, and were selected from 148 samples that were previously screened for a deletion of one of two copies of a nine base-pair (b.p.) repeated sequence located between the COII and lysine tRNA genes (Stoneking *et al.* 1992*b*). All of the Indonesian mtDNAs chosen for sequencing have the deletion.

Amplification of CR hypervariable segments by the polymerase chain reaction (PCR), preparation of single-stranded templates by asymmetric PCR (Gyllensten & Erlich 1988), and dideoxy sequencing were done essentially as described previously (Vigilant *et al.* 1989). Estimates of sequence divergence and associated standard errors (Nei & Jin 1989) were corrected for multiple substitutions by the Jukes–Cantor method (Jukes & Cantor 1969); Kimura's two-parameter method (Kimura 1980) gave essentially identical results. These divergence values, as well as neighbour-joining (NJ) trees (Saitou & Nei 1987), and unweighted pair group method of averaging (UPGMA) trees with associated standard errors of the branch points (Nei *et al.* 1985), were computed with programs kindly provided by M. Nei.

4. RESULTS

(a) Sequences

The CR hypervariable segments span 764 nucleotides; in actuality, an average of 706 nucleotides of DNA sequence was determined from each individual. When combined with the data of Vigilant *et al.* (1991), there were 205 polymorphic nucleotide sites. For the 239 individuals comprising the combined dataset, there were 165 different mtDNA types, including 41 mtDNA types among the 50 PNG sequences and 16 mtDNA types among the 20 Indonesian sequences. Only one type occurred in more than one population, and that type was shared by six individuals from PNG, one Indonesian, and one Philippino.

(b) Comparing Sequences to Restriction Maps

As a means of assessing the information obtained from the CR sequences, we compared the restriction maps that would be inferred from 50 PNG sequences to the restriction maps that were actually determined for these individuals (Stoneking *et al.* 1990). One discrepancy was noted that could be explained by assuming that the restriction site polymorphism in question did not actually map to the sequenced portion of the control region. In every other instance complete concordance was noted between the restriction maps inferred from the CR sequences and the previously determined restriction maps.

We also compared estimates of mean sequence divergence from CR sequences and from restriction maps for each of the 1225 pairs of PNG individuals (figure 3). A clear linear trend is evident, with a moderate correlation coefficient between the two measures of divergence ($r = 0.57$). The slope of the regression line (not shown) indicates that CR sequence divergence values are on average about 13 times bigger than restriction map divergence values (i.e. the CR hypervariable segments are evolving some 13 times faster than the average rate for the entire human mtDNA genome).

Other measures of diversity also indicate that more variation is detected with CR sequences than with high-resolution restriction maps. Among the 50 PNG individuals, CR sequences identified 41 different mtDNA types whereas restriction maps identified only 35 different types. The average probability of identity (that is, the probability of two individuals selected at random having identical mtDNA types) is 3.8% for CR sequences and 4.2% for restriction maps. For individuals with identical CR sequences, the probability that they also have identical restriction maps is 53.8%; for individuals with identical restriction maps, the probability that they also have identical CR sequences is 45.8%.

(c) Phylogenetic Analysis

An abbreviated UPGMA tree relating the 165 CR sequences and rooted with a chimpanzee CR sequence (Foran et al. 1988) is shown in figure 4. Of the 41 PNG types, 35 (85%) fall into one of three groups. An NJ tree for these data was also constructed§; the NJ tree differs in overall branching pattern from the UPGMA tree, but nevertheless retains the three PNG groups (data not shown).

Various characteristics of these three groups (and the other PNG types) are given in table 1. Group 1 differs dramatically from Groups 2 and 3 in three different characteristics (table 1). The frequency of individuals coming from coastal localities, speaking AN languages, and having the 9 b.p. deletion are all significantly elevated in Group 1. The 9 b.p. deletion is particularly noteworthy, as all of the individuals in Group 1 have the deletion, but all other PNG individuals lack the deletion. The distribution of the 9 b.p. deletion in Pacific populations (Hertzberg et al. 1989; Stoneking &

§ UPGMA and NJ trees are not subject to the problems associated with parsimony analysis of these data (Hedges et al. 1992; Templeton 1992; Maddison et al. 1992, Stoneking et al. 1992a).

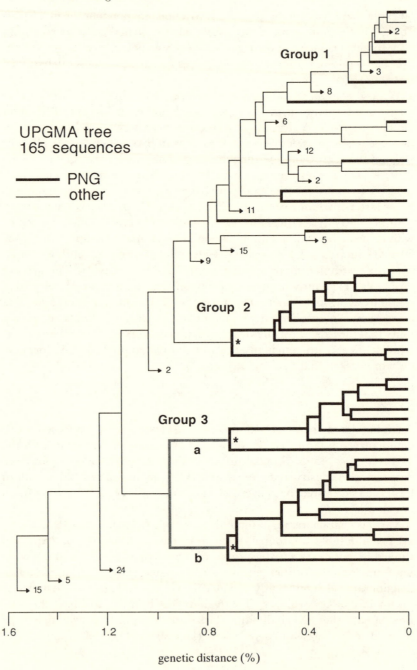

genetic distance (%)

Table 1. *Characteristics of PNG groups defined by* UPGMA *and* NJ *tree analysis*

Group	1	2	3	other	total
number of individuals	11	13	19	7	50
no. of types	6	10	19	6	41
residence (%)					
highland	0.0	84.6	63.2	85.7	58.0
coastal	100.0	15.4	36.8	14.3	42.0
language (%)[a]					
NAN	9.1	92.3	83.3	85.7	69.4
AN	90.9	7.7	16.7	14.3	30.6
9 b.p. deletion (%)					
non-deleted	0.0	100.0	100.0	100.0	78.0
deleted	100.0	0.0	0.0	0.0	22.0

[a] The language affiliation was not known for one member of group 3. NAN, non-Austronesia; AN, Austronesian.

Wilson 1989, Stoneking *et al.* 1992*b*) suggests that it was associated with the primary Austronesian/proto-Polynesian migration that probably began some 3500 to 5000 years ago (Bellwood 1989).

Groups 2 and 3 are similar to each other in residence, language, and 9 b.p. deletion composition. Furthermore, Groups 2 and 3 are each monophyletic groups of PNG mtDNA types, whereas Group 1 is not monophyletic but also includes non-PNG mtDNA types from Asia and Indonesia with the 9 b.p. deletion (including the one case of an identical mtDNA type shared by individuals from PNG, Indonesia, and the Philippines). This is

◄

Figure 4. Abbreviated UPGMA tree for 165 human mtDNA CR sequences, rooted with a chimpanzee CR sequence (Foran *et al.* 1988). Branchpoints are positioned with respect to the scale of genetic (Jukes–Cantor) distance at the bottom of the tree. Thick lines indicate the 41 PNG mtDNA types while thin lines indicate non-PNG types. Thin lines terminating in arrows followed by a number indicate that branching structures involving the indicated number of non-PNG types occur at that location, but the actual detailed branching structure is omitted. The three PNG groups are identified (along with subgroups a and b of Group 3); asterisks indicate the deepest branchpoint and hence the origin of diversity within PNG for Groups 2, 3a, and 3b. The correspondence between PNG groups (based on CR sequences) and PNG mtDNA clans (based on restriction maps (Stoneking *et al.* 1990)) is as follows: Group 1 comprises clans 11–16; Group 2 comprises clan 10; Group 3a comprises clans 3, 4, 6 and 7; and Group 3b comprises clans 2 and 5. PNG CR sequences that do not fall within one of the three groups comprise clans 1, 8, 10, and 18; there is thus no overlap of clans between different groups.

consistent with Group 1 representing a recent migration to PNG, while Groups 2 and 3 represent a more ancient migration, presumably the earliest human colonization of PNG.

(d) Intraspecific Calibration: General Considerations

As outlined previously, the amount of divergence within and between Groups 2 and 3 can be used to estimate the rate of CR sequence evolution (Group 1 is too recent a migration to be used for this purpose). Group 3 consists of two extremely divergent clusters that are designated 3a and 3b (figure 4). For the purpose of calibrating the rate of CR sequence evolution, we consider 3a and 3b to represent separate migrations[||]. If Group 3 is not split up, a faster rate of CR sequence evolution (and hence an even younger age for the common human mtDNA ancestor) will result.

We therefore assumed that divergence within PNG commenced at the deepest points within Groups 2, 3a, and 3b (figure 4), and that these three groups were derived from the earliest migration of humans to PNG. Archaeological evidence places the earliest presence of humans in PNG at about 40 ka ago (Groube et al. 1986), and this date was used previously to calibrate the rate of mtDNA evolution based on restriction maps (Stoneking et al. 1986; Stoneking & Cann 1989). However, the earliest date for humans in Australia is about 53 ka ago (Roberts et al. 1990), at which time Australia and New Guinea formed one land mass. To obtain the slowest rate of CR sequence evolution consistent with the data, and thus the oldest ages for the human mtDNA ancestor, a maximum time of 60 ka was assumed for the initial colonization of PNG. Dates less than 60 ka will result in faster rates, and hence even younger dates for the human mtDNA ancestor.

(e) Intraspecific Calibration: Within-Group Approach

For each of the three groups, the distance to the deepest node and the associated standard error are presented in table 2. These are converted into estimates of the rate of CR sequence evolution by assuming a colonization time of 60 ka, resulting in an average rate of CR sequence evolution of $11.81 \pm 3.11\%$ per Ma. The amount of sequence evolution corresponding to the human mtDNA ancestor in the UPGMA tree (figure 4) is $1.56 \pm 0.21\%$ (for the NJ tree the average amount of sequence evolution to the human mtDNA ancestor was nearly identical, 1.58%). For the within-group approach, then, the best estimate for the age of the human mtDNA ancestor is therefore 133 ka, whereas an approximate 95% confidence interval (based

---

[||] This interpretation is supported by the restriction map analysis, since Groups 3a and 3b comprise different clans (Stoneking et al. 1990).

Table 2. *Calibration of the rate of* CR *sequence evolution and estimates of the age of the common human mtDNA ancestor*

group	distance (%) to the group ancestor	rate (% per Ma) of CR sequence evolution[a]	human mtDNA ancestor[b]	
			age/ka	95% CI/ka
2	0.69 ± 0.18	11.55 ± 3.00	135	65–357
3a	0.71 ± 0.20	11.83 ± 3.27	132	62–374
3b	0.72 ± 0.18	12.03 ± 3.07	130	63–336
average	0.71 ± 0.19	11.81 ± 3.11	133	63–356

[a] Assuming that PNG was colonized 60 ka ago.

[b] Based on an average distance of 1.56 ± 0.21% to the common ancestor.

Table 3. *Estimates of within- and between-group sequence divergence*

(Average divergence (%) within each group is on the diagonal, uncorrected estimates of divergence between each pair of groups (i.e. d_{XY}) are below the diagonal, and corrected estimates of divergence between each pair of group (i.e. d_A) are above the diagonal.)

group	2	3a	3b
2	0.84 ± 0.18	1.34 ± 0.44	1.78 ± 0.42
3a	2.17 ± 0.48	0.81 ± 0.18	1.00 ± 0.03
3b	2.72 ± 0.47	1.93 ± 0.38	1.03 ± 0.19

on 95% confidence intervals for the rate of CR sequence evolution and the amount of sequence evolution corresponding to the human mtDNA ancestor) is 63–356 ka ago.

(f) Intraspecific Calibration: Between-Group Approach

Estimates of d_{XY} and d_A (calculated according to equation (1)) are given in table 3. The average value of d_A is 1.37 ± 0.40%, which (assuming a colonization time of 60 ka) leads to an average rate of $\lambda = 11.42 \pm 3.33\%$. This rate is virtually identical to that estimated above by the within-group approach, and results in an age of the human mtDNA ancestor of 137 ka with an approximate 95% confidence interval of 63–416 ka.

5. Discussion

(a) Caveats

We have presented two different approaches to an intraspecific calibration of the rate of human mtDNA CR sequence evolution; these two approaches yield virtually identical results. Both strategies are based on the divergence of PNG-specific groups of mtDNA types, and thus are not subject to the criticisms that have been levelled at calibrations based on comparing human and chimpanzee mtDNAs. However, the intraspecific calibration does require other assumptions that need to be evaluated.

First, the intraspecific calibration relies on an accurate date for the colonization of PNG. In order to arrive at the slowest possible rate consistent with the data, we have used a date somewhat older than archaeological evidence would suggest, namely 60 ka. However, this date has steadily increased (as now archaeological evidence has come to light), from 30 ka for the first intraspecific calibration (Stoneking *et al.* 1986), to 40 ka for the next calibration (Stoneking & Cann 1989), to 60 ka in the present study. More recent dates are not a problem, as they result in faster rates and hence younger estimates of the age of the human mtDNA ancestor. Older dates, however, will result in slower rates and more ancient estimates for the age of the human mtDNA ancestor.

Given the above trend, can we be confident that the date for the first entry of humans into Sahul (the combined Australia and New Guinea land masses) will not be pushed back even further with future knowledge? It is, of course, impossible to say if earlier dates will be forthcoming from studies of the archaeological and paleontological record in Sahul. However, it does not seem likely that the date will be pushed back much further, as the earliest appearance of anatomically modern humans in the fossil record occurs about 100 ka ago in Africa and the Near East (Stringer & Andrews 1988; Stringer *et al.* 1989). Even if the first entry of humans into Sahul did occur as much as 80 ka ago, the corresponding age of the human ancestor would increase from 133 to just 176 ka, with a maximum age of 464 ka (from the 95% confidence interval). Thus, increasing the age for the colonization of Sahul will not substantially alter our conclusions.

A second assumption is that migration was essentially one-way, so that there was no back-migration from PNG to Indonesia or southeast Asia. However, if undetected back-migration has occurred, then the resulting estimate of the age for the human mtDNA ancestor will be greater than the true age. For example, suppose that the nearest non-PNG neighbour of PNG Group 2 (figure 4) is a back-migrant. If this is the case, then the amount of sequence change observed in the tree for Group 2 will be less than the amount of sequence change that has actually accumulated since colonization. We therefore would underestimate the true amount of sequence evolution, and hence undetected back-migration would lead to an estimated rate that is slower than the true rate.

A third assumption is that the rate of mtDNA sequence evolution is the same in all human populations. One way to check this assumption is to test the pattern of mtDNA variation within each population for departure from neutral expectations. We applied the test developed by Tajima (1989) to the PNG data and found that the mtDNA variation in PNG is consistent with neutrality (data not shown). Vigilant (1990) tested the remaining populations and found three cases in which neutrality was rejected. Two of these probably represent departures from random sampling, as they involve agglomerations of 'Europeans' and 'Asians' that do not reflect known substructure within these continental groups (Horai & Hayasaka 1990; Di-Rienzo & Wilson 1991). The third involves the Herero of Botswana, in which there is historical evidence for a recent bottleneck (Vigilant 1990). We thus find no evidence that selection has distorted the rate of mtDNA evolution within human populations.

Finally, it is assumed that the PNG groups identified by phylogenetic analysis truly are monophyletic clusters, and that further work will not find mtDNA types from outside PNG that fall within these groups. This is a critical assumption, because if the PNG groups are not truly monophyletic, then we have overestimated the amount of sequence evolution that occurred within PNG after colonization. The amount of sequence evolution that we determine to occur within PNG would actually have occurred prior to the colonization of PNG. The result will be an overestimate of the rate of CR sequence evolution, and a corresponding underestimate of the true age of the human mtDNA ancestor.

In order to assess accurately the validity of the PNG groups, it is necessary to sample mtDNAs from locations ancestral to the colonization of PNG. The Indonesian samples were collected for precisely this purpose from populations that exhibit some physical Melanesian characteristics. However, the 20 Indonesian CR sequences analyzed here were pre-selected to have the 9 b.p. deletion that is associated with PNG Group 1, and indeed they all fall within Group 1. Hence, they would not be expected to either be ancestral to or break up PNG Groups 2 or 3. We intend to seek Indonesian samples that might fall within Groups 2 or 3 by using hybridization with sequence-specific oligonucleotide probes (e.g. Stoneking *et al.* 1991) to screen for nucleotide substitutions that characterize the PNG groups. CR sequences will then be determined for any Indonesian sample that might enter into one of the PNG groups. Another future direction to address this problem is to repeat the intraspecific calibration with CR sequences from Australia and other places that would appear to satisfy the requirements of this analysis.

(b) *Comparison With Previous Results*

The results presented herein build on the data of Vigilant *et al.* (1991) with additional CR sequences from PNG and Indonesia. In comparing the present results with the previous work, it is important to note that here amounts and rates of change are expressed in terms of changes observed from an ancestor to an existing type (i.e. as amounts and rates of CR sequence evolution), whereas in Vigilant *et al.* (1991) the corresponding quantities are expressed in terms of changes observed between two existing types (i.e. as amounts and rates of CR sequence divergence). Thus, our values need to be doubled in order to compare them to the values calculated previously. The resulting estimates of the amount of CR sequence divergence since the mtDNA ancestor, the rate of CR sequence divergence, and the age of the human mtDNA ancestor are compared with the previous estimates in table 4. The values from the two studies are in good agreement, even though quite different methods were used to calibrate the rate of CR sequence evolution or divergence.

Table 4. *Comparison of estimates from Vigilant et al. (1991) and the present study for the amount of* CR *sequence divergence since the common ancestor, the rate of* CR *sequence divergence, and the age of the human mtDNA ancestor*

study	divergence (%) from ancestor	rate of divergence (%)	age of the ancestor/ka
Vigilant et al. (1991)[a]	2.87	11.5–17.3	166–249
this study[b]	3.12 ± 0.42	23.62 ± 6.22	63–356
this study[c]	3.12 ± 0.42	22.84 ± 6.66	63–416

[a] The ranges for the rate of divergence and age of the ancestor are derived from using a range of 4–6 Ma for the separation between chimpanzees and humans; these are not confidence intervals.
[b] Based on the average distance to the root of each PNG group.
[c] Based on the corrected divergence between PNG groups.

Vigilant *et al.* (1991) did not estimate confidence intervals for the rate of CR sequence divergence or the age of the human mtDNA ancestor, because methods did not exist for calculating the variance of the transition : transversion ratio, which they used to calibrate the rate of CR sequence divergence. Recently, a method has been developed for calculating the variance of the transition : transversion ratio (M. Nei, personal communication), and the resulting 95% confidence interval for the age of the human mtDNA ancestor is approximately 110–500 ka. Hasegawa & Horai (1991) have also investigated the variance of the substitution rate, using a maximum likelihood method that was applied to subsets of the human CR sequences published by (Greenberg *et al.* 1983; Vigilant *et al.* 1989; Horai & Hayasaka 1990). Their 95% confidence interval for the age of the human mtDNA ancestor was about 180–380 ka. However, they caution that their model may be violated by the different patterns of nucleotide substitution observed in chimpanzee and human CR sequences. Finally, Stoneking & Cann (1989) predicted that a 95% confidence interval for the age of the human mtDNA ancestor would probably be on the order of 50–500 ka ago; this conjecture seems to be borne out by the various methods and datasets that have been used to estimate such confidence intervals.

(c) *Implications and Future Prospects*

There are two important implications of this work. First, the two approaches for intraspecific calibration yielded an average age for the human mtDNA ancestor of about 135 ka. This is more recent than the previous estimates (Cann *et al.* 1987; Hasegawa & Horai 1991; Vigilant *et al.* 1991), which centred around 200 ka ago. In the past it was emphasized that this date is for the human *mtDNA* ancestor, which is not necessarily the same as the actual ancestor of our species, namely anatomically modern humans. There is no requirement for the human mtDNA ancestor to be a member of our species; she might very well have been a member of some preceding species[¶]. However, the dates for the mtDNA ancestor from this work are coming close to the earliest dates ascertained for fossils of anatomically modern humans (Stringer & Andrews 1988; Stringer *et al.* 1989), raising the intriguing possibility that the human mtDNA ancestor might actually have been one of the first anatomically modern humans.

The second major implication of this work is that the oldest age for the human mtDNA ancestor is 356–416 ka ago. Since genetic divergence is expected to precede population divergence (Nei 1987, p. 288), the maximum age of the human mtDNA ancestor places an upper bound on when human populations began to diverge. In other words, if the human mtDNA

[¶] Indeed, based on the 200,000 year old date, she was deemed most likely to be anatomically-archaic (Stoneking & Cann 1989), not modern.

ancestor lived not more than 416 ka ago, then human population differences cannot date back more than 416 ka (and, of course, they could be considerably younger). Therefore, non-African populations that date back more than 416 ka ago could not have contributed any mtDNA types to modern populations. This finding is clearly incompatible with the multiregional evolution hypothesis (Wolpoff 1989), which holds that human population differences should be upwards of 1 Ma old.

However, before we can completely discount the multiregional evolution hypothesis, it must be pointed out that we have analysed variation in only a single gene, namely mtDNA. Although our analysis accounts for the variance in the two components of the age of the human mtDNA ancestor (namely, the rate of CR sequence evolution and the amount of CR sequence evolution since the human mtDNA ancestor), there is a third component that introduces variance into the estimate of when human population divergence actually began. This third component is stochastic variance in the evolutionary history of different genes (Nei & Livshits 1990). Only by analysing different genes can we account for this variance; although mtDNA analyses are valuable for the insights they yield into human evolutionary history, many more genes need to be analysed in similar fashion for a statistically accurate picture of the history of human populations to emerge.

Acknowledgments

We thank K. Bhatia and A. S. M. Sofro for samples, M. Nei and T. Whittam for computer programs, R. Zauhar for computational assistance, and H. Harpending, B. Hedges and M. Nei for valuable discussion and comments. Research supported by NSF grant BNS 90-20567 to M.S.

References

Bellwood, P.S. 1989 The colonization of the Pacific: some current hypotheses. In *The colonization of the Pacific—a genetic trail* (ed. A. V. S. Hill & S. W. Serjeantson), pp. 1–59. Oxford University Press.

Cann, R.L., Stoneking, M. & Wilson, A.C. 1987 Mitochondrial DNA and human evolution. *Nature, Lond.* **325**, 31–36.

DiRienzo, A. & Wilson, A.C. 1991 Branching pattern in the evolutionary tree for human mitochondrial DNA. *Proc. Natn. Acad. Sci. U.S.A.* **88**, 1597–1601.

Foran, D.R., Hixson, J.E. & Brown, W.M. 1988 Comparisons of ape and human sequences that regulate mitochondrial DNA transcription and D-loop DNA synthesis. *Nucl. Acids Res.* **16**, 5841–5861.

Greenberg, B.D., Newbold, J.E. & Sugino, A. 1983 Intraspecific nucleotide sequence variability surrounding the origin of replication in human mitochondrial DNA. *Genetics* **21**, 33–49.

Groube, L.M., Chappell, J., Muke, J. & Price, D. 1986 A 40,000 year-old human occupation site at Huon Peninsula, Papua New Guinea. *Nature, Lond.* **324**, 453–455.

Gyllensten, U.B. & Erlich, H.A. 1988 Generation of single-stranded DNA by the polymerase chain reaction and its application to direct sequencing of the HLA-DQA locus. *Proc. Natn. Acad. Sci. U.S.A.* **85**, 7652–7656.

Hasegawa, M. & Horai, S. 1991 Time of the deepest root for polymorphism in human mitochondrial DNA. *J. molec. Evol.* **32**, 37–42.

Hedges, S.B., Kumar, S., Tamura, K. & Stoneking, M. 1992 Human origins and the analysis of mitochondrial DNA sequences. *Science, Wash.* **255**, 737–739.

Hertzberg, M., Mickleson, K.N.P., Serjeantson, S.W., Prior, J.F. & Trent, R.J. 1989 An Asian-specific 9-bp deletion of mitochondrial DNA is frequently found in Polynesians. *American J. hum. Genet.* **44**, 504–510.

Horai, S. & Hayasaka, K. 1990 Intraspecific nucleotide sequence differences in the major noncoding region of human mitochondrial DNA. *Am. J. hum. Genet.* **46**, 828–842.

Jukes, T.H. & Cantor, C.R. 1969 Evolution of protein molecules. In *Mammalian protein metabolism* (ed. H. N. Munro), pp. 21–132. New York: Academic Press.

Kimura, M. 1980 A simple method for estimating evolutionary rate of base substitutions through comparative studies of nucleotide sequences. *J. molec. Evol.* **16**, 111–120.

Kocher, T.D. & Wilson, A.C. 1991 Sequence evolution of mitochondrial DNA in humans and chimpanzees: control region and a protein-coding region. In *Evolution of life: fossils, molecules, and culture* (ed. S. Osawa & T. Honjo), pp. 391–413. Tokyo: Springer-Verlag.

Maddison, D.R., Ruvolo, M. & Swofford, D.L. 1992 Geographic origins of human mitochondrial DNA: phylogenetic evidence from control region sequences. *Syst. Biol.* (In the press.)

Merriweather, D.A., Clark, A.G., Ballinger, S.W., Schurr, T.G., Soodyall, H., Jenkins, T., Sherry, S.T. & Wallace, D.W. 1991 The structure of human mitochondrial DNA variation. *J. molec. Evol.* **33**, 543–555.

Nei, M. 1987 *Molecular evolutionary genetics.* New York: Columbia University Press.

Nei, M. & Jin, L. 1989 Variances of the average numbers of nucleotide substitutions within and between populations. *Molec. Biol. Evol.* **6**, 290–300.

Nei, M. & Livshits, G. 1990 Evolutionary relationships of Europeans, Asians, and Africans at the molecular level. In *Population biology of genes and molecules* (ed. N. Takahata & J. F. Crow), pp. 251–265. Tokyo: Baifukan.

Nei, M., Stephens, J.C. & Saitou, N. 1985 Methods for computing the standard errors of branching points in an evolutionary tree and their application to molecular data from humans and apes. *Molec. Biol. Evol.* **2**, 66–85.

Roberts, R.G., Jones, R. & Smith, M.A. 1990 Thermoluminescence dating of a 50,000-year-old human occupation site in northern Australia. *Nature, Lond.* **345**, 153–156.

Saitou, N. & Nei, M. 1987 The neighbor-joining method: a new method for reconstructing phylogenetic trees. *Molec. Biol. Evol.* **4**, 406–425.

Stoneking, M., Bhatia, K. & Wilson, A.C. 1986 Rate of sequence divergence estimated from restriction maps of mitochondrial DNAs from Papua New Guinea. *Cold Spring Harb. Symp. quant. Biol.* **51**, 433–439.

Stoneking, M. & Cann, R.L. 1989 African origin of human mitochondrial DNA. In *The human revolution – behavioural and biological perspectives on the origins of modern humans* (ed. P. Mellars & C. Stringer), pp. 17–30. Edinburgh University Press.

Stoneking, M., Hedgecock, D., Higuchi, R.G., Vigilant, L. & Erlich, H.A. 1991 Population variation of human mtDNA control region sequences detected by enzymatic amplification and sequence-specific oligonucleotide probes. *Am. J. hum. Genet.* **48**, 370–382.

Stoneking, M., Jorde, L.B., Bhatia, K. & Wilson, A.C. 1990 Geographic variation in human mitochondrial DNA from Papua New Guinea. *Genetics* **124**, 717–733.

Stoneking, M., Sherry, S.T. & Vigilant, L. 1992*a* Geographic origin of human mitochondrial DNA revisited. *Syst. Biol.* (In the press.)

Stoneking, M., Sofro, A.S.M. & Wilson, A.C. 1992*b* Implications of a mitochondrial marker for the colonization of the Pacific. In *Human evolution in the Pacific Region* (ed. C. K. Ho, G. Krantz & M. Stoneking). Pullman, Washington: Washington State University Press.

Stoneking, M. & Wilson, A.C. 1989 Mitochondrial DNA. In *The colonization of the Pacific: a genetic trail* (ed. A. V. S. Hill & S. Serjeantson), pp. 215–245. Oxford University Press.

Stringer, C.B. & Andrews, P. 1988 Genetic and fossil evidence for the origin of modern humans. *Science, Wash.* **239**, 1263–1268.

Stringer, C.B., Grün, R., Schwarcz, H.P. & Goldberg, P. 1989 ESR dates for the hominid burial site of Es Skhul in Israel. *Nature, Lond.* **338**, 756–758.

Tajima, F. 1989 Statistical method for testing the neutral mutation hypothesis by DNA polymorphism. *Genetics* **123**, 585–595.

Templeton, A.R. 1992 Human origins and analysis of mitochondrial DNA sequences. *Science, Wash.* **255**, 737.

Vigilant, L. 1990 Control region sequence from African populations and the evolution of human mitochondrial DNA. PhD Thesis, University of California, Berkeley.

Vigilant, L., Pennington, R., Harpending, H., Kocher, T.D. & Wilson, A.C. 1989 Mitochondrial DNA sequences in single hairs from a southern African population. *Proc. Natn. Acad. Sci. U.S.A.* **86**, 9350–9354.

Vigilant, L., Stoneking, M., Harpending, H., Hawkes, K. & Wilson, A.C. 1991 African populations and the evolution of human mitochondrial DNA. *Science, Wash.* **253**, 1503–1507.

Wolpoff, M.H. 1989 Multiregional evolution: the fossil alternative to Eden. In *The human revolution – behavioural and biological perspectives on the origins of modern humans* (ed. P. Mellars & C. Stringer), pp. 62–108. Edinburgh University Press.

Southern Africa and Modern Human Origins

H. J. Deacon[1]

SUMMARY

This paper argues that southern Africa was a remote part of the Old World
in the late Pleistocene (125–10 ka ago). Because of this isolated position
there was continuity without significant replacement in the resident population. Isolation and the relatively recent spread of agriculture to the region
has allowed a section of this population to survive into the present. They are
the Bushmen (San). Studies of geographic patterning in conventional genetic markers and mitochondrial DNA indicate that the Bushman clade
has a long evolutionary history in southern Africa. Estimates of more than
100 ka for the continued presence of this population in the region are
supported in archaeological investigations of sites with long sequences such
as Klasies River main site and Border Cave. Human remains dating to the
earlier part of the late Pleistocene have been recovered from these sites and
the samples form a morphological series with the Klasies River remains
possibly 20 ka older than those from Border Cave. There is no fossil record
for the later Pleistocene, however, at a period when selection for a gracile
morphology may have been pronounced. The cultural associations in the
earlier late Pleistocene are with the Middle Stone Age. Expressions of
cultural 'style' and the occurrence of similar artefact design types in the
Middle and Later Stone Ages can be interpreted with reference to the
ethnographic present. Temporal continuity can be shown in the geographical distribution of stylistic markers and this suggests participation in a
shared cognitive system. The inference is that the people in the earlier late
Pleistocene had cognitive abilities that are comparable to those shown by
their Holocene and modern descendants. The presence of the ancestors of a
modern population in the earlier late Pleistocene in this region is perhaps
expected if modern people had their origins in Africa.

1. INTRODUCTION

Southern Africa, in the sense used here, corresponds to a major ecological
zone south of the Miombo woodlands of Central Africa. It is a region of
shrublands and grasslands with a strong climatic gradient from sub-
tropical in the east to hyper-arid in the west. It presents a different and more

[1] Department of Archaeology, University of Stellenbosch, Stellenbosch 7600, South Africa

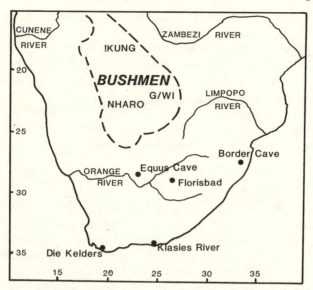

Figure 1. Map of southern Africa showing the location of sites mentioned in the text and the present distribution of the Bushmen.

diverse range of habitats than is found in Central Africa (Cowling *et al.* 1989). The region has been peopled throughout the Pleistocene.

This paper considers the contribution which palaeontological and archaeological studies of the late Pleistocene in southern Africa make to understanding evolution in modern people. The information available from two long-sequence cave sites (figure 1, Klasies River main site and Border Cave) is described as both have provided human remains, claimed to be anatomically modern, in association with archaeological materials. Technical advances have made it possible to date these sequences with reasonable precision. The main human occupation deposits in both sites date to the earlier late Pleistocene, the period between some 60 and 130 ka ago. The archaeological record for the latter half of the late Pleistocene, however, is poor in the whole region (Deacon & Thackeray 1984) and is not well represented at these sites.

Comparisons can be made between the evidence from the earlier late Pleistocene and that from the Holocene and the ethnographic present. The premise that underlies such comparisons is that the people resident in southern Africa in the earlier late Pleistocene were the direct ancestors of the Holocene and present-day Bushmen (the term Bushman is used in preference to San because the people themselves prefer to be called Bushmen (Guenther 1986)) hunter–gatherers. Genetic studies (Nurse *et al.*

1985; Vigilant *et al.* 1989, 1991) show that the Bushmen have a remote ancestry and they are a branch of humankind that evolved in isolation in southern Africa. The advent of agriculture in the last 2000 years (Thomas & Shaw 1991) has broken down the isolation, and replacement by different people has occurred in a large part of the former range. Only that section of the Bushman population, living in areas underlain by Kalahari sands and unsuitable for agriculture, has been able to maintain itself. It is a considerable advantage in the interpretation of the evidence to have an ethnographic as well as an archaeological record from the region.

2. Sites and Evidence

The archaeological evidence for past populations lies in the abundant traces of Stone Age people in the form of stone artefacts in the southern African landscape. The erosion of thin soil mantles and the durability and quantity of artefacts make these traces very obvious. Prominent on this landscape scale of archaeological visibility are artefacts with a distinctive Middle Stone Age ('MSA') typology that date to the late Pleistocene. Caves and rock shelters were frequently used as living sites in the late Pleistocene and there are long sequences that provide a stratigraphic and a chronological framework for the palaeontological and archaeological materials they contain. Although sites are numerous there are few that have yielded human fossils. There are isolated finds of human teeth from Die Kelders Cave (Grine *et al.* 1991) and Equus Cave (Grine & Klein 1985) that have been described as 'modern' in morphology. The sites that have produced the main evidence supporting a high antiquity of modern people in southern Africa are Border Cave and Klasies River main site (figure 1). The Border Cave (Beaumont 1980) human remains are a sample of four individuals. The associations and dating are less well established than the more fragmentary finds representing a larger number of individuals from Klasies River (Singer & Wymer 1982).

An older and possible Middle Pleistocene occurrence, Florisbad, is an open-air site where a human cranium with the puncture mark of a hyaena canine was found by Dreyer in 1932 (Brink 1987). A new reconstruction of this specimen shows it to be similar to the Ngaloba and Omo II finds from East Africa and intermediate in morphology between the archaic Kabwe and Saldanha specimens and those from the earlier late Pleistocene (Kuman & Clarke 1986).

A recent survey (Bräuer & Rösing 1989) has shown that there are no finds of human remains dated with certainty to the latter half of the late Pleistocene. There is a large number of specimens from Later Stone Age contexts dating to the end-Pleistocene and the Holocene, however (Rightmire 1978). Many of these are burials and, in the southern Cape in particular, cave sites were used as cemetries. These remains are not considered in detail but unlike the finds from Klasies River and Border Cave they are so recent in age that they are completely modern in morphology.

3. STRATIGRAPHY AND DATING

Techniques such as uranium–thorium disequilibrium (U/Th), electron spin resonance (ESR) and amino acid racemization (AAR) are being used to date the archaeological deposits in addition to radiocarbon. The most comprehensively dated sequence is the Klasies River main site. This is a 20 m thick cone of sediment resting against a cliff face and filling side caverns in the face. The deposits began to accumulate at the end of the Last Interglacial (130–118 ka ago) as sea levels dropped from their maximum height near to those of the present (Martinson et al. 1987). Sands intercalated with human occupation horizons that include shell and bone food remains, hearths and carbonized patches and artefacts, make up the well stratified sequence (Deacon & Geleijnse 1988).

The culture-stratigraphy at Klasies River mouth has been described by Singer & Wymer (1982) who recognized from the base upwards a Middle Stone Age (MSA) I, MSA II, Howiesons Poort and MSA III levels, with a further sub-stage IV in a wash in a channel (figure 2). Primary Middle Stone Age occupation of the site ended more than 50 ka radiocarbon years ago with the deposition of the Upper stratigraphic member which contains the Howiesons Poort industry and the overlying MSA III. The Howiesons Poort is a distinctive horizon marker that can be assumed to be penecontemporaneous at sites in southern Africa and to represent a limited time interval of some thousands rather than tens of thousands of years (Miller et al., this symposium). In all long sequences with adequate radiocarbon dating, a minimum age of 50 ka has been obtained for this marker horizon. This gives a check on ages estimated by other methods.

The bulk of the human fossils come from two strata. Two maxillary fragments were found in the lowest stratum, the LBS (Light Brown Sand) member. An end-Last Interglacial age is supported by oxygen isotope measurements on shell (Shackleton 1982; Deacon et al. 1988), aspartic acid dating (Bada & Deems 1975) and U/Th dating (Deacon et al. 1988). The second stratum to which most of the finds made by Singer & Wymer (1982) in their excavations in 1967–8 can be referred, and from which a human ulna has been recovered since, is the lower part of the overlying SAS member. The age estimates available suggest a date of the order of 90 ka for this level (Bada & Deems 1975; Deacon et al. 1988; Grün et al. 1990b). The MSA I and II of Singer & Wymer (1982) are found in the SAS member (Thackeray & Kelly 1988).

The RF and Upper members in the Klasies River main site sequence are

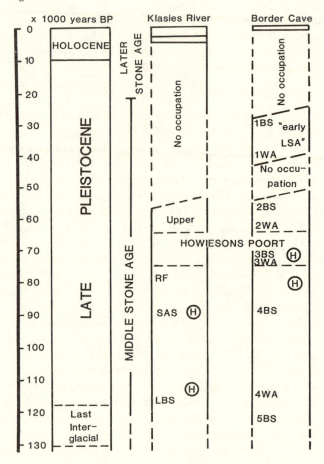

Figure 2. Diagramatic representation of the dating and stratigraphy of Klasies River main site and Border Cave.

considered to be more than 60 ka old. There are few artefacts from the RF deposit but the Upper member includes the Howiesons Poort and MSA III cultural units and these layers have preserved isolated human teeth. The oxygen isotope profile suggests correlation of these members with isotope stages 5b to 4 (Deacon *et al.* 1988). Deacon (1989) has argued that an age centered on 70 ka years is the best estimate for the dating of the Howiesons Poort at Klasies River. This does not accord with the ESR dating of the Upper member by Grün (Grün *et al.* 1990*b*) to the 60 to 40 ka range. The minimum radiocarbon age suggests that these ESR results are an underestimate. The geochemistry of the ground water at Klasies River is complex and locally within the site the uptake of uranium may not fit the models used in age estimations.

Border Cave, high up in the Lebombo range of KwaZulu, is a large cave. The deposits, 4 m in thickness, consist of a series of white ash horizons separated by brown sands. In 1934 the first finds were made there and since 1970 excavations directed by Beaumont (1980) have been designed to establish the age and associations of the human remains. White ash layers are good stratigraphic markers in the sequence and have assisted in reconstructing the horizons from which the specimens were recovered (Beaumont *et al.* 1978). The BC 1 and 2 specimens, a cranium and a mandible, came from a guano pit and have no stratigraphic provenance. However, chemical analyses associate them with an infant skeleton that was excavated in 1942 from below the third white ash (3WA) layer. A further specimen, BC5, found in 1974, came from the 3WA, the layer in which Howiesons Poort artefacts occur. Grün *et al.* (1990a) have dated a large series of bovid tooth enamel fragments and obtained estimates between 90 and 50 ka for the horizons from which the human remains came. Although the ESR dating of the Howiesons Poort to the 75–45 ka range is not in accord with the radiocarbon estimate of the minimum age for an overlying and younger horizon, it is probable that the age of the Howiesons Poort lies within the range estimated by ESR.

The dating of the Border Cave sequence to the earlier part of the late Pleistocene is acceptable on typological correlation with Klasies River. Any reservations regarding the association of the human fossils with these old strata can be resolved only by direct dating of the specimens themselves. They are clearly old, and as Beaumont (1980) has noted, BC1 cannot be younger than 33 ka, the age of the youngest Stone Age horizon. An age of 70 ka for the best provenanced find—the mandible BC5 from the 3WA layer—is not contentious and the other remains may be of similar age. An important consideration to emerge from this survey is that the Border Cave human fossils may be 20 ka younger than those from Klasies River and morphological differences can therefore be expected.

4. Human Remains and Taphonomy

(a) Taxonomic Assessment

The premise adopted in this paper that the resident population in southern Africa has evolved in isolation in the late Pleistocene implies that the fossil materials should represent modern people and should form part of the Bushman clade. What constitutes 'modern' morphology needs to be defined in terms of what is known of evolution in African populations. In recent surveys of the African fossil evidence from the Middle and late Pleistocene (Bräuer 1989; Rightmire 1989) the material from those sites is classified as anatomically modern.

The Klasies River main site material is fragmentary and consists mainly of cranial elements. These consist of upper and lower jaws, isolated teeth, a frontal bone and other cranial pieces. Postcranial remains are limited to an ulna, a vertebra and a clavicle. These remains pose challenges for taxonomic description because they are fragmentary. It is probable that more than ten individuals are represented in the two strata dated to between 120 and 90 ka old. Singer & Wymer (1982) stressed the modern attributes of the mandible (no. 41815) from the 1B part of the site and, more contentiously (Habgood 1989), pointed to features in this and other specimens that could indicate parallels with modern African groups. Rightmire & Deacon (1991) have provided a recent review of the fossil materials from the main site and conclude that the remains differ from those of Neanderthals and other archaic humans. In their assessment the sample shows a degree of robusticity and strong sexual dimorphism that is coupled to a modern morphology. Bräuer *et al.* (1992) have carried out a metrical analysis of a maxilla from the LBS member, the oldest stratum at the Klasies River main site, and the specimen associates with modern and Holocene African populations and not with samples of archaic sapient forms like Kabwe or Omo II. This new study is an answer to the contention of Wolpoff & Caspari (1990) that the Klasies River remains can be associated with archaic rather than modern humans on metrical analysis.

The Border Cave sample has been found comparable to modern groups (de Villiers 1973, 1976; Rightmire 1979, 1989). There is less agreement on the linguistic or ethnic indigenous groups to which the specimens relate. For example, a study by de Villiers & Fatti (1982) used a multivariate statistical approach and concluded that the affinities of the specimens were with black Africans rather than Bushmen. The analytical procedures adopted in the study, however, have been criticized as inadequate to show any specific relationships (Habgood 1989).

The Klasies River specimens, in their robusticity and dimorphism, appear to define what the dominant morphology of the resident population was in the Last Interglacial *sensu lato*, and the Border Cave specimens that of the end of this period. In the later Pleistocene and Holocene there is evidence for large scale environmental changes and population fluxes in southern Africa (Deacon & Lancaster 1988). This suggests that there was marked selection in this period for the morphological traits that are found in the gracile Bushmen. The reduction in stature in the Bushmen appears to be a Holocene phenomenon and may relate to a known period of aridity (Deacon & Lancaster 1988). There is no series of human fossils available at present to document the progression of morphological changes in the latter part of the Pleistocene.

(b) Taphonomy

The human remains from these two South African sites contrast in their degree of completeness. Those from Klasies River main site are broken and burnt and they show cut marks and impact fractures. These finds are associated with domestic waste, bone and shell food remains, that have been discarded in middens. White (1987) has considered the possibility that cannibalism may be involved.

The two maxillary fragments in the LBS member come from the same horizon, a metre apart, but represent different individuals and probably sexes. The association of these specimens with a single horizon prompted re-examination of the context of the specimens recovered in the 1967–8 excavation at the site. The conclusion, detailed in Rightmire & Deacon (1991), is that the human remains excavated by Singer & Wymer (1982) from cave 1 are from the same stratigraphic horizon in the lower part of the SAS member. The direct association with a thin, 20 mm thick, layer with a number of hearths is being investigated further during current excavations. These human materials relate to two episodes in the history of occupation at the site when human materials were discarded.

The role of interpersonal violence seems to be implied by the occurrence of these remains because of the repeated, episodic nature of the occurrences and because individuals of different ages and sex were involved. A functional explanation that the reasons for interpersonal violence were dietary needs to be weighed up against the alternative explanation that interpersonal violence may have had a ritual basis. Ritual killings (Jones 1951; Evans 1992) that are linked to the activities of shamans and are more frequent in times of socio-political uncertainty or stress, still occur widely in southern Africa. The repetition of events is better explained if the practice of interpersonal violence were part of the cognitive system than if the events were a response to catastrophic circumstances.

None of the human remains from Klasies River main site in the late Pleistocene are from deliberate burials. However, at Border Cave the infant skeleton, BC3, is reported to be a burial and BC5 is reported to have been associated with a depression which may be a grave. The recovery of some postcranial material from the dump of the guano pit may be evidence that BC1 and BC2 were also burials. There are no other burials known in this time range in southern Africa and the next oldest are end-Pleistocene and Holocene in age.

5. CULTURAL ASSOCIATIONS

The Klasies River and Border Cave human fossils are associated with Middle Stone Age artefacts. There are good general descriptions of the Middle Stone Age typology in the literature (e.g. Mason 1962; Volman 1984) and descriptions of the artefacts found specifically at Border Cave (Beaumont 1978) and Klasies River (Singer & Wymer 1982; Thackeray & Kelly 1988; Thackeray 1989). The stone artefacts of the Middle Stone Age are predominantly parallel-sided and more rarely convergent-sided flake blades and blades that have prominent dorsal ridges. The low frequency of flakes showing retouch is probably due to their manufacture from very hard materials. Flakes showing reduction of the base and unifacial or bifacial invasive flaking to form leaf-shaped points are a persistent but rare occurrence. There are elements which appear to show clear design 'style', but most notable is the use of backing or blunting, much like that on the blade of a penknife, to make the crescent- and trapeze-shaped pieces that are associated with the Howiesons Poort.

The backed artefacts that characterize the Howiesons Poort are interesting from several viewpoints. They represent design types, standardized in both shape and size, and intended for hafting as replaceable bits or inserts in composite tools. In Later Stone Age sites there are crescents and other backed tools like those found in the Howiesons Poort, but smaller in size. These smaller backed pieces served as armatures for arrows in the Later Stone Age (Clark 1977) and a comparable function, possibly as armatures for spears, can be suggested for the Howiesons Poort backed tools. The parallels with the Later Stone Age 'Wilton' industries, which had a duration from about 8000 years ago until historic times, are quite striking, because crescent-shaped backed tools have a popularity in the middle period of the Wilton sequence much as the Howiesons Poort segments and trapezes have in the middle stages of the Middle Stone Age sequence. Another feature of the Howiesons Poort at Klasies River (Singer & Wymer 1982) and other sites in the region is the increased use of non-local raw materials. Backed pieces were made on local stone as well, but there appears to have been a conscious choice to select more distant materials for non-utilitarian reasons.

The dating of Howiesons Poort horizons with acceptable precision has proved difficult simply because they are too old to date by radiocarbon. However, as noted above, a dating centered on 70 ka for this horizon at various southern African sites is the current best estimate (Deacon 1989; Miller et al., this symposium). At this date, the occurrence of backed inserts for composite tools is significant. In a European context these are the kind of artefacts that would be associated with much more recent Upper Palaeolithic-type industries and with anatomically modern populations. As Clark (1989) has pointed out, there are other regional industries in Africa, like the Aterian, which include unique design types for hafting that may date to the same time range. If the occurrence of design style of this kind can be taken as an indication of modern cognitive abilities, the evidence would be consistent with modern people being present in Africa in the earlier late Pleistocene.

The distinctive typology of the Howiesons Poort industries makes these assemblages a good regional marker. Occurrences of these industries are known only from southern Africa, south of the Zambezi. This bounded distribution is interesting because it defines the geographic limits of a shared concept of artefact style and therefore information exchange. The same geographic distribution is found in the design styles of Later Stone Age artefacts (Deacon 1984) and in rock art motifs that signify a pan-Bushman belief system (Lewis-Williams 1981). It is only by inferring a common cosmology that the maintenance of this regional integrity in the distribution of very specific styles and motifs can be explained. The continuity between the earlier late Pleistocene and modern times suggests not only that the same modern people were involved but also that they had similar cognitive abilities.

Contrary to the argument offered here, a number of researchers (Binford 1984; Klein 1989, 1992; Ambrose & Lorenz 1990) have reasoned that the behaviour of late Pleistocene Middle Stone Age people was not modern because they did not exploit their environment as efficiently as the Later Stone Age Holocene hunter–gatherers did. It is assumed that they were not capable of doing so because of inferior intelligence. However, arguments of this kind imply an innate motivation to optimize the use of resources rather than to satisfy needs. They also ignore differences in access to technology. Middle Stone Age groups, for example, may not have had snares or fish hooks and they did not have the bow: all of which were available in the Holocene to Later Stone Age foragers. The latter in turn lacked boats, guns and other technology introduced by colonial settlers. Comparisons at this level may not be very informative as simpler life styles do not imply a lesser cognitive ability. Later Stone Age people cannot be judged to have been the intellectual inferiors of their Khoikhoi or colonial competitors. A shared cognitive system with their Middle Stone Age ancestors suggests that modern behavioural potentials were achieved at least by the beginning of the late Pleistocene.

6. Whence Modern Humans?

Sites like Klasies River main site and Border Cave have attracted attention because the claims for the early dating of anatomically modern human fossils seemed to run counter to any accepted wisdom on modern human origins even a decade ago. The contribution of molecular biological studies has helped to focus attention on these African sites and to stimulate new investigations here and elsewhere.

Klasies River is as well dated as any late Pleistocene deposit and the context of the human fossils is also well documented. The question is whether these fossils are anatomically modern because, if so, they are among the oldest such remains known. Assessment as modern would provide support for an hypothesis of an African origin of modern people. Where, as in this case, there has been continuity rather than replacement in the population in the late Pleistocene, the diagnosis of 'modern' morphology is to some degree a question of definition. Selection has operated in the late Pleistocene to reduce dimorphism and robusticity. Klasies River documents the presence of a strongly dimorphic population in the Last Interglacial. The retention of some archaic characters (Smith, this symposium) in a non-Neanderthaloid and robust morphology would not rule out assessment of this sample as anatomically modern (Rightmire & Deacon 1991). The gracile specimens, presumed to be female, show characteristics in the area of the chin, frontal and teeth that are impressively modern. The robust male specimens have a more archaic appearance. The Border Cave material which is younger in age does not present the same problem for assessment as modern because of the progression of selection.

The human fossils from these sites are considered to represent the products of evolution in an isolated Late Pleistocene regional population. They can be grouped in a Bushman clade with the implication that the branching of this clade occurred before the beginning of the late Pleistocene. Further support for this contention comes from the genetic evidence that the Bushmen are a long-separate African population (Nurse *et al.* 1985; Vigilant 1989) and the cultural associations that show the region functioned as a bounded entity in the late Pleistocene. Southern Africa thus offers an example of regional continuity without population replacement: but only for the time range of the late Pleistocene. The evidence does not rule out the possibility that the initial evolution of modern people occurred in a single centre, presumably located in sub-Saharan Africa as the early phase of dispersal would have had to include southern Africa. This would have been in the Middle Pleistocene, a period poorly researched in Africa, in part, because of difficulties in dating the evidence. The application of new dating techniques holds the prospect that this critical period of the Middle Pleistocene will soon become better known.

ACKNOWLEDGMENTS

The support by the Centre for Science Development, Pretoria, and the University of Stellenbosch for the research at Klasies River is gratefully acknowledged. I thank Professor O. Bar-Yosef, Mr J. S. Brink, Dr Janette Deacon, Dr Paul Mellars and Ms Ria Schuurman for comments and Mr L. Rossouw for drawing the illustrations. The Struwig Trust has facilitated the research.

REFERENCES

Ambrose, S.H. & Lorenz, K.G. 1990 Social and ecological models for the Middle Stone Age in southern Africa. In *The emergence of modern humans* (ed. P. Mellars), pp. 3–33. Edinburgh University Press.

Bada, J.L. & Deems, L. 1975 Accuracy of dates beyond the C-14 dating limit using the aspartic acid racemization reaction. *Nature, Lond.* **255**, 218–219.

Beaumont, P.B. 1978 Border Cave. M.A. thesis, University of Cape Town.

Beaumont, P.B. 1980 On the age of Border Cave hominids 1–5. *Palaeont. afr.* **23**, 21–33.

Beaumont, P.B., de Villiers, H. & Vogel, J.C. 1978 Modern man in sub-Saharan Africa prior to 49 000 BP: a review and evaluation with particular reference to Border Cave. *S. Afr. J. Sci.* **74**, 409–419.

Binford, L.R. 1984 *Faunal remains from Klasies River Mouth.* Orlando: Academic Press.

Bräuer, G. 1989 The evolution of modern humans: a comparison of the African and non-African evidence. In *The human revolution* (ed. P. Mellars & C. B. Stringer), pp. 123–154. Edinburgh University Press.

Bräuer, G. & Rösing, F.W. 1989 Human biological history of southern Africa. *Rassengeschichte der Menschheit 13, Afrika 2. Südafrika.* München: R. Oldenbourg Verlag.

Bräuer, G., Deacon, H.J. & Zipfel, F. 1992 Comment on the new maxillary finds from Klasies River, South Africa. *J. hum. Evol.* (In the press.)

Brink, J.S. 1987 The archaeozoology of Florisbad, Orange Free State. *Mem. Nas. Mus., Bloemfontein* **24**, 1–151.

Clark, J.D. 1977 Interpretations of prehistoric technology from ancient Egyptian and other sources. Part II. Prehistoric arrow forms in Africa as shown by surviving examples of the traditional arrows of San Bushmen. *Paléorient* **3**, 127–150.

Clark, J.D. 1989 The origins and spread of modern humans: a broad perspective on the African evidence. In *The human revolution* (ed. P. Mellars & C. B. Stringer), pp. 565–588. Edinburgh University Press.

Cowling, R.M., Gibbs Russell, G.E., Hoffman, M.T. & Hilton-Taylor, C.H. 1989 Patterns of plant species diversity in southern Africa. In *Biotic diversity in southern Africa* (ed. B. J. Huntley), pp. 19–50. Cape Town: Oxford University Press.

Deacon, H.J. 1989 Late Pleistocene palaeoecology and archaeology in the southern Cape, South Africa. In *The human revolution* (ed. P. Mellars & C. B. Stringer), pp. 547–564. Edinburgh University Press.

Deacon, H.J. & Geleijnse, V.B. 1988 The stratigraphy and sedimentology of the main site sequence, Klasies River, South Africa. *S. Afr. archaeol. Bull.* **43**, 5–14.

Deacon, H.J., Talma, A.S. & Vogel, J.C. 1988 Biological and cultural development of Pleistocene people in an Old World southern continent. In *Early Man in the Southern Hemisphere* (ed. J. R. Prescott), pp. S23–S31. Adelaide: Department of Physics and Mathematical Physics, University of Adelaide.

Deacon, H.J. & Thackeray, J.F. 1984 Late Quaternary environmental changes and implications from the archaeological record in southern Africa. In *Late Cenozoic palaeoclimates of the southern hemisphere* (ed. J. C. Vogel), pp. 375–390. Rotterdam: Balkema.

Deacon, J. 1984 Later Stone Age people and their descendants in southern Africa. In *Southern African prehistory and paleoenvironments* (ed. R. G. Klein), pp. 221–328. Rotterdam: Balkema.

Deacon, J. & Lancaster, N. 1988 *Late Quaternary palaeoenvironments of southern Africa.* Oxford: Clarendon Press.

De Villiers, H. 1973 Human skeletal remains from Border Cave, Ingwavuma District, Kwa Zulu, South Africa. *Ann. Transv. Mus.* **28**, 229–256.

De Villiers, H. 1976 A second adult human mandible from Border Cave, Ingwavuma District, Kwa Zulu, South Africa. *S. Afr. J. Sci.* **72**, 212–215.

De Villiers, H. & Fatti, L.P. 1982 The antiquity of the Negro. *S. Afri. J. Sci.* **78**, 321–333.

Evans, J. 1992 'Where can we find a beast without hair?' Medicine murder in Swaziland 1970–1988. *Afr. Stud.* **51**.

Grine, F.E. & Klein, R.G. 1985 Pleistocene and Holocene human remains from Equus Cave, South Africa. *Anthropology* **8**, 55–98.

Grine, F.E., Klein, R.G. & Volman, T.P. 1991 Dating, archaeology and human fossils from the Middle Stone Age levels of Die Kelders, South Africa. *J. hum. Evol.* **21**, 363–395.

Grün, R., Beaumont, P.B. & Stringer, C.B. 1990*a* ESR dating evidence for early modern humans at Border Cave in South Africa. *Nature, Lond.* **344**.

Grün, R., Shackleton, N.J. & Deacon, H.J. 1990*b* Electron-Spin-Resonance dating of tooth enamel from Klasies River Mouth Cave. *Curr. Anthrop.* **31**, 427–432.

Guenther, M.G. 1986 *The Nharo Bushmen of Botswana. Tradition and change.* Quellen zur Khoisanforschung 3. Hamburg: Helmut Buske Verlag.

Habgood, P.J. 1989 The examination of regional features of Middle and early Late Pleistocene sub-Saharan African hominids. *S. Afr. archaeol. Bull.* **44**, 17–22.

Jones, G.I. 1951 *Basutoland medicine murder.* London: HMSO.

Klein, R.G. 1989 Biological and behavioural perspectives on modern human origins in southern Africa. In *The human revolution* (ed. P. Mellars & C. B. Stringer), pp. 529–546. Edinburgh University Press.

Klein, R.G. 1992 The archaeology of modern human origins. *Evol. Anthrop.* **1**, 5–14.

Kuman, K. & Clarke, R.J. 1986 Florisbad—new investigations at a Middle Stone Age hominid site in South Africa. *Int. J. Geoarchaeol.* **1**, 103–125.

Lewis-Williams, J.D. 1981 *Believing and seeing.* London: Academic Press.

Martinson, D.G., Pisias, N.G., Hays, J.D., Imbrie, J., Moore, T.C. & Shackleton, N.J. 1987 Age dating and the orbital theory of the Ice Ages: development of a high-resolution 0 to 300,000-year chronostratigraphy. *Quat. Res.* **27**, 1–29.

Mason, R.J. 1982 *Prehistory of the Transvaal.* Johannesburg: Witwatersrand University Press.

Nurse, G.T., Weiner, J.S. & Jenkins, T. 1985 *The peoples of southern Africa and their affinities.* Oxford: Clarendon Press.

Rightmire, G.P. 1978 Human skeletal remains from the southern Cape Province and their bearing on the Stone Age prehistory of southern Africa. *Quat. Res.* **9**, 219–230.

Rightmire, G.P. 1979 Implications of Border Cave skeletal remains for later Pleistocene human evolution. *Curr. Anthrop.* **20**, 23–35.

Rightmire, G.P. 1989 Middle Stone Age humans from eastern and southern Africa. In *The human revolution* (ed. P. Mellars & C. B. Stringer), pp. 109–122. Edinburgh University Press.

Rightmire, G.P. & Deacon, H.J. 1991 Comparative studies of Late Pleistocene human remains from Klasies River Mouth, South Africa. *J. hum. Evol.* **20**, 131–156.

Shackleton, N.J. 1982 Stratigraphy chronology of the Klasies River Mouth deposits: oxygen isotope evidence. In *The Middle Stone Age at Klasies River Mouth in South Africa* (ed. R. Singer & J. Wymer), pp. 194–199. Chicago: Chicago University Press.

Singer, R. & Wymer, J. 1982 *The Middle Stone Age at Klasies River Mouth in South Africa*. Chicago University Press.

Thackeray, A.I. 1989 Changing fashions in the Middle Stone Age: the stone artefact sequence from Klasies River main site, South Africa. *Afr. archaeol. Rev.* **7**, 33–57.

Thackeray, A.I. & Kelly, A. 1988 A technical and typological analysis of Middle Stone Age assemblages antecedent to the Howiesons Poort at Klasies River main site. *S. Afr. archaeol. Bull.* **43**, 15–26.

Thomas, D.S.G. & Shaw, P.A. 1991 *The Kalahari environment*. Cambridge University Press.

Vigilant, L., Pennington, R., Harpending, H. & Kocher, T.D. 1989 Mitochondrial DNA sequences in single hairs from a southern African population. *Proc. natn. Acad. Sci. U.S.A.* **86**, 9350–9354.

Vigilant, L., Stoneking, M., Harpending, H., Hawkes, K. & Wilson, A.C. 1991 African populations and the evolution of human mitochondrial DNA. *Science, Wash.* **253**, 1053–1057.

Volman, T.P. 1984 Early prehistory of southern Africa. In *Southern African prehistory and paleoenvironments* (ed. R. G. Klein), pp. 169–220. Rotterdam: Balkema.

White, T.D. 1987 Cannibalism at Klasies? *Sagittarius* **2**, 6–9.

Wolpoff, M.H. & Caspari, R. 1990 Metric analysis of skeletal material from Klasies River Mouth, Republic of South Africa. *Am. J. phys. Anthrop.* **81**, 319.

Recent Human Evolution in Northwestern Africa

Jean-Jacques Hublin[1]

SUMMARY

The first modern humans in the Maghreb are said to be associated with the Aterian industries which appeared at least 40 ka BP in the northwest. Their predecessors are mainly represented by the Jebel Irhoud (Morocco) specimens. Palaeontological evidence, as well as electron spin resonance (ESR) dating, suggests that this series is older than previously published, and should belong to oxygen isotope stage 5 or even 6. There is no evidence of any Neanderthal apomorphy in this group which can no longer be considered as 'African Nanderthals'. Clear synapomorphies with modern man combined with some plesiomorphic retentions indicate a slightly more primitive (and older?) grade than the Qafzeh–Skhul sample in southwestern Asia. The Northwestern evidence demonstrates that the mediterranean sea was a major biological barrier during the upper Middle and lower Upper Pleistocene and that the rise of anatomically modern features cannot be restricted to a sub-Saharan of eastern African area.

Fossil hominids associated with the Aterian industries in Morocco are usually considered the oldest anatomically modern humans in the Maghreb. The first discovery of human remains related to this industry was made by C. S. Coon in 1939 at Mugharet el Aliya (Tangier). It consists of an isolated and heavily worn left upper second molar and a fragment of a juvenile left maxilla bearing two unerupted premolars and the unerupted canine. These very fragmentary remains were compared with Neanderthals and the juvenile maxilla was said to lack a canine fossa (Senyurek 1940), although a clear *incurvatio inframalaris frontalis* is observed on the specimen. Two other teeth discovered in 1947 remain undescribed. Later the Temara mandible, a more complete specimen, was discovered by J. Roche in 1959 near Rabat and initially attributed to the Acheulean. However, its taxonomic attribution remained unclear and it was described by Vallois & Roche (1958) as bearing 'un ensemble de caractères dont certains rappellent les Néanderthaliens, quelques' uns sont plus avancés, un plus grand nombre est nettement plus primitif'. New excavations at the site have recently demonstrated that the Temara mandible belonged to the Upper

[1] Department of Anthropology, University of California, Berkeley, California 94720, U.S.A. and CNRS, Chaire de Paléoanthropologie du Collège de France, Museum National d'Histoire Naturelle, Paris, France

Aterian levels of the site (Roche & Texier 1976). In 1975 an Upper Aterian level at the same site yielded a rear skull (*squama occipitalis* with part of the parietals) and a piece of the left supraorbital part of the frontal from the same individual. The same year more complete remains were discovered in the Dar-es-Soltane II cave. They were unearthed on top of a marine sand layer below a fallen sand stone block overlaid by Aterian levels. At least three individuals are represented by a partial skull including part of the upper face and an associated hemimandible (Dar-es-Soltane 5), an adolescent mandible lacking its ramus and a juvenile calvaria (Debenath 1975; Ferembach 1976*b*; Debenath *et al.* 1982, 1986). Finally the Zouhra cave (El Harhoura) yielded a mandible in 1977 and a canine in 1978, associated in an 'Aterian with Moroccan points' level (Debenath *et al.* 1982).

The Temara and Dar-es-Soltane II cranial remains were briefly described by Ferembach (1976*a*,*b*) who emphasized the modern status of the Aterian people. Debenath (1991) also provides an illustration of Dar-es-Soltane 5. In Temara the morphology, and the metrical features of the occipital do not show any significant difference from modern series such as those from Afalou or Taforalt. The frontal fragment does not display a supraorbital torus but a flattened *trigonum supraorbitale* (pattern B of Cunningham (1908)). Dar-es-Soltane 5 is a very robust specimen assigned to a mature male individual. The dimensions are large, especially the tranversal ones. Facially the bizygomatic, bijugal, interorbital, orbital and nasal breadths are very large, whereas upper facial height remains moderate, and the orbits and nasal cavities are low. The vault is high (bregma above the biporion axis) but still has wide proportions. One of the most distinctive features of the specimen is the development of the supraorbital relief. The glabella projects, overhanging a deep infraglabellar depression. The *arcus superciliaris* is protuding but well differentiated from the glabella and from the lateral part of the supraorbital area, which is less voluminous and forms a thick *tigonum supraorbitale*. The orbits are voluminous, deep and rectangular. Their axes slightly slope laterally. The nasal opening is pyriform with a sharp inferior border. The face is flattened with the lateral part of the maxilla in a coronal orientation forming a clear angulation with the zygomatic. In *norma lateralis* it is orthognatic with a moderate alveolar prognathism. The temporal squama is rather small and elongated. In *norma basiliaris*, the axes of the tympanic and the petrosal parts of the temporal have the same orientation. The mastoid process is robust and projecting with a marked mastoid crest. The mandible is also very robust. The corpus is thick with great depth anteriorly which decreases markedly posteriorly. The mental foramen is located at mid-height of the corpus, below P4. The ramus is wide and high. None of the mandibular or cranial features observed in Dar-es-Soltane 5 exclude it from modern variation. The Aterian people always display a very robust masticatory apparatus and a pronounced megadonty. These features could explain why the first discoveries (Tangier and Temara), which were represented by mandibular material, were considered as more primitive than they actually are.

The dating of the Aterian in Morocco was reviewed in 1986 by Debenath *et al*. The oldest dated levels seem, unfortunately, beyond the reach of the ^{14}C method. In Temara three dates greater than 40 ka BP, from levels 23 to 19 (Gif 2279, Gif 2588 and Gif 2589), are not considered by Debenath *et al*. (1986), who retain Gif 2277 > 34 550 ± $^{3200}_{2280}$ years BP in level 19 as the *terminus ante quem* of the Moroccan Aterian. Nevertheless, a thermoluminescence (TL) dating BOR56: 41 160 + 3500 years was obtained in the Aterian Level 1 of El Haroura, whereas in this site as well as in Dar-es-Soltane only the upper Aterian seems represented (Debenath *et al*. 1986). These authors, as well as Texier *et al*. (1988), place the chronology of the Aterian industries in northwestern Africa between 40 and 20 ka BP, with a late development toward the South, in North Chad and Niger (Tillet 1983), while the occurence of a hiatus between the Aterian and Iberomaurusian has been argued (Roche 1976).

The question of dating the very first Aterian in North Africa is closely connected with the problem of defining the relationship between this industry and the Mousterian. In Morocco the two 'cultures' seem to evolve one from the other without any discontinuity. The superposition of the two industries was described in the Grotte des Pigeons at Taforalt (Roche 1952). It occurs also at Temara (Debenath *et al*. 1986) and at Rhafas (near Oujda) (Wengler 1986). In both sites a typological transition is observed. At Rhafas, the first genuine Aterian level, with a high percentage of tanged artifacts, still belongs to the 'Lower Soltanian' which is imprecisely identified with the 'Lower Wurm' in the local chronostratigraphy. It overlays a 'proto-Aterian' and a 'final Mousterian'. All the series show a regular technological evolution with an expansion of tanged artifacts and end-scrapers, while side-scrapers decrease. In eastern Morocco, Wengler (1990) observed the same strategy in raw materials exploitation and debitage techniques in both Mousterian and Aterian and subscribed to their 'cultural likeness'.

To the East the situation is more confused. Wendorf *et al*. (1990) assert the Aterian is significantly older than usually accepted, claiming that the only acceptable ^{14}C dates for the Aterian are the infinite or the oldest ones, such as the age near 47 ka BP obtained for one level in Haua Fteah (McBurney 1967), although the Aterian nature of this level might be contested (Debenath *et al*. 1986). Furthermore, according to Wendorf *et al*. (1990), the Mousterian and Aterian may not even be chonologically separated. The antiquity of the Aterian in Algeria may be supported by its occurrence in beach deposits of the last interglacial (Roubet 1969). In El Guettar (Tunisia), a 'typical Aterian tanged point' was discovered in the lowest part of the Mousterian sequence, within an artificial cairn (Gruet 1954). In Egypt, the dating provided for the Bir Tarfawi depression deposits stretches from 160 to 70 ka ago (Wendorf *et al.* 1990). These authors initially assigned most of the excavated sites of this area to a 'Denticulate Aterian' while none of them yielded any tanged pieces in a stratigraphic context. But finally, except for the oldest ones which are considered as 'Mousterian', they assigned the Bir Tarfawi sites to a 'Middle Palaeolithic with denticulates and bifacial foliate points'. However, while in northwestern Africa the later Aterian/Iberomaurusian succession appears to be a clear cut replacement (Roche 1976), perhaps related to a major environmental deterioration (Texier *et al.* 1988), the Mousterian and Aterian succession should, in contrast, be considered as an evolutionary process.

The only North African site which has yielded a rather complete set of Mousterian human remains is the Jebel Irhoud cave, 55 km southeast of Safi (Morocco). The site belongs to the upper part of a karstic network filled with Pliocene and Pleistocene deposits. It was opened in 1960 during the exploitation of a barytine mine. The incidental discovery of a cranium (Irhoud 1) occurred in 1961. Then, an excavation undertaken by E. Ennouchi yielded an adult calvaria (Irhoud 2) at the bottom of the sequence ('ashy level C' of Ennouchi (1963)). In 1968 a juvenile mandible (Irhoud 3) was unearthed 0.6 m lower than Irhoud 2 (Ennouchi 1969). During an excavation by J. Tixier and de Bayles des Hermens in 1969, a juvenile humeral diaphysis (Irhoud 4) was discovered in the lowermost part of the archaeological deposits in level 18 (Hublin *et al.* 1987). The industry studied by Tixier (Hublin *et al.* 1987) is mainly made with flint (54%) or local quartzite (36%). It is characterized by the use of the Levallois technique ('lineal' or 'reccurent') for a quarter of the tools and by 'facettage'. The artifacts are made on flakes without evidence of Quina retouch and very little bifacial rework. Side scrapers are predominant. Unretouched Lavallois tools, notches and denticulates are numerous. The absence of end-scrapers and tanged artifacts is notable.

Biberson (1964) set the Irhoud cave filling near the Presoltanian/Soltanian boundary, i.e. close to oxygen isotope stage 5e. In this view Irhoud would be older than the 'classical' Neanderthals of western Europe. Nevertheless, the contemporaneity of the two groups has been accepted by most palaeoanthropologists (see, for example, Wolpoff (1980); Debenath *et al.* (1982); Bräuer (1984)). This opinion was partly based on the supposed age of all the Mousterian industries and on a ^{14}C dating (greater than 30 ka BP) published by Ennouchi (1966). Actually the date was beyond the reach of the method. To obtain a more accurate age for this site, I provided R. Grün (then at McMaster University in Canada) with three horse teeth and a block of matrix from the Tixier excavation. Five electron spin resonance (ESR) dates were obtained and recently published by Grün & Stringer (1991). EU age estimates range between 90 and 125 ka and LU estimates between 105 and 190 ka. These authors conclude that the site had a long depositional history covering at least oxygen isotope stages 5 and 6 and favour an age within stage 6 (130–190 ka) for the hominids, assuming that they were low in the stratigraphic sequence. Nevertheless, the sediment sample from which the external dose rate was derived does not seem to be representative of the environment of the three teeth, and the close stratigraphic origin of these samples, in the bottom of the stratigraphic sequence, seems inconsistent with the very wide range of ages determined. The fauna yielded by the Tixier excavation was studied by Thomas (1981), and more recently Amani (1991) studied the collections kept in the Faculté des Sciences in Rabat. The faunal association evokes a landscape varying from steppe to desert. The lack of some immigrant species (*Sus*, Cervids) indicates that the deposits predate the major faunal changes affecting the Soltanian, but the accurate age of these changes remains uncertain. According to Jaeger (personal communication) the microfauna is more likely to be 'Ouljian' (i.e. belonging to stage 5 according to this author). Interestingly in the faunal list established by Amani (1991) one finds *Gerbillus grandis*, a species which was described in the Thomas Quarry (Tong 1989) and an Alcelaphinae bearing a primitive dentition (*Rabaticeras?*). These two elements give the fauna a more archaic character than the fauna of Soltanian sites such as Doukala (Morocco). The palaeontological evidence would then support the ESR ages predating stage 4 obtained by Grün.

The Irhoud specimens have been repeatedly allocated to the Neanderthals or designated as bearing Neanderthal features (e.g. Ennouchi 1963, 1969; Howell, 1978; Brauer 1984). This interpretation has been contested by Ferembach (1972), Howells (1974, 1975), Stringer (1974, 1978); Hublin (1978a, 1991), Santa-Luca (1978), Hublin & Tillier (1981) and Hublin *et al.* (1987). Detailed descriptions of Irhoud 3 and 4 were published (Hublin & Tillier 1981; Hublin *et al.* 1987) while the most complete specimens, Irhoud 1 and 2, have been only recently described in detail (Hublin 1991). The main measurements of the Irhoud skull are displayed in table 1.

The Irhoud 3 mandible belonged to an individual about 8-years-old. It is more robust than a present day mandible of an individual of the same age, with some primitive aspects on the posterior side of the symphysis which bears a *planum alveolare* and a *fossa genioglossa*. However, it does not display any clear Neanderthal apomorphy. The anterior teeth are not in alignment. The condyle is not expanded laterally. It can be extrapolated that the retromolar space would have been reduced in the adult. In contrast, modern traits such as the small size of the condyle, the decreasing depth of the corpus posteriorly, the orientation of the digastric fossae, and the association of the four components of a bony chin (*tuber symphyseos, tuber lateralia, fossae mentales* and *incurvatio mandibulae*) are observed. One of the most striking features is the size of the teeth, especially the cheek teeth (Hublin &

Table 1. *Some measurements of Irhoud 1 and 2 discussed in the text, compared with the means and standard deviations observed in European Neanderthals and in the Skhul–Qafzeh group*

(The abbreviations of the measurements are after Martin (1928) or Howells (1973). When the number of individuals measured is below 4, only the range of variation is given).

measurements		Irhoud 1	Irhoud 2	Skhul–Qafzeh	European Neanderthals
maximum length (g-op)	M 1	196.5	194.0 ?	201.0 ± 8.4	203.5 ± 4.4
maximum breadth	M 8	149.5	161.0 ?	144.4 ± 2.7	149.7 ± 6.5
minimum frontal breadth	M 9	105.8	117.0	102.4 ± 4.9	106.8 ± 2.9
maximum frontal breadth	M 10	120.0	131.0 ?	119.4 ± 4.2	120.3 ± 6.8
frontal angle of Schwalbe	M 32a	78.0	84.5	81.6 ± 6.2	65.6 ± 4.4
bregma-glabella-inion angle	M 32(2)	54.3	55.0	56.0 ± 3.4	47.9 ± 2.2
frontal convexity angle	FRA	133.0	131.0	130.5–135	140.9 ± 4.1
parietal sagittal arc (b-1)	M 27	122.0	121.0 ?	132.5 ± 10.3	115.6 ± 5.9
parietal convexity angle	PAA	150.0	145.5	136.6 ± 1.7	139.3 ± 6.2
upper facial height	M 48	76.0	—	72–79	86–92
zygomaticomaxillary angle	SSA	125.0	—	124–133	110.6 ± 4.3
AVR-ZMR		16.5	—	3.0–21	22.1 ± 3.0
nasal height	M 55	52.5	—	53.8 ± 1.3	61–66

123

Tillier 1981). This macrodonty associated with a modern-like chin area and with the persistence of some archaic features on the posterior side of the symphysis evokes the conditions observed in the Skhul–Qafzeh series from the Middle East.

The Irhoud 4 humeral diaphysis is flattened medio-laterally. The lateral supracondylar crest is projecting and the distal epiphysis would have been wide. The deltoid tuberosity is positioned high on the humerus and is frontally oriented. The cresting in the deltoid area forms a very narrow V. The *facies anterior medialis* is flattened and the lateral side of the shaft does not display a *sulcus nervi radialis* but a faint convexity. The cortical part of the bone is thickened relative to the medullary cavity. None of these features, however, need be considered as exclusively Neanderthal but express a great robusticity. The high position of the deltoid tuberosity, the flattening of the diaphysis and the reduction of the medullary cavity are more likely to be plesiomorphic conditions which were common in archaic *Homo sapiens*.

Irhoud 1 (table 1; figures 1 and 2) is a large skull, long and wide but already with an anteriorly positioned maximum width. The vault is low, in the common range of variation of the Neanderthals and the first modern humans. The sagittal profile is elevated in its anterior part but after the bregma it forms a long and moderately convex arc. Thus, the bregmatic index (height of bregma above the glabella-inion line/glabella-inion length) is 51.35, well above the range of variation of the European Neanderthals (36.5–43.1) and near the values of Skhul V (47.8) or Qafzeh 9 (50.2). In posterior view it displays a pentagonal profile flattened at the top; the lateral sides are nearly parallel. The *tuber parietale* are well defined and superiorly positioned. The frontal bone is wide as in the Neanderthals, but also as in the Skhul–Qafzeh group or in Omo 2 or Eliye Springs, but less than in the extremely wide Florisbad frontal. The convexity of the frontal is close to the modern condition. A moderately pneumatized supraorbital torus is present which thins laterally. The parietal arc is long absolutely and relatively to the temporal border of the parietal, but the sagittal convexity remains weak. The squamosal has a rounded and absolutely high outline but it is elongated antero-posteriorly. The root of the zygomatic process is set above the external acoustic meatus. The glenoid fossa is deep and well delimited, with a raised *tuberculum articulare*. The mastoid process is rather small but well defined and projecting downward below the juxtamastoid eminence. The occipital displays low proportions and a flat *planum occipitale* without protruding occipital torus. The endocranial capacity has been estimated to be 1480 cm^3 by Anthony (1966) and 1305 cm^3 by Holloway (1981). The face is wide and low. The prognathism does not exceed the modern condition. The alveolar prognathism is strong but there is no indication of mid-facial prognathism. The orbits are voluminous, rectangular, with axes oriented slightly downward laterally. The nasal cavity is wide in

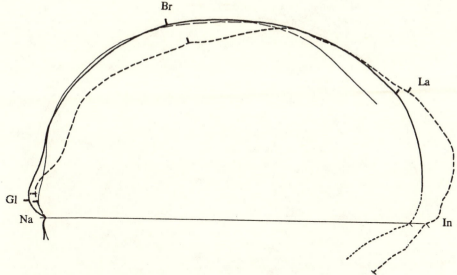

Figure 1. Median outlines of Irhoud 1 (bold continuous line), Irhoud 2 (fine continuous line) and La Chapelle-aux-Saints (discontinuous line). Magn. ×0.53.

its lower part, but narrow upward, and it is very short. The medial part of the zygomatic bone as well as its *facies lateralis* are oriented frontally. The maxilla is of the 'inflexion' type, with an obliquely oriented and moderately wide frontal process. The alveolar arcade is very robust.

Irhoud 2 (table 1; figures 1 and 2) is very similar to Irhoud 1, but the former is metopic, which might explain some difference between the two specimens, including its wider proportions and its more convex frontal bone. This more modern aspect of the frontal is associated with a higher differentiation of the supraorbital elements. Nevertheless, the specimen has no genuine *trigonum supraorbitale*. The cranial bones are thinner than in Irhoud 1 and not far from the modern values. Some other aspects including the higher proportions of the temporal, a more convex parietal arc and the occurrence of an infratemporal crest are more advanced than in Irhoud 1. But in contrast, some other features are more primitive (length of the temporal edge of the parietal, lower proportion of the occipital). This variation seems compatible with the one observed in series such as Qafzeh, Skhul or Shanidar (McCown & Keith 1935; Vandermeersch 1981; Trinkaus 1983). Despite the stratigraphical uncertainties, Irhoud 1 and 2 likely belonged to the same population.

The features observed on Irhoud 1 and 2 are consistent with those already described on Irhoud 3 and 4. No Neanderthalian apomorphies are observed. The skull especially lacks: (i) a round profile ('en bombe') in

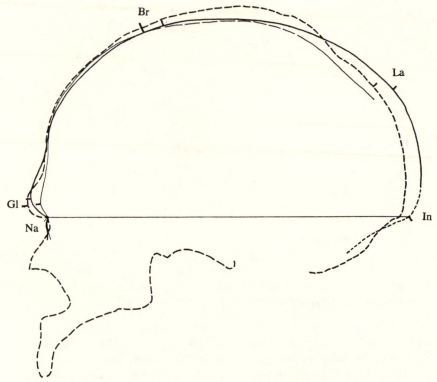

Figure 2. Median outlines of Irhoud 1 (bold continuous line), Irhoud 2 (fine continuous line) and Skhul V (discontinuous line). Magn ×0.53.

norma occipitalis; (ii) a flattening of the mastoid process on the petrous part of the temporal; (iii) a *tuberculum mastoideum anterius* (Hublin 1978*b*); (iv) a projecting juxtamastoid eminence; (v) the bilateral protusion of the occipital torus associated with a developed suprainiac fossa; (vi) a strong convexity of the *planum occipitale* (figure 2); (vii) high and rounded orbits; (viii) mid-facial prognathism and related features: flattening of the antero-lateral part of the maxilla, with no frontal, sagittal or horizontal concavity; a broad and sagitally oriented frontal process of the maxilla; a receding zygomatic; a low subspinale angle (SSA of Howells 1973); and a large difference between M1 alveolus and zygomaxillare radii (AVR and ZMR of Howells 1973).

The only features shared with the Neanderthals are primitive retentions: (i) general robusticity of the skull and of the mandible; and (ii) platycephaly (already reduced), and related features: weak convexity of the parietal; low proportions of the occipital squama; and elongated temporal.

The Irhoud hominids are, therefore, clearly to be excluded from the neanderthal clade. Moreover, they display clear affinities to the first modern humans of the Skhul–Qafzeh group, combining modern apomorphies (especially the development of a bony chin on the mandible, the convexity and orientation of the frontal squama, the dissociation of the supraorbital elements in Irhoud 2) and some plesiomorphies (general robusticity, macrodonty, strong supraorbital relief, a wide, low and flattened face (?)) which allow an ancestor–descendant relationship with late Upper Pleistocene modern humans.

When compared with the Skhul–Qafzeh group, the Irhoud specimens are only slightly more primitive. The cranial vaults of Irhoud 1 and 2 are lower than Skhul 5 (figure 2), mainly in their posterior parts. The rotation of the occipital is less advanced, with a series of consequences such as moderate sagittal convexity of the parietal, a still rather elongated temporal, and the low proportions of the occipital squama. In some morphological aspects, as for example the supraorbital morphology, Irhoud 1 and 2 are similar to the most primitive specimens from Skhul and Qafzeh. When comparing Irhoud with the Aterian specimens, the latter display a more advanced morphology. Nevertheless, no anatomical argument would demonstrate any evolutionary discontinuity between the two groups, a statement already emphasized by Ferembach (1976*b*) and which is consistant with the archaeological record. Furthermore, as with Irhoud, the Aterian hominids display a comparable combination of modern features in association with the same primitive retentions, i.e. the supraorbital relief, the broad braincase and megadonty (Ferembach 1976*b*; Hublin & Tillier 1981; Hublin 1991).

CONCLUSIONS

Anatomically it seems difficult to advocate the 'Neanderthal' or 'Neanderthaloid' nature of the Irhoud material. More likely the few primitive retentions that the Irhoud specimens share with the Neanderthals are explained by their age which probably antedates oxygen isotope stage 4. Furthermore, some of these primitive retentions are still present in the first modern humans from the Middle East. The Mediterranean Sea appears, therefore, as a major biological barrier during at least the second half of the Middle Pleistocene. Although we see in Europe a steady accretion of Neanderthal features from around 300 ka at least, the northwestern African series differs considerably (Hublin 1991). As a result, by the beginning of the Upper Pleistocene two very different populations are separated by the Straits of Gibraltar. This statement is not consistent with substantial exchanges between North Africa and Spain during low sea level periods, an hypothesis regularly proposed mainly on the basis of cultural evidence (Alimen 1975). Tixier (Hublin *et al.* 1987), in describing the Irhoud industries, noted some typological similarities with the Cova Negra industry, and without endorsing a crossing via the Gibraltar straits, stated that the Irhoud Mousterian would not come as a surprise in western Europe. However, some cultural exchanges could have occured without massive human displacement. If the similarities tentatively demonstrated in the Palaeolithic industries North and South of the Gibraltar Straits did not result from simple technical convergence, then whatever population exchanges took place were not substantial enough to allow significant biological change.

Another important aspect of this evolutionary process is that the Irhoud hominids should be considered as a grade immediately preceding the first modern humans of the Middle East and probably predating this group (Valladas *et al.* 1988; Schwarcz *et al.* 1988; Stringer *et al.* 1989). In this view, no anatomical or chronological argument would exclude them from possible ancestry of this group or later still modern Europeans. If an African origin for modern humans is assumed, the 'cradle' is rather large and should be extended from the Atlantic coast of Morocco to South Africa, and should probably include also the Middle East. This scheme rather contradicts the initial 'Out of Africa' genetic model which emphasized the role of the sub-Saharan area (Cann *et al.* 1987; Cavalli Sforza *et al.* 1988; Vigilant *et al.* 1989) nor does it strictly fit the 'Afro-European hypothesis' (Bräuer 1984) which also allocated the origin of modern European to a southeastern part of Africa.

Finally the Irhoud hominids highlight the vexing question of subspecific taxonomy within *Homo sapiens*. The fossil evidence would support the regular, even if accelerated, incrementation of modern features in the late Middle Pleistocene and early Upper Pleistocene in Africa rather than a quick and clear cut emergence of an Adamic 'anatomically modern man'. The attempts to define grades within our species, as for example those by Stringer *et al.* (1979) or Bräuer (1984, 1989) seem unable to resolve this problem. To remain with the North African record, how can we classify together as 'archaic *Homo sapiens*', such a primitive specimen as Salé (which indeed already displays some '*sapiens*' derived features) together with the very different Irhoud specimens, which are already phenetically very near to the middle-eastern forerunners of modern Europeans?

ACKNOWLEDGMENTS

I am grateful to J. Benslimane, F. Z. Alaoui, M. Touri, M. El Ajraoui, A. Debenath, J. P. Raynal and D. Penot for their decisive help. The study and publication of the adult specimens of Jebel Irhoud were allowed by INSAP (Rabat). My research in Morocco has been funded by the Chaire de Paléoanthropologie du College de France (Professor Y. Coppens).

REFERENCES

Alimen, M.H. 1975 Les 'isthmes' hispano-marocain et siculo-tunisien aux temps acheuléens. *Anthropologie* **79**, 399–436.

Amani, F. 1991 *La faune du gisement à hominidés de Jebel Irhoud (Maroc)*. Thesis, University of Rabat.

Anthony, J. 1966 Premières observations sur le moulage endocrânien des hommes fossiles de Jebel Irhoud (Maroc). *C. r. Acad. Sci., Paris* **262**, 556–558.

Biberson, P. 1964 La place des hommes du Paléolithique marocain dans la chrono-logie du Pleistocene atlantique. *Anthropologie* **68**, 475–526.

Bräuer, G. 1984 A craniological approach of the origin of anatomically modern *Homo sapiens* in Africa and implications for the appearance of modern Europeans. In *The origin of modern humans* (ed. F. H. Smith & F. Spencer), pp. 327–410. New York: Alan Liss.

Cann, R.L., Stoneking, M. & Wilson, A.C. 1987 Mitochondrial DNA and human evolution. *Nature, Lond.* **325**, 31–36.

Cavalli-Sforza, L.L., Piazza, A., Menozzi, P. & Moutain, J. 1988 Reconstruction of human evolution: bringing together genetic, archeological and linguistic data. *Proc. natn. Acad. Sci. U.S.A.* **85**, 6002–6006.

Cunningham, D.J. 1908 The evolution of the eyebrow region of the forehead, with special reference to the excessive supraorbital development in the Neanderthal race. *Trans. R. Soc. Edinb.* **46**, 283–311.

Debenath, A. 1975 Découverte de restes humains probablement atériens a Dar Es Soltane (Maroc). *C. r. Acad. Sci., Paris* **281**, 875–876.

Debenath, A. 1991 Les atériens du Maghreb. *Les dossiers d'Archéologie* **161**, 52–57.

Debenath, A., Raynal, J.P. & Texier, J.P. 1982 Position stratigraphique des restes humains paléolithiques marocains sur la base des travaux recents. *C. r. Acad. Sci., Paris* **294**, 1247–1250.

Debenath, A., Raynal, J.P., Roche, J., Texier, J.P. & Ferembach. D. 1986 Position, habitat, typologie et devenir de l'atérien marocain: données récentes. *Anthro-pologie* **90**, 233–246.

Ennouchi, E. 1963 Les néandertaliens du Jebel Irhoud (Maroc). *C. r. Acad. Sci., Paris* **256**, 2459–2460.

Ennouchi, E. 1966 Essai de datation du gisement du Jebel Irhoud (Maroc). *C. r. Somm. Soc. Geol. France* **10**, 405–406.

Ennouchi, E. 1969 Présence d'un enfant néandertalien au Jebel Irhoud (Maroc). *Ann. Paleont. (Vertebres)* **55**, 251–265.

Ferembach, E. 1972 L'ancêtre de l'homme du paléolithique supérieur était-il néandertalien? In *Origine de l'homme moderne* (ed. F. Bordes), pp. 73–80, Paris: Unesco.

Ferembach, D. 1976a Les restes humains de Temara (Campagne 1975). *Bull. Mém. Soc. Anthrop. Paris* **3**, 175–180.

Ferembach, D. 1976b Les restes humains de la grotte de Dar-es-Soltane 2 (Maroc). *Bull. Mém. Soc. Anthrop. Paris* **3**, 183–193.

Gruet, M. 1954 Le gisement moustérien d'El Guettar. *Karthago* **5**, 1–79.

Grün, R. & Stringer, C.B. 1991 Electron spin resonance dating and the evolution of modern humans. *Archaeometry* **33**, 153–199.

Holloway, R. 1981 Volumetric and asymetry determinations on recent hominid endocasts: Spy 1 and 2, Djebel Irhoud I, and the Sale Homo erectus specimens, with some notes on the Neanderthal brain size. *Am. J. phys. Anthrop.* **55**, 385–393.

Howell, F.C. 1978 Hominidae. In *Evolution of African mammals* (ed. V. J. Maglio & H. B. S. Cooke), pp. 154–258. Cambridge: Harvard University Press.

Howells, W.W. 1973 Cranial variation in man. *Pap. Peabody Mus.* **67**, 1–259.

Howells, W.W. 1974 Neanderthals: names hypothesis and scientific method. *Am. Anthrop.* **76**, 24–38.

Howells, W.W. 1975 Neanderthal man: facts and figures. In *Paleoanthropology, morphology and paleoecology* (ed. R. H. Tuttle), pp. 389–407. The Hague: Mouton.

Hublin, J.J. 1978a *Le torus occipital transverse et les structures associées: évolution dans le genre Homo.* Thèse 3e cycle, University of Paris VI.

Hublin, J.J. 1978b Quelques caracteres apomorphes du crâne neandertalien et leur interpretation phylogenetique. *C. r. Acad. Sci., Paris* **287**, 923–925.

Hublin, J.J. 1991 L'émergence des Homo sapiens archaiques: Afrique du Nord-Ouest et Europe occidentale. Thèse d'Etat, Université de Bordeaux 1.

Hublin, J.J. & Tillier, A.M. 1981 The mousterian Juvenile Mandible from Irhoud (Morrocco): a phylogenetic interpretation. In *Aspects of human evolution* (ed. C. B. Stringer), pp. 167–185. London: Taylor and Francis.

Hublin, J.J., Tillier, A.M. & Tixier, J. 1987 L'humérus d'enfant moustérien (Homo 4) de Jebel Irhoud (Maroc) dans son contexte archéologiques. *Bull. Mém. Soc. Anthrop. Paris* **4**, 115–142.

Martin, R. 1928 *Lehrbuch der Anthropologie.* Stuttgart: Fisher.

McBurney, C.B.M. 1967 *The Haua Fteah (Cyrenaica) and the Stone Age of the South-East Mediterranean.* Cambridge University Press.

McCown, H.T. & Keith, H.A. 1939 *The stone age of Mount Carmel II. The fossil human remains from the Levalloiso-Mousterian.* Oxford: Clarendon Press.

Roche, J. 1976 Cadre chronologique de l'épipaléolithique marocain. *IX Congress of UISPP, Colloque II, Pretirage*, pp. 153–167, Nice.

Roche, J. & Texier, J.-P. 1976 Découverte de restes humains dans un niveau atérien supérieur de la grotte des Contrebandiers, à Temara (Maroc). *C. r. Acad. Sci., Paris* **282**, 45–47.

Roubert, F.E. 1969 Le niveau atérien dans la stratigraphie cotière à l'ouest d'Alger. In *Paleoecology of Africa*, vol. IV (ed. E. M. van Zinderen Bakker), pp. 124–129 Cape Town: Balkema.

Santa Luca, A.P. 1978 A re-examination of presumed Neanderthal-like fossils. *J. hum. Evol.* **7**, 616–636.

Schwarcz, H.P., Grün, R., Vandermeersch, B., Bar-Yosef, O., Valladas, H. & Tchernov, E. 1988 ESR dates for the hominid burial site of Qafzeh in Israel. *J. hum. Evol.* **17**, 733–737.

Senyurek, M.S. 1940 Fossil Man in Tangier. *Pap. Peabody Mus. Am. Archeol. Ethnol.* **16**, 1–27.

Stringer, C.B. 1974 Population relationships of Later Pleistocene Hominids; a multivariate study of available crania. *J. archeol. Sci.* **1**, 317–342.

Stringer, C.B. 1978 Some problems in Middle and Upper Pleistocene hominid relationships. In *Recent advances in primatology*, vol. 3 (*Evolution*) (ed. D. Chivers & K. Josey), pp. 395–418. London: Academic Press.

Stringer, C.B., Grün, R., Schwarcz, H.P. & Goldberg, P. 1989 ESR dates for the hominid burial site of Es Skhul in Israel. *Nature, Lond.* **338**, 756–758.

Texier, J.P., Hustable, J., Rhodes, E., Miallier, D. & Ousmoi, M. 1988 Nouvelles données sur la situation chronologique de l'Atérien du Maroc et leurs implications. *C. r. Acad. Sci., Paris* **307**, 827–832.

Tillet, T. 1984 *Le Paléolithique du bassin tchadien septentrional (Niger, Tchad)*. Paris: Ed. du C.N.R.S.

Thomas, H. 1981 La faune de la grotte à néandertaliens du Jebel Irhoud (Maroc). *Quaternaria* **23**, 191–217.

Tong, H. 1989 Origine et évolution des Gerbillidés (Mammalia, Rodentia) en Afrique du Nord. *Mem. Soc. Geol., France* **155**, 1–120.

Trinkaus, E. 1983 *The Shanidar Neandertals*. New York: Academic Press.

Valladas, H., Reys, J.L., Joron, J.L., Valladas, G., Bar-Yosef, O. & Vandermeersch, B. 1988 Thermoluminescence dating of Mousterian 'Proto-Cro-Magnon' remains from Israel and the origin of modern man. *Nature, Lond.* **331**, 614–616.

Vallois, H.V. & Roche, J. 1958 La mandibule acheulénne de Temara. *C. r. Acad. Sci., Paris* **246**, 3113–3116.

Vandermeersch, B. 1981 *Les hommes fossiles de Qafzeh (Israel)*. Paris: C.N.R.S. (Cahiers de Paléoanthropologie).

Vigilant, L., Pennington, R., Harpending, H., Kocher, T. & Wilson, A. 1989 Mitochondrial DNA sequences in single hairs from a southern African population. *Proc. natn. Acad. Sci., U.S.A.* **86**, 9350–9354.

Wendorf, F., Close, A.E., Schild, R., Gautier, A., Schwarcz, H.P., Miller, G.H., Kowalski, K., Krolik, H., Bluszcz, A., Robins, D. & Grün, R. 1990 Le dernier interglaciaire dans le Sahara oriental. *Anthropologie* **94**, 361–391.

Wengler, L. 1986 Position chronologique et modalités du passage Moustérien-Atérien en Afrique du Nord. L'exemple de la grotte du Rhafas au Maroc oriental. *C. r. Acad. Sci., Paris* **303**, 1153–1156.

Wengler, L. 1990 Economie des matières premières et térritoire dans le Moustérien et l'Atérien Maghrébins. Exemple du Maroc oriental. *Anthropologie* **94**, 335–360.

Wolpoff, M. 1980 *Paleoanthropology*. New York: Knopf.

The Role of Western Asia in Modern Human Origins

O. Bar-Yosef[1]

SUMMARY

Western Asia provides the best collection of human skeletal remains relevant to the two basic models for the emergence of modern humans, namely the 'rapid replacement' and the 'regional continuity' models. Regardless of the taxonomies of particular hominids, their chronology is of crucial importance. Thermoluminescence (TL) and electron spin resonance (ESR) dates demonstrate that the Acheulo–Yabrudian and Mousterian entities and their associated fossils (Zuttiyeh, Tabun, Skhul, Qafzeh, Kebara, Shanidar, Amud) span the late Middle and Upper Pleistocene period. These new dates initiated major chronological revisions and renewed discussion of the cultural–archaeological implications. One of the most important conclusions is that the Middle to Upper Palaeolithic transition (or Revolution) 45–40 ka ago has nothing to do with the appearance of anatomically early modern humans in western Asia, which occurred some 100 ka ago or more.

The Levant, the coastal region of the eastern Mediterranean, was both a corridor for movement of humans and animals as well as a refugium during climatically harsh periods. The mixture of morphological characteristics among the available Middle Palaeolithic human fossils is interpreted as reflecting the presence of immigrant and local populations. Archaeologically observable behavioural changes are taken as hints to the pre-adaptations of the Middle to Upper Palaeolithic revolution.

The archaeological record of western Asia can contribute significantly to explaining the Middle to Upper Palaeolithic revolution. This region was the core area where the 'Neolithic Revolution' took place. The shift to systematic cultivation and the domestication of animals occurred within a short time. Population increase resulted from predictable supplies of food, and growth initiated the expansion of early Neolithic communities first northward and then westward and eastward. The westward dispersal into Europe was by demic diffusion and acculturation. I recommend adopting the same research strategy employed to resolve the 'where' and 'when' of the Neolithic revolution for the Middle to Upper Palaeolithic transition. Once the source region is identified and dated, the search for causes can be more focused.

[1] Department of Anthropology, Peabody Museum, Harvard University, Cambridge, Massachusetts 02138, U.S.A.

1. INTRODUCTION

The current debate concerning the origins of modern humans is centred on two models, the 'multi-regional continuity' model (e.g. Wolpoff 1989) and the 'rapid replacement' model, focusing in particular on Africa as source area (e.g. Stringer 1989). The first implies a regional continuity in the evolution of local populations, whereas the second derives all modern humans from a sub-Saharan population. Studies of mitochondrial and nuclear DNA tend to support the second model and suggest that the founder population lived in sub-Saharan Africa some 200–150 ka ago (e.g. Cavalli-Sforza *et al.* 1988; Vigilant *et al.* 1991). Some doubts concerning the interpretation of some of the mitochondrial data have recently been raised (Maddison *et al.* 1992). Note that the 'out of Africa' model suggests that the lineage leading to modern humans emerged 200–150 ka ago while the demic diffusion and replacement of earlier and archaic European populations by incoming modern humans ('Cro-Magnons') took place from around 45–35 ka.

The supposed resemblances between European Cro-Magnons and the early modern fossils from Qafzeh and Skhul were thought to reflect their close temporal relationship (e.g. Howell 1952; Howells 1976; Vandermeersch 1981). It is for this reason that the Qafzeh-Skhul fossils were sometimes termed 'Proto Cro-Magnons'. This view began to change during the 1980s. Chronological assignments based on faunal bio-zones and palaeoenvironmental interpretations preceded the use of TL and ESR in questioning the validity of the accepted model. However, ending the discussion with dated fossils alone, the classification of which is hardly acceptable by all bio-anthropologists, is far from satisfactory.

The main problem now is to uncover the behavioural patterns and changes that took place during the past 200 ka, leading to the emergence of modern cultures as expressed in Upper Palaeolithic archaeological contexts. The main sources of information are Middle Palaeolithic sites.

As in other geographic regions most of the excavations in Levantine caves centred on establishing stratigraphies, and uncovering rich lithic and faunal assemblages as well as human remains. Behavioural information was rarely sought by early excavators who centred their efforts on elaborate lithic studies. However, if we are to understand the cultural changes that reflect behavioural changes which were not caused by the introduction of a new hominid species or a hypothetical neurological mutation, we need to gather behavioural information from such diverse sources as spatial distributions of bones and artefacts on occupational surfaces, hearths, burials, use of red ochre, hunting techniques, choices of plant foods and fire wood, season of site occupation, and so on. Much of the debate concerning the classification of fossils, their dates and the associated lithic industries, diverts our attention from these important issues and at the same time seems to assume that these are the most important data sets available for discussion. Also, the observations concerning so-called 'bio-mechanical' differences among the skeletal remains assume that by scrutinizing the information from lithics or subsistence strategies, as based on faunal studies, we will be able to tell what were the behaviours that resulted in the observable variability, for example, in the shape and thickness of the cortical bone of the lower limbs (e.g. Trinkaus 1989). It is not impossible that such biological traits resulted from activities not registered in the archaeological remains, such as excessive dancing.

The current debate is greatly influenced by the new TL and ESR dates (e.g. Grün & Stringer 1991) which are summarized for the Levant in figure 1. These dates span the late Middle and Upper Pleistocene in the Levantine cave sites (figures 1 and 2) and raise a series of questions.

(1) Can the dated archaeological sequence of Tabun cave serve as a techno-cultural yardstick for the entire Levantine Mousterian?

(2) What is the nature of the Mousterian and its chronological range in the Taurus–Zagros region?

(3) Are there any inferable behavioural differences between the archaeological association of the two human groups (Skhul–Qafzeh versus Kebara–Amud–Shanidar)?

(4) Can the Near Eastern fossils be interpreted as evidence for human movements from Africa to Eurasia? How good is the evidence for the movement of Mediterranean Neanderthals into the Levant? Alternatively, might the fossils represent an evolving regional population?

(5) Does the Middle Palaeolithic archaeological record provide clear evidence for pre-adaptations that were later of critical importance to initiating the Middle to Upper Paleolithic revolution?

The current unresolved debate about the interpretation of the hominid morphological and metrical data and whether the available fossils record one or two Middle Palaeolithic species or simply several populations cannot affirm, as mentioned above, that the bio-mechanical differences in the skeletal remains resulted from, or were caused by, known patterns of behaviour. I therefore suggest we should look for the behavioural aspects as recorded in the archaeological residues (not only in the stone artifacts) and feel that the following questions need to be resolved first.

▶

Figure 1. Radiocarbon, TL and ESR dates from the Levantine sites. Sources: Grün & Stringer (1991); Goren-Inbar (1990); Bar-Yosef (1989); Huxtable (1990). For some of the TL and ESR measurements the oldest and the youngest dates obtained for samples of each level are indicated (by bars and circles respectively) with associated error limits for those samples. The average dates for each level, as published, are also shown.

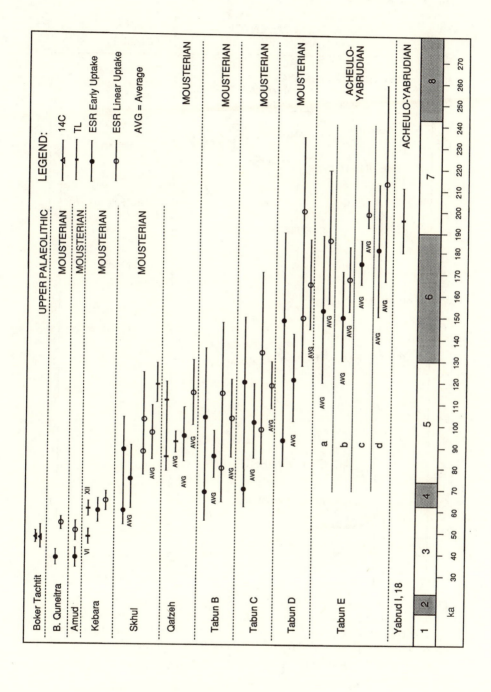

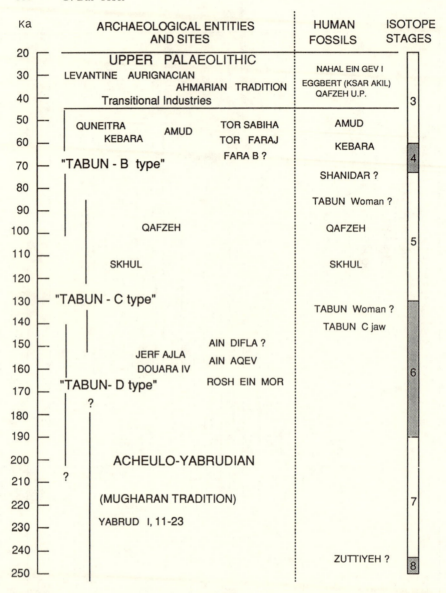

Figure 2. A proposed chronology for Levantine sites and human fossils. Question marks indicate the uncertain position of fossils or those which are not yet dated. The apparent overlapping of the Mousterian industries reflects the standard deviations on the age measurements and conflicting dates. These industries are stratified and therefore cannot be contemporary with each other.

(1) What if some kind of difference can be inferred when comparing features that occur in both Middle and Upper Palaeolithic contexts such as the spatial organization of features and dumping zones in occupation sites, burials, hearths, use of red ochre or other pigments, collection of marine shells when not a subsistence activity, etc.?

(2) Do differences between faunal assemblages in frequencies of mammalian species, distribution of body parts, fragmentation indices and cut marks represent shifts in hunting strategies, hunting techniques and opportunistic scavenging through time?

(3) Are there any functional differences between sites evidenced in the bio-data? Can patterns of site distributions across the region be used to reconstruct the seasonal or annual movements in each period?

(4) What do operational sequences (*chaînes opératoires*) in stone tool production reflect when good quality flint was available in the vicinity of the site, a situation that characterizes most Levantine sites? Is there any evidence for curation of stone artifacts? Are there any correlations between blank types, frequencies of retouched items, and a set of preferred activities?

Several brief answers to a few of these questions are outlined below, while others are still under study.

2. THE CULTURAL SEQUENCE, ASSOCIATED FOSSILS AND THE DATES

The large number of lithic studies from stratified Mousterian assemblages indicates that one may employ the archaeological sequence of Tabun cave as a basic scale, at least for the Levant (Garrod & Bate 1937; Copeland 1975; Jelinek 1982; Bar-Yosef 1989). This site contains the longest stratigraphic record in the region, and the trend exhibited by the published TL and ESR dates supports the contention that it can serve as an archaeological yardstick (figure 2). The following summary is based on several studies of operational sequences (*chaîne opératoire*) for the production of blanks (e.g. Meignen & Bar-Yosef 1988) and incorporates the human fossils for which the stratigraphic provenance is reasonably secure.

1. The pre-Mousterian layers in Tabun contain the Upper Acheulian levels (not discussed here) covered by the thick deposit of the archaeological entity known as 'Acheulo–Yabrudian' or 'Mugharan Tradition' (Jelinek 1982). Three lithic facies were defined on the basis of quantitative studies in these levels (e.g. Jelinek 1982). The 'Yabrudian facies' contains numerous side-scrapers, often made on thick flakes, which, following extensive resharpening, resulted in high frequencies of scaled retouch, together with a few Upper Palaeolithic tools, rare blades and a very few or total absence of Levallois products. The 'Acheulian facies' has up to 15% bifaces with numerous Yabrudian scrapers. The 'Amudian facies' (known also as 'pre-Aurignacian') with end scrapers,

burins, backed knives and rare bifaces, contains the evidence for limited practice of Levallois technique (Jelinek 1982). The observation that the use of the Levallois technique increased rapidly during the time of the Transitional Unit (Unit X) in Tabun can be interpreted as the result of Mousterian occupation in an erosional basin accompanied by redeposition of Acheulo–Yabrudian material.

The geographic distribution of the Acheulo–Yabrudian is limited to the northern and central Levant and it has not yet been reported from the Taurus–Zagros area. A TL date of 195 ± 15 ka (Huxtable 1990) for layer 18 in Yabrud Rockshelter I tentatively supports the ESR dates from Tabun that the Acheulo–Yabrudian is older than 200 ka. The earliest age for the Acheulo–Yabrudian is unknown but could have been in the range of 330–300 ka. In addition, if Michelson (1970), who studied the Pleistocene shorelines of Mount Carmel was right in his observations and tentative correlations, then the sandy deposits in Tabun cave, layers G, F (Upper Acheulian) and E (Acheulo–Yabrudian) could have accumulated beginning in the earliest Tyrrhenian or Isotope Stages 13–11 (*ca.* 500–400 ka). An Acheulo-Yabrudian industry was associated with the fragmentary skull from Zuttiyeh which, on the basis of Th/U dates, had previously been assigned to *ca.* 150 ka or more, but should be now placed within the range of 250–350 ka, similar to Petralona, Bodo, and other archaic *Homo sapiens*.

2. Tabun Layer D (Jelinek's Unit IX and Copeland's Mousterian 'phase 1') is characterized by uni-directional core reduction management and the production of Levallois blade blanks that display either a triangular shape or parallel edges. The 'Tabun D-type' industry (as represented also at Rosh Ein Mor, Douarah layer IV and Jerf' Ajla) could have been as early as 120–130 to 180–200 ka as indicated by the ESR readings at Tabun (figure 2). This early entity is as yet poorly dated and additional determinations are required before a satisfactory chronology can be accepted. No human fossils are associated with this industry.

3. Tabun Layer C (Jelinek's units I–VII or Mousterian 'phase 2') is dominated by ovate, radially prepared Levallois flakes with low frequencies of points. The 'Tabun C-type' industry, such as in Qafzeh, Naamé and Hayonim cave, could have been as old as 85 to 120–130 ka. The relevant fossils are from Qafzeh and Skhul as well as the Tabun CII jaw.

4. Tabun Layer B (or Mousterian 'phase 3') is represented by the production of flakes that are long and narrow, along with short, broad-based Levallois points derived from uni-directionally or radially prepared cores. The 'Tabun B-type' industry seems to have lasted from 80–100 ka to 48–46 ka TL (e.g. Quneitra, Kebara, Tabun B, Amud, Tor Faraj, Tor Sabiha). Human fossils were found in Amud and Kebara caves. It is worth noting that the exact location of the 'woman' from Tabun Cave, known as Tabun I, is not well established. Garrod herself suggested that its attribution to Layer C was uncertain and that it could have come from Layer B (Garrod & Bate 1937, p. 64).

Until quite recently the chronological foundations for the Levantine Lower and Middle Palaeolithic were based on the identification of micro- and macro-mammalian bio-zones and on geological observations. The study of micro-mammals is considered a useful check on the radiometric chronology as proposed by ESR and TL dates, at least within the Mount Carmel–Galilee region (*ca.* 2500 km²). Without repeating previously published summaries, it is worth stressing that the Qafzeh assemblage would, on palaeontological grounds, be best placed after Tabun E or D and clearly before Tabun C (Tchernov 1988). Thus there is a contradiction between the bio-chronological status of Tabun D and the published dates for Qafzeh (figure 2). Unfortunately, the information concerning the community composition of the micromammals of Tabun D is based on a very small sample and we hope that these uncertainties may be resolved by the forthcoming excavations at Hayonim cave where a deposit rich in microvertebrates contains a Tabun D-type industry.

4. The Implications of the New Dates

Mediterranean Neanderthals in the Galilee–Mount Carmel area (at Kebara and Amud) are associated with the Tabun B-type industry between 100 and 46 ka. The Qafzeh–Skhul group of anatomically modern hominids produced the earlier Tabun C-type industry and were present earlier sometime during early Isotope Stage 5, 125 to 100 ka. Given this chronology, there is no close temporal relationship between the so-called 'Proto-Cro-Magnons' of the Levant in the Mousterian and the European (or even Levantine) Cro-Magnons, and a direct population relationship between these two groups would be difficult to sustain. In the past, the evolution of the Qafzeh–Skhul group into the Upper Palaeolithic European Cro-Magnons was generally seen as correlated with the Middle to Upper Palaeolithic cultural transition. The new TL and ESR dates illustrate that this association can no longer be sustained. The Skhul and Qafzeh hominids did not differ from other producers of Mousterian industries such as those in North Africa producing the Aterian, or in East and South Africa, where the Mousterian-like industries are known as Middle Stone Age.

Moreover, the search for behavioural differences by looking at daily activities and motions as, for example, reflected in the edge damage of stone artifacts disclosed similar patterns for the two groups of industries (Shea 1989). The only difference between the Kebara and the Qafzeh assemblages is the higher frequencies of points in the former. These Levallois points, which were apparently sometimes hafted and used as spear heads, were obtained by a specific core reduction strategy. Frequent evidence for woodwork in both assemblages may hint that both human groups used wooden spears, known already from Lower Palaeolithic contexts in Europe (e.g. at Clacton-on-Sea and Lehringen). Intentional burials are found among both groups, and the only recorded difference to date is the presence of *Glycymeris* shells at Qafzeh and Skhul and red ochre at Qafzeh and with the Tabun C-type industry at Hayonim cave.

5. EARLY HUMAN MIGRATIONS

During milder climatic episodes, the Levant would have been particularly important as a two-way corridor for movement of humans and animals between Africa and Eurasia. The region always enjoyed higher temperatures relative to adjacent areas, and plant and animal food resources that were more predictable, stable, and reliable than those of most European environments. The Levant would therefore have been attractive to nearby human groups living under conditions of diminishing resources and increasing social stress in, for example, the Balkans, the Anatolian plateau and the Taurus–Zagros ranges. Those who occupied the Caucasus area had their own refugium in the lowlands near the Black Sea and the Caspian Sea.

The movement of *Homo erectus* out of Africa was not a unique event, but rather a series of repeated efforts. In the course of colonizing the temperate zone, which is subject to major seasonal fluctuations, failures probably occurred. Colonization by *Homo erectus* of the temperate zone of Eurasia indicates that humans were equipped with the technological and social adaptations necessary for such long-range dispersals.

Under these circumstances movements of Middle Palaeolithic human groups during a period that lasted at least 150 ka (Isotope Stages 6, 5, 4 and early 3) is quite plausible. The view that prehistoric populations were stable and well established in each region assumes their ability to adapt to every environmental fluctuation. But if Middle Palaeolithic humans had the capacity to endure the climatic vagaries of the northern latitudes why did they not move farther on and colonize the New World? The European stratigraphic records clearly indicate that during a cold period, such as Isotope Stage 4, large areas were deserted. If people did not die out they moved to nearby territories, closer to the Mediterranean shores and the Black Sea. It seems that the range of variability of physical features among the Middle Palaeolithic Levantine fossils resulted from the region serving as a refugium for several different groups during periods of environmental stress.

6. THE MIDDLE TO UPPER PALAEOLITHIC TRANSITION IN THE LEVANT

The sequence of the Levantine Upper Palaeolithic begins with a 'Transitional Industry' known from Ksar Akil and Boker Tachtit (Marks 1983;

Ohnuma & Bergman 1990). This industry is characterized by the diminishing use of the flat unipolar and bipolar Levallois core reduction with increasing frequencies of prismatic cores. Blanks were modified into end-scrapers, chamfered pieces (in Ksar Akil and other Lebanese sites), burins, and rare Emireh points. This industry evolves directly into the full-blown, blade-dominated Ahmarian tradition.

The question of whether the technological transition occurred in place was first raised when an increase of radial core preparation was observed in late Mousterian deposits (e.g. Ksar Akil, Kebara). The excavations in Boker Tachtit documented, on the basis of numerous refitted cores (Marks 1983), a local developmental sequence. Thus, Boker Tachtit seems to support an autochtonous transition from the Middle to the Upper Palaeolithic with radiocarbon dates of 47–46 ka before present (BP) for the earliest level (figure 1). However, the lack of a characteristic Mousterian assemblage stratified immediately under the Boker Tachtit layers cautions against uncritical acceptance of this conclusion. The appearance of Upper Palaeolithic technology in the Levant could have been the result of rapid acculturation similar to that of the Châtelperronian industry in Europe, if contemporary or earlier Upper Palaeolithic sites were discovered in the region. This transitional phase seems to be absent or poorly dated in the adjacent Anatolian–Iranian or the Caucusus regions.

The Upper Palaeolithic entity that follows in the Levant is characterized by a series of blade or bladelet industries named the Ahmarian Tradition; its early part is radiocarbon dated to about 38–35 ka through 22–20 ka BP. What seems to be an otherwise continuous sequence is interrupted by a different industry commonly referred to as the 'Levantine Aurignacian' (35–28 ka BP). The Levantine Aurignacian assemblages have been uncovered only in the central Levant. Its early phase is characterized by the dominance of blade and bladelets with carinated and nosed scrapers as well as retouched bladelets and El-Wad points, together with a few bone and antler objects. The later phase ('Levantine Aurignacian B') is increasingly dominated by flake production, with nosed and carinated scrapers, El-Wad points and a more abundant bone and antler industry.

The main behavioural differences between the Middle and the Upper Palaeolithic assemblages (as reflected in the latter) are as follows: production of bone and antler objects, use of worked marine shells (possibly for body decorations), very rare art objects, frequent use of red ochre, systematic presence of a few grinding tools, stone encircled hearths and use of rocks for warmth banking. Observable differences between the two sets of sites include the appearance of clear occupational horizons in the Upper Palaeolithic that indicate less frequent re-occupations of the same locale and therefore are interpreted as reflecting greater mobility, possibly within larger territories.

7. THE MIDDLE TO UPPER PALAEOLITHIC REVOLUTION

Major socio-economic revolutions are more clearly understood after they have happened than during their revolutionary period. This is certainly true for the Middle–Upper Palaeolithic revolution. Most authorities agree that the change is clearly reflected in the lithic industries and, in western Europe, by the appearance of body decorations, bone and antler industry, craft specialization and long distance exchange of raw material (e.g. Klein 1989; Mellars 1989). The rate of cultural change during the Upper Palaeolithic was faster than in the Middle Palaeolithic. Human groups were more mobile and their ranges covered larger territories. More complex social organization, both locally and spatially, is also inferred. A series of inventions and innovations enabled some groups to move into the northern latitudes and thence colonize the Americas. In lower latitudes the ability to cross waterways allowed the colonization of Australia (e.g. Jones 1989). The dates for these major changes support a temporal and geographic distribution, from early to late, along an east-west axis beginning in the Near East through to western Europe. Unfortunately no dates are available for northeast Africa or eastern Asia (Klein 1989). Moreover, the emergence of the Upper Palaeolithic cannot be well correlated with a known climatic change.

The archaeological evidence for the transition is best known in western Europe and is employed by many scholars as a model for other regions although most would now agree that this is an atypical sequence. The Châtelperronian seems to represent a cultural continuation of the Mousterian of Acheulian Tradition, as originally proposed by Bordes, and its assemblages were probably produced by the latest Neanderthals (Mellars, this symposium). These humans were capable of producing blades through a complex *chaîne opératoire* (Pelegrin 1990) which implies that their technological abilities were not limited by innate physical or mental constraints, as has sometimes been suggested.

The long-claimed contemporanity between the Aurignacian (generally seen as the product of Cro-Magnon populations), and the Châtelperronian is supported by TL dates from St. Césaire (Mercier *et al*. 1991) and the dates for the early Aurignacian in Spain (Straus 1990). Thus, in this region the phenomenon of an immigrating population seems well documented. Unfortunately, the exact relationship between the two is not well established because the sites in question were dated by different radiometric techniques and laboratories. Furthermore, no human remains have so far been recovered in the earliest Aurignacian levels, only in the somewhat later ones. Similar archaeological generalizations have been inferred from central and eastern European sequences (e.g. Kozlowski 1988), where the period of overlap may be longer.

The question that intrigues everyone is 'why' and 'where' did this behavioural transition happen? The easiest answer is that it was caused by a biological change, which almost certainly means accepting the 'replacement' hypothesis—originally known as the 'Noah's Ark' scenario (Howells 1976). The advocates of biological change agree that it did not take place in Europe, perhaps not even in Asia (although see Stringer (1989) for a potential western Asia locus). The evidence from the Levant as presented above indicates that a rapid change in lithic technology and settlement patterns is observed in this region around 47–46 ka (Marks 1990), a date that needs to be supported by additional readings. This leads to the conclusion that if the biological or cultural change did not emerge from the Levant then it should be traced to northeast Africa, East or Central Africa. The available record suggests that Egypt and the Sudan were probably not the source area. The Nile valley could have been the route of Upper Palaeolithic humans to Asia but supportive archaeological evidence is needed. No archaeological information is available at present from the northeast African coastal belt or the alternative route through the Ethiopian–Arabian Peninsula. The relevant records from the vast region of East and Central Africa are as yet poor, although discoveries such as in Katanda in Zaire, where a Middle Stone Age industry contained barbed and unbarbed bone points (A. Brooks and J. Yellen, personal communication), may suggest that the core area where the cultural change began was in equatorial Africa. The Howieson's Poort industry in South Africa, now dated to 75 to 65–45 ka, is a remote option as the origin of the Eurasian Upper Palaeolithic and is often overlain by Middle Stone Age assemblages (e.g. Border Cave, Klasies River Mouth) (Deacon, this symposium).

But locating the core area where the Middle to Upper Palaeolithic Revolution took place does not differ in principle from any other problem of identifying a core area. The model suggested here is adopted from the study of the 'Neolithic Revolution'. To materialize this approach we need to summarize the available evidence and draw a chronogeographical 'Gap Chart', similarly to the one compiled by R. Braidwood in the 1940s, that will indicate where the sites needed to fill in the chronological and archaeological gap might be found.

To employ the lessons learned from research on the 'Agricultural Revolution' as a tool for studying an earlier one, the following contentions are, in my view, accurate and based on the most recent archaeological, archaeozoological and archaeobotanical evidence (Bar-Yosef 1991; Bar-Yosef & Belfer-Cohen 1992, and references therein).

1. The 'Neolithic Revolution' took place within a single species, i.e. within modern *Homo sapiens*, and was not caused by a biological change.
2. The shift to intentional and systematic cultivation of cereals and legumes in

the southern Levant occurred within a short time (*ca.* 10 300–9900 years BP) while the domestication of animals (goat, sheep, cattle, pig) happened next, as part of the activities of the agricultural communities (*ca.* 9–8 ka BP).

3. Population increase, expressed in a shift in average site size from 0.2 to 2.0–3.0 hectares, was coincident with the establishment of cereal cultivation and was probably the result of having predictable supplies of weaning food stuffs. Increased sedentism and secured supplies caused a drop in the age of menarche of better fed women and shorter inter-birth intervals, and thus to population increase.

4. The expansion of early Neolithic communities was initially northward and eastward. The introduction of cereal cultivation to Anatolia was rapid and led in the new environment to a population explosion that drove demic diffusion further westward.

5. The Neolithic economy spread throughout the Mediterranean basin by coastal navigation and inland movement along the Danube valley. Both demic diffusion and acculturation were the processes responsible for the 'Neolithization' of Europe (Ammerman 1989).

6. The eastward expansion of Neolithic subsistence systems reached Pakistan within 1500 radiocarbon years. It is noteworthy that it took about 2000 radiocarbon years for agriculture to penetrate into the 'next door' Nile valley that can be reached from the Jordan valley within a one-week walk.

The Middle to the Upper Palaeolithic revolution can also be explained as resulting from the introduction of new technologies, both inventions and innovations. These include new or improved techniques for food acquisition, such as spear throwers and even archery, perhaps basketry, and new tools for food preparation such as grinding stones. Possibly, new trapping and storing techniques became available, although the evidence is yet meagre. The improved food acquisition techniques and food processing led to better nourishment and greater survival of newborns who reached adulthood. A slight increase in life expectancy perhaps secured the survival of older members of the group, thus extending the 'living memory' of the group which would have meant a better monitoring of the environment and of more distant regions. Long range social alliances were developed in order to overcome seasonal or annual economic disasters. These are expressed, among others, in the transportation of objects and raw materials over long distances. The self-identification of groups is probably reflected in specialized lithic artifacts and body decorations.

The continuous reproductive success of one group would probably cause the decline of another group. The demographic modelling by Zubrow (1989) indicates that it does not take long for a less successful population, for example the Neanderthals, to disappear. Even if his suggestion for 'kinless' social groups among Neanderthals is untenable (as no such relationship is known among human societies nor, indeed, among apes), it is useful in showing how human groups could rapidly become extinct.

As with the Neolithic Revolution there may have been dramatic changes within a single human population. On the basis of the behavioural interpretation of the archaeological residues (burials, spatial organization, hearths, planning depth reflected in core reduction strategies, use of red ochre, etc.), we may plausibly argue (e.g. Deacon 1989, this symposium; Arensburg *et al.* 1990) that there is no need to look for a biological threshold for explaining the emergence of the Upper Palaeolithic, such as a sudden mutation that resulted in the capacity of humans for modern languages (e.g. Klein 1989). If this is so, then we urgently need to identify the core area where the Middle to Upper Palaeolithic revolution took place, and identify the routes by which it spread across the Old World.

Acknowledgments

I am grateful to David Pilbeam (Peabody Museum, Harvard University) for his numerous constructive comments on an earlier version of this manuscript and to Sally Shearman for her editorial help. Due to space restrictions only selected references, where more complete lists are available, are given here.

References

Ammerman, A.J. 1989 On the Neolithic transition in Europe: a comment on Zvelebil and Zvelebil (1988). *Antiquity* **63**, 162–165.

Arensburg, B., Schepartz, L., Tillier, A.M., Vandermeersch, B. & Rak, Y. 1990 A reappraisal of the anatomical basis for speech in Middle Palaeolithic hominids. *Am. J. phys. Anthrop.* **83**, 137–146.

Bar-Yosef, O. 1989 Upper Pleistocene cultural stratigraphy in Southwest Asia. In *The emergence of modern humans* (ed. E. Trinkaus), pp. 154–179. Cambridge University Press.

Bar-Yosef, O. 1991 The Early Neolithic of the Levant: recent advances. *Rev. Archaeol.* **12**, 1–18.

Bar-Yosef, O. & Belfer-Cohen, A. 1992 From foraging to farming in the Mediterranean Levant. In *Transitions to agriculture in prehistory* (ed. A. B. Gebauer & T. D. Price), pp. 21–48. Prehistory Press.

Cavalli-Sforza, L.L., Piazza, A., Menozzi, P. & Mountain, J. 1988 Reconstruction of human evolution: bringing together genetic, archaeological, and linguistic data. *Proc. Natn. Acad. Sci. U.S.A.* **85**, 6002–6006.

Copeland, L. 1975 The Middle and Upper Palaeolithic of Lebanon and Syria in the light of recent research. In *Problems in prehistory: North Africa and the Levant* (ed. F. Wendorf & A. E. Marks), pp. 317–350. Dallas: Southern Methodist University Press.

Deacon, T.D. 1989 The neural circuitry underlying primate calls and human language. *Hum. Evol.* **4**, 367–401.

Garrod, D.A.E. & Bate, D.M. 1937 *The Stone Age of Mount Carmel.* Oxford: Clarendon Press.

Goren-Inbar, N. 1990 *Quneitra: a Mousterian site on the Golan Heights.* Jerusalem:

"Qedem", Monographs of the Institute of Archaeology, The Hebrew University of Jerusalem.

Grün, R. & Stringer, C.B. 1991 Electron spin resonance dating and the evolution of modern humans. *Archaeometry* **33**, 153–199.

Howell, F.C. 1952 Pleistocene glacial ecology and the evolution of 'classic Neanderthal' man. *Southwest. J. Anthrop.* **8**, 377–410.

Howells, W.W. 1976 Explaining modern man: evolutionists versus migrationists. *J. hum. Evol.* **5**, 477–495.

Huxtable, J. 1990 Burnt flint date for Yabrud Shelter I. *Ancient TL Date Lists No. 4.* Entry 43.

Jelinek, A.J. 1982 The Middle Palaeolithic in the southern Levant with comments on the appearance of modern *Homo sapiens*. In *The Transition from the Lower to the Middle Paleolithic and the Origin of Modern Man* (ed. A. Ronen), pp. 57–104. Oxford: British Archaeological Reports International Series 151.

Jones, R. 1989 East of Wallace's line: Issues and problems in the colonisation of the Australian continent. In *The Human Revolution: behavioural and biological perspectives on the origins of modern humans* (ed. P. Mellars & C. Stringer), pp. 743–782. Edinburgh University Press.

Klein, R.G. 1989 *The human career*. University of Chicago Press.

Kozlowski, J. 1988 The transition from the Middle to the Early Upper Paleolithic in central Europe and the Balkans. In *The Early Upper Paleolithic; evidence from Europe and the Near East* (ed. J. F. Hoffecker & C. A. Wolf), pp. 193–235. Oxford: British Archaeological Reports International Series 437.

Maddison, D.R., Ruvolo, M. & Swofford, D.L. 1992 Geographic origins of human mitochrondrial DNA: phylogenetic evidence from control region sequences. *Syst. Biol.* (In the Press.)

Marks, A.E. (ed.) 1983 *Prehistory and Paleoenvironments in the Central Negev, Israel*. Vol. III. Dallas: Southern Methodist University Press.

Marks, A.E. 1990 The Upper and Middle paleolithic of the Near East and the Nile Valley: the problem of cultural transformations. In *The emergence of modern humans: an archaeological perspective* (ed. P. Mellars), pp. 56–80. Edinburgh University Press.

Meignen, L. & Bar-Yosef, O. 1988 Kebara et le Paléolithique Moyen du Mont Carmel. *Paléorient* **14**, 123–130.

Mellars, P. 1989 Major issues in the emergence of modern humans. *Curr. Antropol.* **30**, 349–385.

Mercier, N., Valladas, H., Joron, J.L., Reyss, J.L., Lévêque, F. & Vandermeersch, B. 1991 Thermoluminescence dating of the Late Neanderthal remains from Saint-Césaire. *Nature, Lond.* **351**, 737–739.

Michelson, H. 1970 *Geology of the Carmel coast*. Tahal: Water Planning for Israel, Tel-Aviv. Report No. HG/70/025. [in Hebrew.]

Ohnuma, K. & Bergman, C.A. 1990 A technological analysis of the Upper Palaeolithic levels (XXV–VI) of Ksar Akil, Lebanon. In *The emergence of modern humans: an archaeological perspective* (ed. P. Mellars), pp. 91–138. Edinburgh University Press.

Pelegrin, J. 1990 Observations technologiques sur quelques séries du Chatelperronien et du MTA B du Sud-Ouest de la France; une hypothèse d'évolution. In

Paléolithique Moyen récent et Paléolithique Supérieur ancien en Europe (ed. C. Farizy), pp. 195–202. Nemours: Memoires du Musée de Préhistoire d' Ile de France.

Shea, J.J. 1989 A functional study of the lithic industries associated with hominid fossils in the Kebara and Qafzeh Caves, Israel. In *The human revolution: behavioural and biological perspectives on the origins of modern humans* (ed. P. Mellars & C. Stringer), pp. 611–625. Edinburgh University Press.

Straus, L.G. 1990 The Early Upper Palaeolithic of Southwest Europe: Cro-Magnon adaptations in the Iberian peripheries, 40,000–20,000 BP. In *The emergence of modern humans* (ed. P. Mellars), pp. 276–302. Edinburgh University Press.

Stringer, C.B. 1989 The origin of Early Modern Humans: a comparison of the European and non-European evidence. In *The human revolution: behavioural and biological perspectives on the origins of modern humans* (ed. P. Mellars & C. Stringer), pp. 232–244. Edinburgh University Press.

Tchernov, E. 1988 Biochronology of the Middle Paleolithic and dispersal events of hominids in the Levant. In *L'Homme de Néandertal*, Vol 1 (ed. M. Otte), pp. 153–168. Liége: Etudes et Recherches Archéologiques de l'Université de Liège **34**.

Trinkaus, E. 1989 The Upper Pleistocene transition. In *The emergence of modern humans* (ed. E. Trinkaus), pp. 42–66. Cambridge University Press.

Vandermeersch, B. 1981 *Les hommes fossiles de Qafzeh (Israel)*. Paris: Editions CNRS.

Vigilant, L., Stoneking, M., Harpending, H., Hawkes, K. & Wilson, A.C. 1989 African populations and the evolution of human mitochrondrial DNA. *Science, Wash.* **253**, 1503–1507.

Wolpoff, M.H. 1989 Multiregional evolution: The fossil alternative to Eden. In *The human revolution: behavioural and biological perspectives on the origins of modern humans* (ed. P. Mellars & C. Stringer), pp. 62–108. Edinburgh University Press.

Zubrow, E. 1989 The demographic modelling of Neanderthal extinction. In *The human revolution: behavioural and biological perspectives on the origins of modern humans* (ed. P. Mellars & C. Stringer), pp. 212–231. Edinburgh University Press.

African and Asian Perspectives on the Origins of Modern Humans

J. Desmond Clark[1]

SUMMARY

The ways in which the cultural evidence—in its chronological context—can be used to imply behavioural patterning and to identify possible causes of change are discussed. Improved reliability in dating methods, suites of dates from different regional localities, and new, firmly dated fossil hominids from crucial regions such as northeast Africa, the Levant, India and China, are essential for clarification of the origin and spread of the modern genepool. Hominid ancestry in Africa is reviewed, as well as the claims for an independent origin in Asia. The cultural differences and changes within Africa, West and South Asia and the Far East in the later Middle and early Upper Pleistocene are examined and compared, and some behavioural implications are suggested, taking account of the evolutionary frameworks suggested by the 'multiregional evolution' and 'Noah's Ark' hypotheses of human evolution. A possible explanation is proposed for the cultural differences between Africa, West Asia and India on the one hand, and southeast Asia and the Far East on the other. The apparent hiatus between the appearance of the first anatomically modern humans, *ca.* 100 ka ago, and the appearance of the Upper Palaeolithic and other contemporaneous technological and behavioural changes around 40 ka ago, is discussed. It is suggested that the anatomical changes occurred first, and that neurological changes permitted the development of fully syntactic language some 50 ka later. The intellectual and behavioural revolution, best demonstrated by the 'Upper Palaeolithic' of Eurasia, seems to have been dependent on this linguistic development—within the modern genepool—and triggered the rapid migration of human populations throughout the Old World

1. INTRODUCTION

The main thrust of this paper is the way the cultural evidence in its chronological context may be seen to imply behavioural patterning and to discuss the possible causes and effects of the transition from Middle to Upper Palaeolithic technology that followed the appearance of anatomically modern humans and the disappearance of all other archaic hominid populations.

[1] Department of Anthropology, University of California at Berkeley, Berkeley, California 94720, U.S.A.

Possible models for understanding this transition can be no better than the data on which they are based and it must be readily apparent that it is absolutely essential to have more complete fossil remains in contexts dated by several proven and accepted methods, in situations where there is no question of the archaeological associations, and where evidence of prehistoric use of space is preserved. Within the straitjacket of the limited data at present available, therefore, the cultural evidence in context and its possible behavioural implications will be discussed.

There is now no doubt that the hominid lineage evolved initially in Africa and the record of evolutionary change from *Australopithecus* to *Homo habilis* to *Homo erectus* grades is clear although the ramifications of speciation events that gave rise to this are still open to much debate. The oldest *H. erectus* fossils from Africa date to between 1.8 and 1.6 Ma. The first stone artifacts intentionally shaped to a recurring pattern, the Oldowan tradition, are found with *Homo habilis* fossils between 2.4 and 2.0 Ma in East Africa. By 1.4 Ma or more the Oldowan tradition had been supplemented by a tradition, the Acheulian Techno-complex, characterized by large bifaces: hand-axes and cleavers. These are not (although some may still disagree) distinct and separate tool-kits made by morphologically different populations but are variable components of the technological products of a single hominid grade: *Homo erectus*. In some occurrences the dominant tool is the biface, in others the (now Developed) Oldowan, core/chopper and flake tools predominate, sometimes to the exclusion of bifaces entirely. However, the great majority of Lower Palaeolithic assemblages in Africa, the Near East and India with which I am familiar combine varying percentages of both Acheulian and Oldowan components (Clark 1975; Gowlett 1988; Jayaswal 1982). It is important to recognize the extent of this variability in composition in the African Lower Palaeolithic when seeking to explain those artifact assemblages in Europe and eastern Asia where the Acheulian biface component appears to be missing. There is much speculation but, as yet, no testable explanation as to why this should be so. Climate and environment may have dictated the use of one preferred technology over another for the exploitation of particular resources. Different social and economic organization or mobility with limited and intermittent interaction between otherwise isolated communities could be another factor and, in the earlier Pleistocene, biologically distinct populations have also been invoked to explain the technological differences which will be discussed again later in this paper.

The spread of *Homo erectus* into tropical and sub-tropical Asia took place around 1.0 Ma; even as early as 1.2 Ma on the evidence of the micro-fauna from 'Ubeidiya, the earliest well-researched and dated stone tool locality outside Africa. *Homo erectus* spread through the Asian tropics into southeast Asia—represented by the classic fossils from Java—and to the sub-tropics and temperate regions of the Far East, as evidenced by the Pekin Man fossils from China. No acceptable stone artifacts are as yet known to be associated with Java Man but with Pekin Man at Zhoukoudian and other sites, a long cultural record is present that is technically similar to the African Developed Oldowan (Wei Qi 1988).

In Africa, by about 0.5 Ma, *Homo erectus* had been replaced by fossils showing more advanced characteristics grouped within a grade known as early or archaic *Homo sapiens* and showing a considerable amount of morphological variability combining archaic and modern features. These makers of the Acheulian and Developed Oldowan techno-complex in Africa had by this time spread from the believed original homeland in the dry tropical savannas into almost all ecological niches in the continent other than evergreen tropical forest. The earliest hominid fossils in Europe are generally assigned to this archaic grade (Stringer 1989) and are associated with both Acheulian and Oldowan-type tool-kits. Archaic *Homo sapiens* fossils are known from the Levant (Zuttiyeh) (Vandermeersch 1989), India (Hathnora) (de Lumley & Sonakia 1985), southeast Asia (Ngandong and Sambung-machan) (Rightmire 1990, pp. 34–52), and China (Dali, Maba, Jinnushan, Xujiayao, Yunxian) (Wu Rukang & Olsen 1985, pp. 79–165). Do these derive from this later expansion out of Africa into Europe and the Levant? Or are they the outcome of autochthanous biological evolution from the original *Homo erectus* populations in eastern Asia, as is generally thought to be the case?

All these fossils are poorly dated, but faunal associations suggest a later Middle Pleistocene or earlier later Pleistocene context: 0.5–0.2 Ma is considered approximate and is also suggested by the artifacts, where these are present. At Zuttiyeh, the stone industry is an evolved Acheulian (Jabrudian); at Hathnora it is also a typical later Acheulian. In China, where artifacts are associated, they are of the core/chopper and flake tradition. The Acheulian biface has disappeared and nowhere in eastern Asia is there any evidence of the specialized core techniques or the standardization of form and flaking pattern found with the Acheulian in Africa, West Asia and Europe. A variable heavy-duty pick component is present at some Chinese sites in the south and centre of the country but these almost never resemble Acheulian bifaces, rather are they comparable to the sub-Saharan Sangoan tradition from Africa with which they are most likely contemporary.

2. INDEPENDENT HOMINID ORIGINS IN ASIA

At this point the claim for a separate origin for the hominid lineage in Asia must be briefly considered. This is mainly supported by some Chinese palaeontologists and archaeologists and is based on the possibility that the late Neogene hominoids, exemplified by the fossils from the Yuanmou

Basin (Banguo Basin), did not become extinct without leaving descendants. The upper part of the long Yuanmou fluvio-lacustrine sequence yielded two hominid incisor teeth (one *in situ*), a tibia from another site and what are believed to be a small number of intentionally flaked stone artifacts (Wen 1978). The incisors were first thought to be Australopithecine on the basis of palaeo-magnetic dating suggesting an age of between 1.67 and 1.87 Ma (Chen *et al.* 1977). Later palaeomagnetic sampling, however, suggested a Bruhnes epoch age of 0.73 Ma or later. Resampling (Qian 1985) confirmed that a reversed polarity exists above the incisor-bearing sediments, putting the whole of the long Yuanmou sequence between 0.73 and 3.40 Ma. The associated stone pieces (Wen 1978) are, in my opinion, very doubtful artifacts. They are abraded with no unquestionable evidence of artificial fracture and they and the fossils are in secondary context. Clearly, further interdisciplinary field research and more precise dating are essential but, in any case, the age of the incisor-bearing strata puts them in the range of *Homo erectus* in Asia. The Java fossils may date between 0.9 and less than 0.7 Ma but there are, as has been said, no certain stone artifacts associated with them (Bartstra 1982). The Zhoukoudian (Choukoutien) Cave *Homo erectus* fossils date between ~0.7 and 0.24 Ma ago on latest estimates and the long and deep deposits in this cave preserve irrefutable evidence of sporadic occupation by hominids. The core/chopper and flake tool assemblages are technically comparable to the Developed Oldowan of Africa. Lantian (Gongwangling) is probably the oldest evidence for *Homo erectus* in China and is dated to between 1.2 and 0.8 Ma. Again, it is in secondary context but with a small number of stone artifacts (Wu & Olsen 1985, pp. 148–150) from adjacent localities. Other fluvial sediments with artifacts (e.g. Xihoudu) in China are not sufficiently well dated to be considered here.

In northern Pakistan there have been recent claims for stone artifacts in conglomerates of the Upper Siwalik Group that may be more than 2.0 Ma. The palaeomagnetic dating is convincing and so are the three flaked stone pieces I have seen (Dennell & Rendell 1988; Rendell *et al.* 1989, pp. 96–126). Tectonic folding and compression can, however, produce simulated artifacts and those forces have been at work in the Soan incline where the specimens were found. In peninsular India to my knowledge the earliest stone artifact assemblages belong to a later, not an earlier Acheulian (Misra 1989; Jayaswal 1982) and in our survey of the Middle Son Valley in 1980–82, we found no sediments older than Middle Pleistocene (Clark & Williams 1990). However, reconsideration is necessary if a possible artifact from below a tephra at Bori in Maharastra, dated to 1.4 Ma is confirmed by further finds (Korisettar *et al.* 1989). In this case an earlier movement into south Asia before 1.0 Ma will have to be considered.

Mention should be made here also of a claim for an age of 1.5–2.0 Ma for a core/chopper assemblage from a terrace of the Lena River in Siberia.

Even more significant, however, is the very recent discovery of a hominoid mandible from Dmanisi, an open site in south Georgia, associated with a Villafranchian fauna suggesting an age of 1.6 Ma.

Admittedly, there has not been nearly so much detailed interdisciplinary survey for fossil hominoids and associated cultural and faunal remains in eastern and southern Asia as there has been in Africa, and often the sites are without fauna, but the surveys carried out have produced no evidence for an Australopithecine grade nor for *Homo habilis*. The *Sivapithecus* hominoids becoming extinct shortly after 7.0 Ma appear to have left no Australopithecine or *Homo habilis* descendants and at present it must be accepted that the first hominid in eastern and southern Asia, *Homo erectus*, moved into eastern Asia around 1.2–1.0 Ma, or a little earlier, from an origin in Africa, bringing with him the inherited technological skills for tool manufacture in stone and other raw materials.

3. Late Middle Pleistocene and Early Later Pleistocene Hominids and Their Stone Tool Assemblages in Africa

It is now necessary to review the situation in Africa that led up to the appearance of anatomically modern humans 200 ka or more years ago, and the innovative technologies of the Middle Palaeolithic–Middle Stone Age. At about the same time (200 ka) a crucial change took place wherever the Acheulian biface tradition was found. This was the disappearance of the large biface cutting tools from assemblages that had always included an important flake tool component, little distinguishable from the Mousterian. There can be little doubt that in Africa the Middle Palaeolithic–Middle Stone Age is directly derived from the terminal Acheulian, both north and south of the Sahara.

Assemblages of small bifaces and Middle Palaeolithic flake technology: Fauresmith in South Africa (Volman 1984); Lake Langano (Chavaillon 1979) in the Ethiopian Rift Valley; Akka (Rodrigue 1987) and other Moroccan spring sites and the Dakhla Oasis spring sites in Egypt (Schild & Wendorf 1977) can be seen as transitional assemblages, like the Jabrudian or Mugharan Traditions in the Levant (Bar-Yosef 1988) and other such occurrences in the Caucasus (Adamenko & Gladiline 1989) and Crimea (Kolossov 1988). The disappearance of bifaces represents, it is suggested, a very significant behavioural–technological change and I believe it is due to the major technological invention of hafting with the greater efficiency which that gives to tool-use. These flake tools were lighter, more economical in raw material and could be easily resharpened or replaced. It is, therefore, likely to be in the time range of the late Acheulian and the contemporary later Archaic populations of Africa and western Asia that the ancestral stock of modern humans will be found. The degree of regional variability shown by the early modern human fossils implies that the speciation event that triggered the human revolution may have been completed some considerable time before 100 ka ago.

Others have discussed the fossil and cultural evidence in its chronological and palaeoenvironmental context as it relates to the modern genotype in the African continent and the technical innovations that can be recognised in the time range of 100 to 50 ka ago and immediately precedes and anticipates the upper Palaeolithic. I would like to discuss these and their behavioural implications more generally here. The South African evidence from Klasies River Mouth Caves (Deacon & Geleijinse 1988; Deacon 1989, this symposium) and Border Cave (Beaumont *et al.* 1978) shows that the Middle Stone Age began in the Last Interglacial (oxygen-isotope Stage 5e) and that the Middle Stone Age–Later Stone Age transition dates between 35 and 30 ka before present (BP) (Deacon 1989). This is supported by the long sequences in Umhlatuzana Rock Shelter (Kaplan 1990), Boomplaas (Deacon 1979) and Nelson Bay Caves (Klein 1972) and other sites (Volman 1984) although the dating needs to be more precise. The anatomically modern human fossils from Klasies River Mouth (Rightmire & Deacon 1991) have a minimum age of 90 ka ago and those from Border Cave are of comparable age.

The most significant innovation in the Middle Stone Age tool assemblages is the basic blade technology and the blade tradition or facies that characterises the Howieson's Poort Industry which probably dates between 60 000 and 75 000 years ago.

In East Africa, the Middle Stone Age is at least 100 ka old and, if dates from Ethiopia are confirmed, the beginning could be twice that age (Clark 1988). This is in accord with the variable fossil evidence. Some fossil crania are robust but fully modern (Omo I and Ngalaba) whereas other fossils (Omo II, Lake Eyasi, Singa, DireDawa and Bodo: this last now dated to 260 ka although confirmation is needed) show varying amounts of archaic and modern traits (Bräuer 1989; Stringer & Andrews 1988). The East African Middle Stone Age also shows early emphasis on the use of blades, especially in the Horn where obsidian and flint are the materials used (Brandt & Gresham 1989). It can be demonstrated (figure 2) that blade technology grew out of the Levallois Point and Nubian core forms, as has already been shown so well in the Negev and other Levantine sites (Marks 1977; Volkman 1983). Especially important is an occurrence comparable to that of the Howieson's Poort which is stratified in the Mumba Rockshelter in the Lake Eyasi Rift. Named the Mumba Industry, it comprises backed flakes and blades, including trapezes and short, stubby but usually well made bifacial and unifacial points. At Mumba the Middle Stone Age (Kisele Industry) that lies below is dated to *ca.* 100–130 ka ago and the Mumba Industry to between about 30 ka BP by radiocarbon, and 65 ka by Uranium series (Mehlman 1991).

In North Africa, the evidence from the Maghreb is strongly suggestive of an origin for the modern hominid fossils from Dar-es-Soltan, Tamara and other sites (Debénath *et al.* 1986), in the archaic lineage represented by Ternifine, Salé and Jebel Irhoud (Hublin 1985). There is general agreement that none of these later Pleistocene African fossils can be classified as 'Neanderthal' but that they are representative of the first anatomically modern peoples in that part of the continent. They, in turn, are direct ancestors of the Mechta-Afalou race (Arambourg *et al.* 1934) which, by 20 ka BP was widely spread in northern Africa.

The earliest Middle Palaeolithic in North Africa is Mousterian, usually with the Levallois technique and other regional variations (Balout 1955, pp. 269–335; Van Peer 1991). This was succeeded in the northwest and Sahara, relatively quickly it would seem, by an evolved Middle Palaeolithic known as the Aterian Industrial Complex (Tixier 1967) of which the greater part if not the whole is older than 40 ka BP and beyond the range of radiocarbon dating. On the evidence from the eastern Sahara sites of Bir Tarfawi, the Middle Palaeolithic sequence associated with five lacustrine episodes appears to date between 160 and 70 ka ago: the last occurrence has been named Aterian (Wendorf *et al.* 1990). The Aterian is spread throughout the Maghreb and the whole of the Sahara up to the Nile Valley (Tillet 1983, pp. 191–265). It is absent from the northeast and in Cyrenaica the contemporary industry is a Levallois–Mousterian (McBurney 1967, pp. 105–134). This is dated between more than 46 and 40 ka BP, when it is succeeded by a true Upper Palaeolithic blade industry: the Dabban (McBurney 1967, pp. 135–184). Below the Levallois–Mousterian in the warm episode of the Last Interglacial (perhaps oxygen–isotope Stage 5e) the artifact assemblage is a blade industry (pre-Aurignacian). This could be as old as 80–60 ka and resembles the Amudian Facies of the Mugharan Tradition in the Levant, with which it is believed to be contemporary. It should be noted here that the Acheuleo–Jabrudian in Israel, Syria and Lebanon is essentially non-Levallois whereas, if the chronology is correct, that in the Negev and northern and eastern Africa generally, the Middle Palaeolithic, is Levallois-based with emphasis on the production of Levallois points, where the raw material permits. I believe this has significance in view of the demonstrated derivation of blade technology from the Levallois point core as shown at Boker Tachtit between 47 and 38 ka BP (Marks 1977, pp. 61–80).

There can, therefore, be no doubt that the anatomically modern fossils with no Neanderthal traits, in South, East and North Africa, are associated with Middle Stone Age–Middle Palaeolithic industries and that they are as old as, or older than, those in western Asia. They are contemporary with the Neanderthal fossils and Mousterian industries of Europe and the Levant and they show very considerable variation, probably due to broad, re-

▶

Figure 1. Middle Palaeolithic–Middle Stone Age regional variants in Africa.

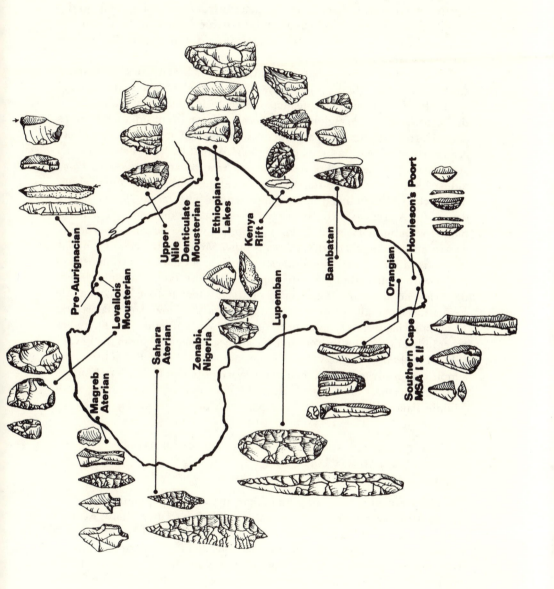

Pre-Aurignacian

Levallois Mousterian

Magreb Aterian

Sahara Aterian

Zenabi Nigeria

Upper Nile Denticulate Mousterian

Ethiopian Lakes

Kenya Rift

Lupemban

Bambatan

Orangian

Howieson's Poort

Southern Cape MSA I & II

155

gional, behavioural adaptation to ecological diversity that induced the emergence of specialized technologies (Van Peer 1991). These need to be briefly reviewed as they emphasise the ability of these populations to develop regional identities which are nowhere in evidence in the Lower Palaeolithic (Acheulian) or with the chopper/flake traditions of the Lower and Middle Pleistocene.

The extent of this regional variability can, for brevity, best be demonstrated on a map (figure 1) to show some of the characteristic regional assemblages which can be considered as ecologically adapted tool-kits. In the hornfels, quartzite regions of southern Africa, in the obsidian, flint areas of the Horn, and where flint and silcrete were used in northern Africa, there is an early emphasis on blade production, from at least as early as 100 ka ago. Facies such as the Pre-Aurignacian, Mumba and Howieson's Poort industries emphasize the importance of hafting and this becomes abundantly clear in the tanged point component of the Aterian. Tixier (1967) defines the Aterian as a Mousterian facies of Levallois debitage, often multi-bladed with many facetted striking platforms, with a larger proportion of end-scrapers, often on blades, than any other Mousterian facies. An important part of the tool-kit, sometimes as much as a quarter, is composed of pieces with a bifacial tang located proximally. This tang is irrefutable evidence for mounting the stone working parts of a tool in some kind of handle or shaft. The small segments and trapezes of the Howieson's Poort and Mumba facies can only have been used efficiently if mounted. There are other indications of hafting of Mousterian pieces especially from the Levant (Shea 1989) and it is likely that, by the end of the Middle Palaeolithic, the simple composite tool was a regular piece of equipment for modern humans and Neanderthals alike. Certainly, although there are facies changes, all Middle Palaeolithic industries are part of a broad, technological entity.

4. CLIMATIC CHANGE AND ENVIRONMENTAL IMPACT ON LATER
   PLEISTOCENE HUMAN POPULATIONS
   (FIGURE 2)

The impact of climatic change on human and animal population distribution in Africa was significant especially in relation to the Sahara. Most of the evidence comes from the later Pleistocene and the Holocene but it is not unreasonable to extrapolate cautiously from this for earlier episodes. Effects were not as dramatic as in high latitudes, but in the tropics and subtropics were still profoundly significant. For example, during the time of the Last Glacial maximum, the tropics were 5–8°C cooler, tropical evergreen forest retreated to a few refugia and its place was taken by wood- and grassland and montane vegetation descended 1000 m or more below its present altitudinal range. It was at such a time, probably in the Penultimate Glacial, that the Congo Basin was first permanently occupied by humans

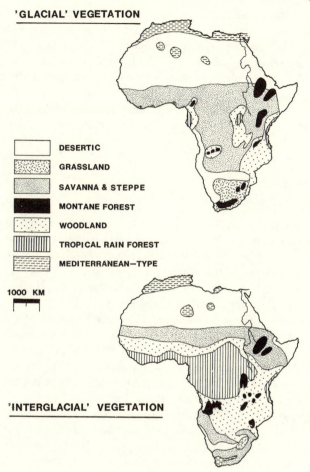

'GLACIAL' VEGETATION

DESERTIC

GRASSLAND

SAVANNA & STEPPE

MONTANE FOREST

WOODLAND

TROPICAL RAIN FOREST

MEDITERRANEAN—TYPE

1000 KM

'INTERGLACIAL' VEGETATION

Figure 2. Hypothetical vegetation patterns for Africa under glacial and interglacial climates. (After *The historical atlas of Africa*. Longman's (1985).)

(Hamilton 1976; Clark 1980). The crucial region that controls movements of animals and humans between North and South Africa is the Sahara. Evidence is well preserved there for both more intensive desertification and also more humid periods when streams flowed, lakes filled and much of the desert was replaced by a Sudanic tree or grassland highly favoured for occupation by the large Ethiopian fauna and by humans (Clark 1989).

Clearly, when the Sahara was green it was occupied and, when aridification set in, animal and human populations moved out to the peripheries and to montane refugia. When the desert became hyperarid it was virtually unoccupied by man or beast. It is this climatic rhythm of more humid to more arid habitats that had, I believe, a major effect on interaction and exchange between northern and southern Africa and on movements and migrations within and outside the continent. The First was the Miocene ape migration to Eurasia; the next of which we have record is that of *Homo erectus* into Eurasia around one million or more years ago. I stress this to emphasize that, if modern humans evolved in Africa and moved out after 200 ka as the DNA data suggest (Stoneking & Cann 1989), then this is a repetition of a pattern and not the first migratory movement of such magnitude.

5. THREE HYPOTHETICAL SCENARIOS FOR AFRICAN AND WEST ASIAN INTERACTION

Figure 3 presents three hypothetical scenarios to show possible movements and interaction between North African and West Asian populations in response to climatic and environmental changes between the late Middle Pleistocene and the early last glacial.

Figure 3*a*: If the Uranium series dates for the mound-springs and 'radar rivers' in the eastern Sahara are reliable, the makers of the late Acheulian industries occupied the desert during the humid oxygen-isotope Stage 7, around 245–190 ka ago (Wendorf *et al.* 1990). The desertification of the Sahara during the penultimate glacial that followed triggered, it is suggested, a northward movement out of the desert into the Mediterranean littoral and eastward into the Nile valley; a movement that, it can be conjectured, turned the North African littoral into an Interaction Zone and, following the onset of the last interglacial (isotope Stage 5), once again permitted population expansion and movement into the desert and over the Isthmus of Suez to and from the Levant; and perhaps also movement by some narrow sea-crossings into the Arabian peninsula and western Europe when sea levels were lower by 100 m or more during the maximum of a glacial.

Figure 3*b*: With the rapid onset of the warmer last interglacial, between *ca.* 125 and 74 ka ago, sea levels rose and the available space in the coastal plain became more restricted. Population densities are also likely to have increased following readaptation to new habitats, including the earliest use of sea-foods, the grinding of plant foods and innovations in technology. This last resulted in the disappearance of bifaces and experimentation with both early blade and more refined prepared core technologies in conjunction with the invention of hafting which permitted the production of simple, but more efficient, composite tools.

Figure 3*c*: The evidence from the Levant suggests that the first anatomically modern humans were present there about 90–100 ka ago and that they probably came from Africa. The northern African human populations

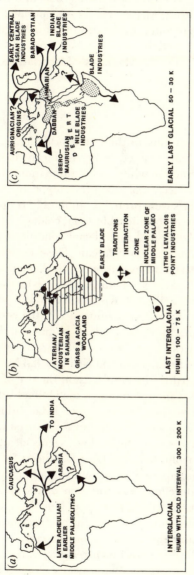

Figure 3. Hypothetical scenarios to show possible movements and interaction between northern Africa and western Asia. (*a*) Initial spread of later Acheulian and early Middle Palaeolithic from Africa to Eurasia under interglacial conditions, 300–200 ka ago. (*b*) To show early blade traditions in Africa and the Levant; the 'Nuclear Region' with heavy emphasis on Levallois point production and the 'Interaction Zone' between northeast Africa and the Levant during the humid period of the last interglacial, 100–75 ka ago. (*c*) The spread of Upper Palaeolithic blade industries from northeast Africa and the Levant during the cold and dry climates of the last glacial, 50–30 ka ago.

159

associated with the Middle Palaeolithic, early Upper and Epi-Palaeolithic belong to the Mechta–Afalou race (described first from Epi-Palaeolithic sites in eastern Algeria) that, as has been said, had its roots in the ancient *Homo erectus* population of northwest Africa. The closest parallels to the Mechta–Afalou physical type were found to be with the Cro-Magnon fossils of western Europe. The early modern human fossils from Qafzeh and Skhul have been described as 'Proto-Cro-Magnons'. The relationship between the Levant and North Africa was clearly a close one at this time.

6. THE EXPANSION INTO ASIA

Looking at a simplified vegetation map of the Old World (figure 4) it is apparent that montane regions have tended to be significant barriers to north–south movement and interaction while, at the same time, favouring movement from west to east and vice versa along the steppe and savanna corridors. The central Asian deserts were probably similar filters north and south as was the Sahara. Of course, considerable zonal changes in vegetation must be projected under glacial and interglacial conditions and the elevation of the Himalayas and the Thibetan plateau. The evergreen forest was an effective barrier to the eastward extension of the Acheulian, even though much of the Far East may have seen a much greater extension of the dry tropical and sub-tropical forest (Prell & Kutzbach 1987).

The Levantine evidence underscores the significance of the contemporary co-habitation of the Levant by early modern humans and Neanderthals and their stone industries. There do not seem to be any major technological differences between the modern and Neanderthal Middle Palaeolithic tool-kits except in regard to the emphasis on the use of the Levallois method in the southern Levant and more on the Quina tradition in the north (Bar-Yosef 1988). That the earliest Upper Palaeolithic blade tradition—the Ahmarian (*ca.* 37 ka BP)—in the Levant evolved from the southern Mousterian with Levallois point technology, seems clear, as also that it is the earliest Upper Palaeolithic in the Levant (Gilead 1991). It is comparable to and broadly contemporary with the Dabban in Cyrenaica (*ca.* 40 ka BP). Comparable antecedents can be seen in the 'Levallois–Idfuan' and Nazlet Khater industries along the Upper Nile (Vermeersch *et al.* 1990; Van Peer 1991). As at present, therefore, the evidence once again suggests that northern Africa and the Levant could be considered as a single 'culture area' (figure 3), albeit with much regional variability, the material products of which were made by anatomically modern humans (see figure 3*b*).

▶

Figure 4. Simplified vegetation map of the Old World. (After *The Times concise atlas of the world*. Times Books (1974).)

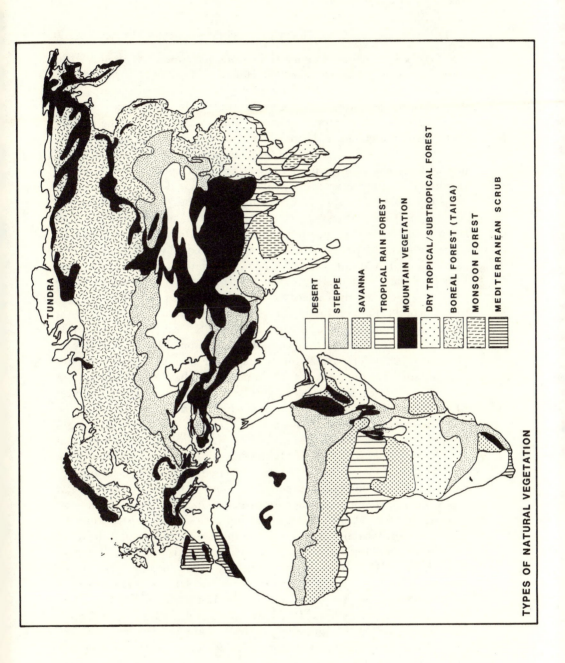

TYPES OF NATURAL VEGETATION

DESERT
STEPPE
SAVANNA
TROPICAL RAIN FOREST
MOUNTAIN VEGETATION
DRY TROPICAL/SUBTROPICAL FOREST
BOREAL FOREST (TAIGA)
MONSOON FOREST
MEDITERRANEAN SCRUB

TUNDRA

161

7. The Middle and Early Upper Palaeolithic in the Middle East

The Lower Palaeolithic dichotomy in stone tool traditions, well seen in Europe (Wymer 1982; Svoboda 1989; Howell & Arsebük 1989), and Africa (Kleindienst 1961; Clark 1975; Gowlett 1988) continues eastwards. The Acheulian biface tradition is present in Arabia and the Indian peninsula and even in Nepal, but the Indian assemblages are closest to the African pattern with both biface and core/chopper traditions being represented in a single assemblage but without the Levallois method. The Acheulian biface does not occur anywhere in or eastward of the tropical forest zone first encountered in northeast India (Lubine *et al.* 1985).

To the north of Arabia in the Crimea (Kolossov 1988), Georgia and Azerbaijan (Golovanova *et al.* 1990; Adamenko & Gladiline 1990) only the late or terminal Acheulian appears to have penetrated and the basal assemblage in the cave deposits in these regions might equally well be considered as transitional to Middle Palaeolithic; they are dated to the later part of the Last Interglacial. The same prondnik-type of bifacial knife occurs in the Crimea as it does at the eastern Sahara mound spring sites.

The Middle Palaeolithic in the Middle East (Iraq and Iran) is best known for the long sequence in Shanidar Cave (Solecki 1971) with its clear association with Neanderthal hominids; and from Warwasi (Dibble & Holdaway 1990). The artifact assemblages are from cave and open sites and, because they differ in artifact composition, it has been suggested that they represent seasonal patterning. The assemblages resemble Typical Mousterian but the Levallois method is rarely used. Points, side-scrapers, denticulates and borers are the most usual tool types and these assemblages show resemblances to both the northern Mousterian of the Levant and that from Central Asia. The earliest Middle Palaeolithic is thought to date from 80–100 ka and to continue to 40 ka. The environment was cold and dry with two more humid episodes between 80 and 62 ka and 56 and 42 ka; it was a desertic steppe with some forest in refugia. The Baradostian—the succeeding earlier Upper Palaeolithic industry known mostly from the Zagros sites in Iran and Iraq—is one of the earliest recorded, if the dates are correct (38–33 ka BP) and is clearly contemporary with the Ahmarian in the Levant. It is a blade-based technology with some micro-blades, the dominant tool types being burins, scrapers on flakes (some carinated), delicate points (Font Yves) and small, retouched bladelets with rare choppers, picks and grindstones. It follows directly on the Mousterian in the rockshelters and caves, suggesting that its appearance was abrupt. A derivation from the local Mousterian is not ruled out, however (Smith 1986). Regional specialization is very apparent. The steep scrapers of the Baradostian find parallels in the Levantine Aurignacian and with the Upper Palaeolithic industries in the Caucasus and Transcaucasia. In Central Asia and Afghanistan, however, Upper Palaeolithic prismatic blade technology seems to have made only a later appearance (Smith 1986).

8. THE INDIAN PENINSULA

In northeastern Pakistan, Acheulian handaxes have been dated between 730 and 400 ka by palaeomagnetism (Rendell *et al.* 1989). The late Acheulian is known from many open sites (Misra 1989) and also from caves (Misra 1985). The transition from Acheulian to Middle Palaeolithic in India took place sometime not less than 100 ka, and appears to follow the pattern observed in Africa and Europe where the bifaces disappear and the flake tool component takes over (Clark & Williams 1990). In general the Middle Palaeolithic in peninsular India is a flake-based technology with only a modified form of the Levallois method and, especially where quartzites were used, characterized by a lack of regular retouch. Only where cherts and other homogeneous materials were used is there evidence for regular retouching. Thermoluminescence and Uranium-series dates from Rajasthan range from 150–100 ka while radiocarbon dates indicate ages between 40 and 10 ka BP. The former are likely to be more correct. The climate shows a change from humid at the beginning to cold and dry with open vegetation and much grassland later.

The time of the introduction of Upper Palaeolithic blade technology into India is, as yet, unknown and such assemblages as have been dated range in age between *ca.* 26 and 10 ka BP. However, large blades in secondary and abraded context occur stratified in gravels at the base of the early Upper Pleistocene Baghor Formation in the Son Valley and are likely to be older. The Upper Palaeolithic is a blade and bladelet techno-complex dominated by backed blades and with lower percentages of scrapers in regionally varied contexts. Blade tools are reminescent of those of the Ahmarian in the Levant and this relationship is reinforced in terminal Pleistocene contexts in both India and Iraqi Kurdistan (see figure 3*c*).

9. CENTRAL ASIA

In cave and palaeosol sites in the loess in Central Asia (figure 5) in Uzbekistan (Islamov 1990) and Tadjikistan (Ranov & Davis 1979; Davis *et al.* 1980) the Acheulian biface facies of the Lower Palaeolithic is unknown and the assemblages are characterised by core-choppers and flake tools not infrequently with steep retouch; Levallois typology is not present. Heavier duty forms are rare and in no way resemble an Acheulian biface. The age— on palaeomagnetic evidence—appears to be between 250 and 130 ka

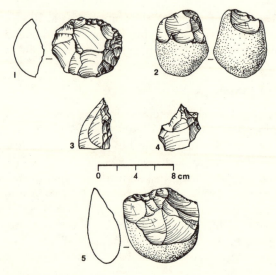

Figure 5. Core/chopper and flake tools from Lakuti I (nos. 1–4) and Karata (no. 5) sites in the loess in Kazakstan, Central Asia. (After Davis *et al.* 1980.)

(Davis *et al.* 1980). All are associated with episodes of warmer, more humid, though nevertheless dry climate supporting a forest–steppe vegetation.

The succeeding Middle Palaeolithic in Central Asia can be seen as a derivative of the Lower Palaeolithic Industry, as elsewhere, and is characterized by retouched scrapers and points, but this retouching may be the outcome of resharpening and related to raw material procurement and availability (Dibble 1988). The little that is known of the Lower Palaeolithic in Iran and Iraqi Kurdistan is comparable and probably dates to not less than 100 ka, indicating that the assemblages are similar to those in Central Asia (Smith 1986, pp. 14–17) but at Barda Balka (Braidwood & Howe 1960) a few poorly made handaxes are associated with the core/choppers and flake tool components. It seems likely that the distribution of bifaces in the more tropical south and of the core/chopper and flake tool tradition in the north has a basis in climatic and environmental differences.

10. Northern Asia

Research during the last decade has produced evidence of what is considered to be Lower Palaeolithic occupation in southern and western Siberia (Dolitsky 1985) but there is no general agreement as to the age of these assemblages, although even claims of 70 ka ('Makarovo Horizon') have been put forward. However, because some of the assemblages are surface finds, there is room for doubt. Similar problems arise in the dating of the Middle Palaeolithic except for cave sites in the Altai (Ust-'Kanskaya: Strashnaya and Denisova Caves) which are clear evidence for a stratified Mousterian, although claims for a Levallois component of the assemblages seem unproven (Larichev *et al.* 1987). The three sites are dated between 40 ka and 20 ka BP and are, therefore, late for a Middle Palaeolithic. At Denisova, although blades are absent from the assemblages, it is claimed that in each layer except one, Upper Palaeolithic and Mousterian types of artifact occur together. In sites west of Lake Baikal, the 'Makarovo Horizon', thought to date more probably to more than 40 ka BP, comprises cores and choppers, flakes and blades, 'micro-flaking' and prismatic cores and combines Middle and Upper Palaeolithic technology. It is said to be contemporary with the Mousterian in the Altai (Larichev *et al.* 1988; 1990, pp. 354). Such assemblages have led to claims for a direct transition of the Siberian Upper Palaeolithic from the regional Mousterian. Early Upper Palaeolithic prismatic blade technology is found at three sites west of Lake Baikal and is dated to between 32 and 28 ka BP. East of the Lake, four other sites are ascribed to the early Upper Palaeolithic and two have been dated between 35 and 26 ka BP and provide evidence of dwelling foundations and hearths (Larichev *et al.* 1990, p. 365). Russian investigators claim that true Upper Palaeolithic assemblages exist (Igetey Ravine I: Ust'-Kova) that predate (25–28 ka BP) the 'classic' Siberian Upper Palaeolithic (Mal'ta and Bur'et) which is dated to 20–21 ka BP, and a strong case for regional continuity has been made. Notwithstanding, in view of the traits shared with some of the south Russian sites, especially in the art and bone and ivory working, it is difficult not to see a connection that could imply an eastward and northward movement of the first modern human populations around 22 ka BP.

Given the severity of the climatic oscillations during the Glacial maximum, population movements might be expected but the direct antecedents of the classic Upper Palaeolithic remain uncertain. Is it, as some researchers claim, an autochthonous development out of the local Middle Palaeolithic, or is it intrusive? These assemblages in the Lake Baikal region described as early Upper Palaeolithic, that combine Middle and Upper Palaeolithic technological features, might also be seen as a comparable regional response to ecological change by technological innovation or by interaction as are those blade/flake industries such as the Châtelperronian, Uluzzian, Szeletian, Howieson's Poort, Amudian and other industries that may be the final expression of the Mousterian rather than the beginning of the Upper Palaeolithic (Mellars 1989).

11. EASTERN ASIA

In the tropical forest habitats of mainland southeast Asia, the chopper/chopping tool tradition, as it has been called by Movius (1948), is completely dominant but very poorly dated. Most of the assemblages are of late Pleistocene or later age although there is a claim that needs to be substantiated for a date of 0.8–0.6 Ma (Pope *et al.* 1986). From the Island of Java, the oldest artifacts that are not proven to be of late Pleistocene age are, perhaps, the small flake tools, surface finds from a fluvial context at Sangiran (von Koenigswald 1978) and, on the evidence from China, would not be inappropriate examples of the stone tools that could have been made by Java Man.

In China the core and flake tool facies is everywhere dominant and is well documented by numerous investigators (Ikawa-Smith 1978; Aigner 1978*a*, *b*; Pei Wenzhong & Zhang Senshui 1985; Jia Lanpo 1980). Here, in late Middle and early later Pleistocene contexts (not less than 100 ka) a heavy duty component is sometimes added to the core/flake traditional artefacts, as at Dingcun and Baisur (Huang Weiwen, 1987). These also occur in South Korea (e.g. at Chongokni (Bae 1988)) but their presence most likely has a functional explanation, as does the African Sangoan which this Far Eastern tool component resembles.

The core/chopper and flake tradition of southeast and East Asia is part of the very extensive techno-complex that stretched from Africa and western Eurasia to the Far East and is not an independent autochthonous development unrelated to the other parts of the Old World. It reflects the choice of the hominid populations that this was the preferred stone equipment in the forest and steppe environments of those regions from Central Asia eastwards to the Far East. The longest stratigraphic record covering the late Middle and Upper Pleistocene in the Far East comes from Locality 1 at Zhoukoudian (Pei & Zhang 1985) but this is supplemented by other, less extensive, sequences dated by fauna, palaeomagnetic, U-series and radiocarbon methods (Wei Qi 1988). Work by a joint Chinese–U.S. team in the Nihewan Basin in northern China has produced sealed activity sites with much fauna dated by palaeomagnetism to around 1.0 million years ago. This is a flake and core/chopper industry that exhibits modification but only minimal retouch. It is closely comparable to the assemblages from Zhoukoudian where flakes predominate but there, unlike the Nihewan sites, bipolar flaking is well in evidence (Schick *et al.* 1991). This tradition continues up to the coming of the Upper Palaeolithic micro-blade industries that appear to have spread into northern China between 30 and 20 ka BP. There is very little change in technology and artifact types from bottom to top at Zhoukoudian but rare, retouched racloirs and borers, or stubby points, occur with the later assemblages and increasing use was being made

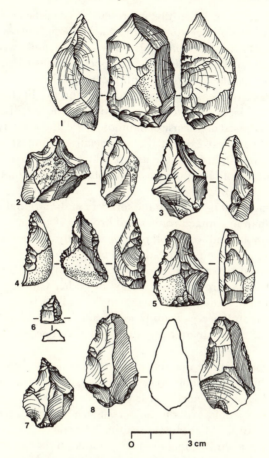

Figure 6. 'Middle Palaeolithic' core/chopper and Light Duty modified and retouched flake tools from Xujiuyao (Hsu-chia-yao), Yangkao County, Shanxi Province. (After Jia & Wei 1976.)

of finer-grained raw materials. This is well seen both at cave sites (e.g. Hsiao-nan-hai (Aigner 1978*b*, pp. 167–172) and the Upper Cave at Zhoukoudian (Aigner 1978*b*, pp. 186–192)) and at open air sites such as Xujiayo (Jia & Wei 1976) (figure 6) and Ban Jing in the Nihewan (Xie Fei, personal communication) that date from *ca.* 100 ka or later. The industries remain technologically unspecialized, even where the heavy duty point tools and picks are present and it is apparent that there was no necessity for retouching and resharpening of artifacts and that the supply of raw materials was adequate for what they were used on, as they show very little evidence of heavy usage. The great majority of flakes show little or no modification and, even when this is present, it consists usually of simple micro-chipping of an edge due to use. Such a long unspecialized stone industry suggests that the materials on which the tools were used were mostly soft, not hard and resistant. It has been suggested since the 1930s that in the Far East the tools of Palaeolithic hominids may have been made of bamboo. A strong case can be made out for the likelihood that the technology of the forest and steppe populations in the late Middle and later Pleistocene was based on the use of bamboo, wood and their by-products. If this was so, it can best explain the unspecialized, almost opportunistic, nature of the stone industries, the uses of which would have been confined to the basic needs of chopping, sawing, splitting and scraping these raw materials.

A recent study (1991) of montane foragers and marginal cultivators in southern Yunnan in a mixed conifer and broad-leafed, open forest habitat, shows that bamboo and wood still provide virtually all their material needs today with the exception of the addition of a short iron machete. Experiments with flaked stone tools (chopper and flakes) made on the spot and comparable to those from Zhoukoudian and other Chinese sites, showed that they were fully adequate for carrying out all the tasks necessary for preparing the many pieces of equipment made by these people from bamboo. Studies of use-wear and phytoliths on the edges of these tools are proceeding.

If, as we believe will be demonstrated, the main raw materials and food sources for which stone tools were needed by Pleistocene populations in southeast and East Asia northwards to the 'Bamboo Line', were obtained from plants, this would explain the persistence of the unspecialized stone industries: a tradition that later spread to Australasia.

In the Far East, this techno-complex is found in the time range of *Homo erectus*, archaic *Homo sapiens* fossils (Dali, Xujiayao (Wu & Olsen 1985), Yunxian (Li & Etler 1992) and Jinnuishan (LüZune 1990)) and with some later Pleistocene modern human fossils. Because no major changes can be seen in the technological base, this has been used to support a claim for regional continuity between the *Homo erectus* and anatomically modern populations. If the early modern fossils from China (e.g. Salawusu, Liuchiang, Laipin (Wu & Olsen 1985)) were more precisely dated and their morphology better known, it would strengthen this model. However, the latest report on the 'Old Man' from the Upper Cave at Zhoukoudian shows it to be late in time and not to be Mongoloid (Kamminga & Wright 1988). Whereas in Africa and western Europe, the abrupt transition from Middle to Upper Pleistocene is marked by major technological changes, this does not seem to have been the case in China. If this can be seen as an argument for regional evolution and continuity in the human population, it might equally be seen as a highly successful behavioural and technological adaptation of anatomically modern populations moving from the west some 40 ka ago, bringing with them such Upper Palaeolithic traits as ornamentation and bone tools (e.g. Upper Cave, Zhoukoudian). The association of fully modern fossils with the core/flake tradition in Australia and the lack of fossil connections linking the southeast Asian evolved *Homo erectus* with modern Australian remains inadequately demonstrate that either model is tenable. However, when considered in relation to the molecular and cultural evidence respectively, especially the art, the 'Noah's Ark' model appears at the present time to be the most likely.

12. Behavioural Implications of The Middle Palaeolithic–Middle Stone Age

This review of the artifact assemblages of Africa and Asia and their place in space and time has demonstrated the ancient dichotomy present in Lower Palaeolithic technology that, most probably, under climatic and environmental restraints, dictated the emphasis on one or other of these great techno-complexes. Whatever the explanation, it is clear that, when the choice has been made, the technology successfully fulfilled the need for survival. The transition and continuity between the Lower and Middle Palaeolithic appears clear, especially in the west and south, though in eastern Asia, while the continuity is clear, any significant transition is not easily seen or dated.

The climatic fluctuations in northern Africa and sequential drastic environmental changes in the Sahara and the Levant due to the effects of the continental glacial advance, initiated technological and attendant behavioural changes manifest in the transition from Acheulian to Middle Palaeolithic. The Middle Palaeolithic in the southern Levant and northeast Africa have much in common as exemplified in the early experimentation with blade technology during the Last Interglacial and later the development of the true Upper Palaeolithic blade technology more than 40 ka. The DNA evidence (Stoneking and Cann 1989) and the associated fossils of anatomically modern humans show that these technological changes are most likely to have been associated with the modern genotype and not with Neanderthals. The review of the Middle Palaeolithic–Upper Palaeolithic cultural evidence from central and eastern Asia is unfortunately ambiguous, though associated fossils with the Middle Palaeolithic are described as 'Neanderthal'. There are claims for both regional continuity and catastrophic replacement of technological traditions for explaining the replacement of Middle by Upper Palaeolithic technology. More chronological precision is essential, however. Modern humans were in Israel around 100 ka ago. Why, if they possessed the same intellectual and physiological capabilities as ourselves, did not the behavioural changes of the 'Cultural

Revolution' manifest themselves at the same time? They did not, and early modern and Neanderthal tool-kits show no very significant differences in the Levant for some 50 ka when, first, the Ahmarian blade tradition made its appearance followed, some millennia later, by the Aurignacian. The hiatus seems unexplainable on the cultural and fossil evidence alone.

The technological and organisational complexity of the Upper Palaeolithic–Later Stone Age, always associated with the modern genotype, is sharply contrasted with that of the Middle Palaeolithic–Middle Stone Age. Much has been written about the richness of Upper Palaeolithic culture and there is no need to repeat it here. The evidence for the beginnings of a broader perception of the nature of their world is, however, hinted at in the Middle Palaeolithic but is remarkably limited and unconvincing where symbolic behaviour is concerned (Chase & Dibble 1987; Chase 1991). Early moderns and Neanderthals buried their dead (Qafzeh, Kebara) (Smirnov 1989). There is some slight suggestion also, from associated grave goods, of a possible belief in an afterlife. Use of pigment (Wreschner 1980) might, perhaps, be seen as a means of symbolic expression but there is no evidence for ritual behaviour now that the skull and context of the Monte Circeo Neanderthals have been reinvestigated. Similarly, the caches of bear skulls in caves in the Alps must be eliminated. There is also little or no use of bone for equipment although, in the tropics, hardwood took the place of bone, even in the Later Stone Age. There is minimal evidence for ornamentation, although a few rare examples do exist in both Europe and Africa. Art, with the possible exception of notched bones, and incised ostrich egg-shells in southern Africa, does not exist. The bone 'flute' from Haua Fteah is now seen as more likely to be the result of hyaena chewing than of human modification (Davidson 1991). Evidence for dwelling structures comes from French Châtelperronian contexts, from southern Russia and from Morocco.

Unless it be the diversity in the Middle Palaeolithic–Middle Stone Age tool traditions in Africa, implying ecologically adapted specialisations, little difference in behaviour can be seen between the technologies of the Neanderthals and those of early moderns. The Howieson's Poort industries and related occurrences in Africa do seem to anticipate the Later Stone Age blade traditions but they may not be all that different in age and grade from the Châtelperronian and similar industries in Europe which were, at one time, thought to be the earliest Upper Palaeolithic but are now seen as more likely to represent a terminal stage of the Middle Palaeolithic and are regarded as attempts by the last Neanderthals to adjust their technology and behaviour to those of the first modern peoples that they encountered (Mellars 1989, this symposium). This interpretation is, no doubt, strengthened by the Neanderthal burial in a Châtelperronian level at St Cesaire.

Anatomically modern humans like ourselves are expected to have possessed the same potential for intellectual ability as does our own kind. Their technology and behaviour, therefore, should be very different from that of the Neanderthals who, although possessing considerable ability to survive inimical environments, nevertheless became extinct. Thus, the fact that the technology and behaviour of the first modern humans in Africa and the Levant do not appear to be all that different from those of the Neanderthals, poses a major problem. It should, however, not necessarily be assumed that these similar tool-kits were used in the same way by the two groups, and some tool forms may have been used very differently by moderns and Neanderthals occupying similar habitats. Therein lies the importance of the Middle Stone Age regional variability in technology and the Strategies for resource procurement for which they were adapted. If the chronology is correct, there were some 50 ka between the time when the first moderns appeared in the Levant and the time when Upper Palaeolithic technology, symbolic behaviour and social organization spread so rapidly throughout the world. What was going on behaviourally, intellectually and technologically during that time? Until more of the hard data—excavated localities, fossil and cultural evidence in well-dated environmental contexts—are available it is possible only to speculate. More basic data from key areas and key sites are essential. I see every reason to accept that anatomically modern humans evolved in Africa at the time suggested by the molecular record (Stoneking & Cann 1989) but that they had not yet acquired the unique intellectual abilities that made possible the complex social organisation and symbolic behaviour of the Upper Palaeolithic populations. The catalyst that made the Upper Palaeolithic possible was, I have believed for a long while, the development of a full language system like our own, which opens up a new world of ever-broadening horizons and opportunities, the ability to convey specific information, to distinguish between past, present and future, to think abstractly, to use symbolism and, in short, to be psychologically similar to ourselves (Clark 1970: 146–7; Cavalli-Sforza *et al.* 1989, 1991; Mellars 1989, 1991; Davidson 1991). The threshold must be in that time range when Middle Palaeolithic technology was replaced by the Upper Palaeolithic, the cultural complexity of which is seen in the circumstantial evidence of the activity areas or settlements and the proliferation of technological variability and in elaborate artistic expression.

Whether the ability to speak is a physical or neurological phenomenon, or both, is for the anatomists and linguists to decide. The hyoid bones of *H. erectus* and other archaic hominids are not available for comparison but a Neanderthal hyoid bone, similar to our own, does not necessarily imply that Neanderthals could talk, though it does imply that they had the anatomic ability to do so. Broca's area can be identified even on crania assigned to *H. habilis* and, while this is related to the ability to speak, it is unclear what degree of vocal communication was represented. Emotional vocalizations, gesturing and posturing of chimpanzees have enabled them to develop an efficient proto-culture that could have some analogous relationship to the communication system and behaviour of *H. habilis*, the maker of the Old-owan stone tools. The culture of *H. erectus* is certainly more elaborate but it does not appear to this author to have needed any *complex* communication system and the ability to make even 'refined' stone tools can be mastered by observation, experiment and practice with minimal vocal instruction. Bickerton (1990) suggests that the neural structure of the brain could have allowed early hominids to extract from their perceptions a 'secondary representation' that improved the efficiency of their use of the environment. His contention is that 'primitive language' would have had a vocabulary of words signifying meaning but lacking the grammatical elements of syntax. He sees the jump from 'primitive' language to syntactic language as rapid and considers that it emerged as a single genetic event. If the first anatomically modern humans evolving in Africa already had a syntactic language system, why do we not see this most significant development reflected in the cultural evidence associated with the early modern fossils, which we do not? If, however, full language developed only later and suddenly between 40 and 50 ka ago, this would account for the lag in the appearance of the cultural revolution represented by the Upper Palaeolithic traditions and the very rapid spread of modern humans throughout the world from 40 ka BP onwards. If Africa, as the preponderance of the evidence now suggests, was the home of anatomically modern humans—the continent, moreover, where these modern traits made their appearance early in the Middle Pleistocene—it would seem that this evolutionary event need not have been accompanied by the ability to speak syntactically, as we do. This may well have been a later development for which modern humans were pre-adapted. Whether this event also took place in Africa, or elsewhere, remains to be shown but, if there were two genetic events and not one, this would explain the undifferentiated nature of Middle Palaeolithic stone technology associated with the first anatomically modern humans in North Africa and the Levant and the experimentation with new technologies represented by the Pre-Aurignacian, the Amudian, the Howieson's Poort and similar technological manifestations in South and East Africa and Equatoria. It might also be connected with the division of Caucasoids and Mongoloids on the genetic tree.

It is of interest that the early modern fossils from eastern Asia and Europe are closer morphologically to each other than are the modern fossils from eastern Asia to the antecedent hominid fossils of the region. This suggests the migration hypothesis, though some gene flow between seems to be observable (Stringer 1990).

The first humans to enter Australia around 40–60 ka (Roberts *et al.* 1990) were anatomically fully modern and carried with them a tool-kit that resembled that which had been in use in China since the days of *Homo erectus*. If, however, there is no compelling evidence for the direct descendancy of the modern Mongoloid and Australoid populations of eastern Asia and Australasia from the then existing archaic genepool in the East, it is equally possible that modern humans pushing eastwards were quick to readapt their technology and behaviour to that best suited for exploiting the resources of the new regions into which they moved.

13. CONCLUSIONS

To summarize: the palaeontological and archaeological evidence points to an early emergence of anatomically modern humans—the 'African Eve'— associated with regionally and ecologically specialized tool-kits that were evolving in Africa from around 200 ka ago. By 100 ka ago, modern groups had spread into western Asia where they lived for some 50 ka contemporaneously with Neanderthals. Although it is to be expected that behavioural adaptations of modern humans and Neanderthals grew increasingly different, this does not appear to be reflected in the cultural associations, though meaningful variation may, perhaps, be obscured by the too-generalized level of the approach we are using. Some time subsequent to the move into the Levant and possibly further afield, the modern human genotype developed a syntactic language system that, by 40 ka ago, had revolutionized social organization, communication and symbolic relationships, leading to this genotype's rapidly replacing, as they moved out in EuroAsia—without receiving from them any significant genetic input— the archaic human races they encountered in their population of the world.

REFERENCES

Adamenko, O.M. & Gladiline, V.N. 1989 Korolevo: un des plus anciens habitats Acheuléens et Moustériens de Transcarpatie Soviétique. *Anthropologie* **93** (4), 689– 712.

Aigner, J.S. 1978*a* Pleistocene Faunal and Cultural Stations in South China. In *Early Palaeolithic in South-East Asia* (ed. F. Ikawa Smith), pp. 129–160. The Hague: Mouton.

Aigner, J.S. 1978*b* Important archaeological remains from North China. In *Early Palaeolithic in South-East Asia* (ed. F. Ikawa Smith), pp. 163–232. The Hague: Mouton.

Arambourg, C., Boule, M., Vallois, H. & Verneau, R. 1934 Les Grottes paléolithiques des Beni Ségoval (Algérie). *Archs Inst. Paléont. hum.* **13**.

Bae, Kidong 1988 The significance of the Chongokni Stone Industry in the tradition of the Palaeolithic cultures of East Asia. Ph.D thesis, University of California, Berkeley.

Balout, L. 1955 *Préhistoire de l'Afrique du Nord*. Paris: Arts et Métiers Graphiques.

Bartstra, G.J. 1982 *Homo erectus*: the search for his artifacts. *Curr. Anthrop.* **23**, 318– 320.

Bar-Yosef, O. 1988 Le Paléolithique d'Israel. *Anthropologie* **92**, 769–795.

Beaumont, P.B., de Villiers, H. & Vogel, J.C. 1978 Modern man in sub-Saharan Africa prior to 49,000 BP: A review and evaluation with particular reference to Border Cave. *S. Afr. J. Sci.* **74**, 409–419.

Bickerton, D. 1990 *Language and species.* University of Chicago Press.

Braidwood, R.J. & Howe, B. 1960 Prehistoric investigations in Iraqi Kurdistan. In *Studies in ancient oriental civilisation*, vol. 31. Chicago University Press.

Brandt, S.A. & Gresham, T.H. 1989 L'Age de la Pierre en Somalie. *Anthropologie*, **94**(3), 459–482.

Brauer, G. 1989 The evolution of Modern humans: a comparison of the African and non-African evidence. In *The human revolution* (ed. P. Mellars & C. Stringer), pp. 123–154. Edinburgh University Press.

Chase, P.G. 1991 Symbols and Palaeolithic artifacts: style, standardization and the imposition of arbitrary form. *J. anthrop. Archaeol.* **10**, 193–214.

Chase, P.G. & Dibble, H.L. 1987 Middle Palaeolithic symbolism: a review of current evidence and interpretations. *J. anthrop. Archaeol.* **6**, 263–296.

Chavaillon, J. 1979 Un site Acheuléen près du Lac Langano (Ethiopie) *Abbay Documents pour servir à l'histoire de la civilisation ethiopienne* **10**, pp. 57–74. Paris: CNRS.

Chen Guoliang, Li Suling & Lin Jinlu 1977 Discussion of the age of *Homo erectus yuanmouensis* and the event of early Matuyama. *Scient. Geol. Sinica* **1**, 34–43.

Clark, J.D. 1975 A comparison of the Late Acheulian Industries of Africa and the Middle East. In *After the Australopithecines* (ed. K. W. Butzer & G. Ll. Isaac), pp. 604–659. The Hague: Mouton.

Clark, J.D. 1980 Early human occupation of African savanna environments. In *Human ecology in savanna environments* (ed. D. R. Harris), pp. 41–72. London: Academic Press.

Clark, J.D. 1988 The Middle Stone Age of East Africa and the beginnings of regional identity. *J. World Prehis.* **2**(3), 235–303.

Clark, J.D. 1989 The origins and spread of modern humans: a broad perspective on the African evidence. In *The human revolution* (ed. P. Mellars & C. Stringer), pp. 565–588. Edinburgh University Press.

Clark, J.D. & Williams, M.A.J. 1990 Prehistoric ecology, resource strategies and culture change in the Son Valley, Northern Madhya Pradash, Central India. *Man Environ.* **15**(1), 13–24.

Davidson, I. 1991 The archaeology of language origins: a review. *Antiquity* **65**, 39–48.

Davis, R.S., Ranov, V.A. & Dodonov, A.E. 1980 Early Man in Soviet Central Asia. *Scient. Am.* **243**, 130–137.

Deacon, H.J. 1979 Excavations at Boomplaas Cave: a sequence through the Upper Pleistocene and Holocene in South Africa. *World Archaeol.* **10**, 241–257.

Deacon, H.J. 1989 Late Pleistocene Palaeoecology and Archaeology in the Southern Cape, South Africa. In *The human revolution* (ed. P. Mellars & C. Stringer), pp. 547–564. Edinburgh University Press.

Deacon, H.J. & Geleijinse, V.B. 1988 The stratigraphy and sedimentology of the Main Site sequence, Klasies River, South Africa. *S. Afr. archaeol. Bull.* **43**, 5–14.

Debénath, A., Raynal, J.-P., Roche, J., Texier, J.-P. & Ferembach, D. 1986 Stratigraphie, habitat, typologie et devenir de l'Atérien Marocain: Données récentes. *Anthropologie* **90**(2), 233–246.

Dennell, R.W. & Rendell, H.M. 1988 Late Pliocene artifacts from northern Pakistan. *Curr. Anthrop.* **29**(3), 495–498.

Dibble, H.L. 1988 The interpretation of Middle Palaeolithic scraper reduction patterns. In *L'Homme de Néandertal*, vol. 4 (*La technique*) (ed. L. Binford & J-Ph. Rigaud), pp. 49–58. Liège: ERAUL.

Dibble, H. & Holdaway, S. 1990 Le Paléolithique moyen de l'Abris sous roche de Warwasi et ses relations avec le Moustèrien du Zagros et du Levant. *Anthropologie* **94**(4), 619–642.

Dolitsky, A.B. 1985 Siberian Palaeolithic archaeology: approaches and analytic methods. *Curr. Anthrop.* **26**(3), 361–378.

Gilead, I. 1991 The Upper Palaeolithic period in the Levant. *J. World Prehist.* **5**(2), 105–154.

Golovanova, L.V., Levkovskaya, G.M. & Barychinikov, G.F. 1990 Le nouveau site Moustérien en Grotte de Matouzka, Caucase septentrional (Résultats des Fouilles de 1985–1987). *Anthropologie* **94**(4): 739–762.

Gowlett, J.A.J. 1988 A case of Developed Oldowan in the Acheulian. *World Archaeol.* **20**, 13–26.

Hamilton, A. 1976 The significance of patterns of distribution shown by forest plants and animals in tropical Africa for the reconstruction of Upper Pleistocene palaeoenvironments: a review. In *Palaeoecology of Africa, 1972–1974*, vol. 19. (ed. E. M. van Zinderen Bakker), pp. 63–97. Cape Town: Balkema.

Howell, F.C. & Arsebök, G. 1989 *Yarimburgaz Cave, 1988*: Report on the investigations in the Cave of Yarimburgaz (Marmora, Turkey). Report to the National Geographical Society, Washington.

Huang Weiwen 1987 Bifaces in China. *Acta anthrop. Sinica* **6**(1), 61–68.

Hublin, J.-J. 1985 Human fossils from North African Middle Pleistocene and the origin of *Homo sapiens*. In *Ancestors: the hard evidence* (ed. E. Delson), pp. 238–288. New York: Alan Liss.

Ikawa Smith, F. 1978 *Early Palaeolithic in South and East Asia*. The Hague: Mouton.

Islamov, Y.I. 1990 Sel'oungour, un nouveau site du Paléolithique inférieur en Asie centrale. *Anthropologie* **94**(4), 675–688.

Jayaswal, V. 1982 *Chopper-chopping component of the Palaeolithic in India*. Delhi: Agam Kala Prakashan.

Jia Lanpo 1980 *Early Man in China*. Beijing: Foreign Language Press.

Jia Lanpo & Wei Qi 1976 A Palaeolithic site at Hsu-chia-yao in Yangkao County, Shansi Province. *Acta archaeol. Sinica* **2**, 97–114.

Kamminga, J. & Wright, R.V.S. 1988 The Upper Cave of Zhoukoudian and the origins of the Mongoloids. *J. hum. evol.* **17**(8), 739–767.

Kaplan, J. 1990 The Umhlatuzana Rockshelter sequence: 100,000 years of Stone Age history. *Natal Mus. J. Human.* **2**, 1–94.

Klein, R.G. 1972 Preliminary report on the July through September, 1970 excavation at Nelson Bay Cave, Plettenberg Bay (Cape Province, South Africa). *Palaeoecol. Africa* **6**, 177–208.

Kleindienst, M.R. 1961 Variability within the Late Acheulian Assemblage in Eastern Africa. *S. Afr. archaeol. Bull.* **16**(62), 35–52.

Kolossov, I.G. 1988 Les débuts du Paléolithique en Crimée. *Anthropologie* **92**(3), 809–838.

Korisettar, R., Mishra, S., Rajaguru, S.N., Gogte, V.D., Ganjoo, R.K., Venkatesan, T.R., Tandon, S.K., Somayajulu, B.L.K. & Kale, V.S. 1989 Age of the Bori volcanic ash and Lower Palaeolithic culture of the Kukdi Valley, Moharashtra. *Bull. Deccan Coll. Res. Inst.* **47**, 135–137.

Larichev, V., Khol'ushkin, U. & Laricheva, I. 1987 Lower and Middle Palaeolithic of Northern Asia: achievements, problems and perspectives. *J. World Prehist.* **1**(4), 415–464.

Larichev, V., Khol'ush kin, U. & Laricheva, I. 1988 The Upper Palaeolithic of Northern Asia: achievements, problems and perspectives I. Western Siberia. *J. World Prehist.* **2**(4), 359–396.

Larichev, V., Khol'ushkin, U. & Laricheva, I. 1990 The Upper Palaeolithic of Northern Asia: achievements, problems and perspectives II. Central and Eastern Siberia. *J. World Prehist.* **4**(3), 347–385.

Li Tianyuan & Etler, D.A. 1992 New Middle Pleistocene hominid crania from Yunxian, Hubei Province, The People's Republic of China. *Nature, Lond.* (In the Press.)

Lubine, V.P., Tcherniachovski, A.G., Barychnikov, G.F., Levkovskaia, G.M. & Selivanova, N.B. 1985 La Grotte de Koudaro I: (Résultats de recherches pluridisciplinaires). *Anthropologie* **89**(2), 159–180.

de Lumley, H. & Sonakia, A. 1985 Contexte stratigraphique et archéologique de l'Homme de la Namada, Hatnora, Madhya Pradesh, Inde. *Anthropologie* **89**, 3–12.

Lü Zun-E. 1990 La Découverte de l'Homme fossile de Jing-niu-shen: Première Etude. *Anthropologie* **94**(4), 899–902.

Marks, A.E. 1977 The Upper Palaeolithic sites of Boker Tachtit and Boker: A preliminary report. In *The prehistory and palaeoenvironments in the central Negev, Israel*, vol. 2 (ed. A. E. Marks). Southern Methodist University Press.

McBurney, C.B.M. 1967 *The Haua Fteah (Cyrenaica) and the Stone Age of the Southeast Mediterranean*. Cambridge University Press.

Mehlman, M.J. 1989 Later Quarternary archaeological sequences in northern Tanzania. Ph.D. Thesis, University of Illinois.

Mehlman, M.J. 1991 Context for the emergence of Modern man in Eastern Africa: Some new Tanzanian evidence. In *Cultural beginnings: approaches to understanding early hominid lifeways in the African savanna* (ed. J. D. Clark), pp. 177–196. Mainz: Römisch-Germanisches Zentralmuseum.

Mellars, P. 1989 Major issues in the emergence of modern humans. *Curr. Anthrop.* **30**(3), 349–385.

Mellars, P. 1991 Cognitive changes and the emergence of modern humans in Europe. *Cambr. archaeol. J.* **1**(i), 63–76.

Misra, V.K. 1985 The Acheulian succession at Bhimbetka, central India. In *Recent advances in Indo-Pacific Prehistory* (ed. V. N. Misra & P. Bellwood), pp. 35–48. Oxford and New Delhi: IBH.

Misra, V.N. 1989 Stone Age India: an ecological perspective. *Man Environ.* **14**(1), 17–64.

Movius, H.L. 1948 The Lower Palaeolithic cultures of southern and eastern Asia. *Trans. Am. phil. Soc.* **38**(4), 329–420.

Pei Wenzhong & Zhang Senshui 1985 A study of the lithic artifacts of *Sinanthropus*. *Palaeontol. Sinica* **12**, 1–277.

Pope, G., Barr, S., MacDonald, A. & Nakabanlang, S. 1986 Earliest Radiometrically dated artifacts from Southeast Asia. *Curr. Anthrop.* **27**, 275–279.

Prell, W.L. & Kutzbach, J.E. 1987 Monsoon variability over the past 150,000 years. *J. geophys. Res.* **92**(D.7) 8411–8425.

Qian Fang 1985 On the age of "Yuanmou Man": A discussion with Liu Tung-Sheng *et al. Acta anthrop. Sinica* **4**(4), 324–331.

Ranov, V.A. & Davis, R.S. 1979 Towards a new outline of the Soviet Central Asian Palaeolithic. *Curr. Anthrop.* **20**(2), 249–270.

Rendell, H.M., Dennell, R.W. & Halim, M.A. 1989 *Pleistocene and palaeolithic investigations in the Soan Valley, Northern Pakistan.* Oxford: BAR International Series, **544**.

Rightmire, G.P. 1990 *The evolution of Homo erectus.* Cambridge University Press.

Rightmire, G.P. & Deacon, H.J. 1991 Comparative studies of Late Pleistocene human remains from Klasies River Mouth, South Africa. *J. hum. Evol.* **20**, 131–156.

Roberts, R.G., Jones, R. & Smith, M.A. 1990 Thermoluminescence dating of a 50,000 year old human occupation site in northern Australia. *Nature, Lond.* **345**, 153–156.

Rodrigue, A. 1987 Nouveaux éléments sur le Moustérien du Maroc: La station d'Akka (Maroc Saharien). *Anthropologie* **91**, 483–496.

Schick, K.D., Toth, N., Qi, Wei, Clark, J.D. & Etler, D. 1991 Archaeological perspectives in the Nihewan Basin, China. *J. hum. Evol.* **21**(1), 13–26.

Schild, R. & Wendorf, F. 1977 *The prehistory of Dakhla Oasis and adjacent desert.* Warsaw: Polska Academia Nauk.

Shea, J.T. 1989 A functional study of the lithic industries associated with hominid fossils in the Kebara and Qafzeh Caves, Israel. In *The human revolution* (ed. P. Mellars & C. Stringer), pp. 611–625. Edinburgh University Press.

Smirnov, Y. 1989 Intentional human burial: Middle Palaeolithic (Last Glaciation) Beginnings. *J. World Prehist.* **3**(2), 199–233.

Smith, P.E.L. 1986 *Palaeolithic archaeology in Iran.* University Museum, University of Pennsylvania.

Solecki, R.S. 1971 *Shanidar: the first flower people.* New York: Alfred A. Knopf.

Stoneking, M. & Cann, R. 1989 African origins of Human Mitochondrial DNA. In *The human revolution* (ed. P. Mellars and C. Stringer), pp. 17–30. Edinburgh University Press.

Stringer, C.B. 1989 The origin of early modern humans: A comparison of the European and non-European evidence. In *The human revolution* (ed. P. Mellars & C. Stringer), pp. 232–244. Edinburgh University Press.

Stringer, C.B. 1990 The emergence of modern humans. *Scient. Am.* **263**(6), 98–104.

Stringer, C.B. & Andrews, P. 1988 Genetic and fossil evidence for the origin of modern humans. *Science, Wash.* **239**, 1263–1268.

Svoboda, J. 1989 Middle Pleistocene adaptations in Europe. *J. World Prehist.* **3**(1), 33–70.

Tillet, T. 1983 *Le Palaéolithique du Bassin Tchadien septentrional (Niger-Tchad).* Paris: CNRS.

Tixier, J. 1967 Procédés d'analyse et questions de terminologie concernant l'étude des ensembles industriels du Paléolithique récent et de l'Epipaléolithique dans l'Afrique du nordouest. In *Background to evolution in Africa* (ed. W. W. Bishop & J. D. Clark), pp. 771–812. University of Chicago Press.

Vandermeersch, B. 1989 The evolution of Modern humans: recent evidence from south-west Asia. In *The human revolution* (ed. P. Mellars & C. Stringer), pp. 155–164. Edinburgh University Press.

Van Peer, P. 1991 Interassemblage variability and Levallois styles: The case of the Northern African Middle Palaeolithic. *J. anthrop. Archaeol.* **10**, 107–151.

Vermeersch, P.M., Paulissen, E. & Van Peer, P. 1990 Le Paléolithique de la Vallée du Nil égyptien. *Anthropologie* **94**, 435–458.

Volkman, P. 1983 Boker Tachtit core reconstruction. In *The Prehistory and Palaeoenvironments in the central Negev, Israel*, vol. 3 (ed. A. E. Marks), pp. 129–190. Methodist University Press.

Volman, T.P. 1984 Early prehistory of southern Africa. In *Southern African prehistory and palaeoenvironments* (ed. R. G. Klein), pp. 169–220. Rotterdam: Balkema.

von Koenigswald, G.H.R. 1978 Lithic industries of *Pithecanthropus erectus* of Java. In *Early Palaeolithic in Southeast Asia* (ed. F. Ikawa Smith), pp. 23–27. The Hague: Mouton.

Wei Qi 1988 Le cadre stratigraphique, géochronologique et biostratigraphique des sites les plus anciens connus en Chine. *Anthropologie* **92**(3), 931–938.

Wen Benheng 1978 Palaeolithic artifacts found in the Yuanmou Basin, Yunnan. In *Gurenlei Lunwanji* (Collected papers of palaeoanthropology) (ed. Institute of Vertebrate Palaeontology and Palaeoanthropology), pp. 126–133. Academia Sinica. Beijing: Science Press.

Wendorf, F., Close, A.E., Schild, R., Gautier, A., Schwarcz, H.P., Miller, G.H., Kowalski, K. Krolik, H., Bluszcz, A., Robbins, D. & Grün, R. 1990 Le dernier interglaciaire dans le Sahara Oriental. *Anthropologie* **94**, 361–391.

Wreschner, E. 1980 Red ochre and human evolution: A case for discussion. *Curr. Anthrop.* **21**, 631–644.

Wu Rukang & Olsen, J.W. 1985 *Palaeoanthropology and palaeolithic archaeology in the People's Republic of China*. Orlando: Academic Press.

Wymer, J. 1982 *The Palaeolithic Age*. London: Croom Helm.

Reconstructing Recent Human Evolution

Christopher B. Stringer[1]

SUMMARY

The two most distinct models of recent human evolution, the multiregional and the recent African origin models, have different retrodictions concerning specific archaic–recent population relationships. The former model infers multiple regional archaic–modern connections and the ancient establishment of regional characteristics, whereas the latter model implies only an African archaic–all modern relationship, with recent (late Pleistocene) development of regionality. In this paper, four late archaic groups from Europe, southwest Asia, Africa and East Asia are compared with various fossil and recent *Homo sapiens* crania or cranial samples. The results of Penrose shape comparisons narrowly favour a late archaic African–modern special relationship over an East Asian–modern one, with European and southwest Asian Neanderthal groups much more distant. No specific archaic–recent regional relationships are indicated in the shape analyses, nor in separate examinations of patterns of regionality, which indicate a recent origin for present day regionality. The Skhul–Qafzeh sample provides an excellent shape intermediate between the archaic and recent samples.

1. INTRODUCTION

Debate on recent human evolution over the past few years has been focused on the contrasting models of multiregional evolution (regional continuity) and a recent African origin ('Out of Africa') to explain the evolutionary origins of anatomically modern *Homo sapiens* (hereafter *Homo sapiens* or modern humans). At their most basic, these different models have quite different retrodictions for the fossil record (Stringer & Andrews 1988; Wolpoff 1989).

From the multiregional evolution model, geographic 'clades' should be identifiable from the Early Pleistocene or earlier middle Pleistocene leading from local archaic populations to modern ones in the same regions. However, these 'clades' were not completely distinct genetically or phylogenetically, since they shared a common gene pool through gene flow and could even be regarded as representing early examples of our own species (*Homo sapiens sensu* Wolpoff & Thorne) following the last cladogenetic event,

[1] The Human Origins Group, The Natural History Museum, Cromwell Road, London SW7 5BD, U.K.

taken as the late Pliocene origin of what is usually termed *Homo erectus*. Grade changes can be recognized in the multiregional evolution of '*Homo sapiens*', with the gradual predominance of 'modern' morphological features occurring in the late Pleistocene.

In contrast, the recent African origin model has no specific retrodictions for middle Pleistocene hominid relationships. However, a monophyletic clade consisting of the (African) last common ancestor of all *Homo sapiens* plus all descendant hominids should be recognized. There would be no special clade relationship between regional *Homo sapiens* variants and non-*Homo sapiens* populations except via an Africa ancestor. There would be both a grade and clade relationship between *Homo sapiens* populations, with possible nested clades representing the results of late Pleistocene regional diversification.

Two related critical tests of the models concern the identification of a single or multiple archaic ancestral population for *Homo sapiens* in the late middle or early late Pleistocene, and the identification of specific regional affinities to modern *Homo sapiens* populations in any archaic samples. I have previously presented both phenetic and cladistic data in support of an African ancestral population for *Homo sapiens*. However, most of the evidence considered was from western Eurasia or Africa. Here I would like to use phenetic cranial data to investigate late middle Pleistocene: recent human relationships for all the major regions and to test whether one or more archaic populations are closest to recent populations as a whole or whether there are instead specific archaic–modern regional links. The main method used is the Penrose Shape Distance and it will be used to assess possible grade and clade similarities and differences in overall cranial shape comparing within and between archaic and modern samples. By comparing shape distances, it may be possible to assess which archaic group provides the best 'shape ancestor' for *Homo sapiens*.

I will also briefly examine the establishment of patterns of regionality in *Homo sapiens* as this provides a further test of the two evolutionary models. For the multiregional model these patterns had been established since the middle Pleistocene at least, and hence should be very evident even in early modern samples, whereas from the recent African model such patterns would have been poorly developed or absent in early *Homo sapiens*.

2. Cranial Samples

The comparisons given here will be presented for three different sets of material.

1. The first set consists of 'archaic' (i.e. non-anatomically modern) material from the late middle–early late Pleistocene of four regions: Europe (late Neanderthals), southwest Asia (late Neanderthals), Africa and China. The samples for crania used are as follows.

EuNea (actual or presumed European late Neanderthals): Saint-Césaire; Sala; La Chapelle-aux-Saints; La Quina 5; Forbes' Quarry; Feldhofer; Spy 1, 2; La Ferrassie 1; Guattari 1.

AsNea (actual or presumed late southwest Asian Neanderthals): Shanidar 1, 5 (data from Trinkaus (1983) and personal communication); Amud 1.

Af lmP (actual or presumed late middle Pleistocene African crania, excluding Omo-Kibish 1): Ngaloba–Laetoli hominid 18: Irhoud 1, 2; Eliye Springs ES-11693 cast; Singa; Omo Kibish 2.

DaMa (actual or presumed late middle Pleistocene Chinese crania): Dali (data from de Lumley & Sonakia (1985), Wu (1981) and a cast); Maba. Although not presented here, comparisons were also performed using Dali alone, with very similar results.

2. A set of early anatomically modern crania are also analysed, with samples as follows.

SQ (Skhul–Qafzeh): Qafzeh 3, 6, 9; Skhul 5, 9.

UP (European actual or presumed early Upper Palaeolithic): Vogelherd 1; Mladeč 1, 2, 5, 6 (casts or originals); Brno 2; Dolni Vestonice 3; Pavlov 1 cast; Predmostí 3, 4 (casts); Cro-Magnon 1, 2, 3; Grotte des Enfants 6 (cast); Abri Pataud 2.

Af Taf (North African Afalou and Taforalt): Afalou 9, 10, 29; Taforalt 11, 17.

RAus ('Robust early Australian') Cohuna (cast); Coobol Creek (a male individual).

Keil: Keilor (Australia) cast.

Wad: Wadjak 1 (Java, Indonesia) (Stringer/Parsons reconstruction).

UC: Upper Cave Zhoukoudian, 101, 102, 103 (casts, only selected data taken from the distorted and immature 102 cranium).

3. A third set of data consists of modern regional 'controls' consisting of overall means (=mean of male and female means) for the following *Homo sapiens* samples from Howells (1989).

No: Mediaeval Norse (110 individuals). Zalavar values had to be used for BRR, as this was not measured for the Norse sample.

Zu: South African Zulu (101 individuals).

Aus: Lower Murray River Australian (101 individuals).

SCr: Santa Cruz Island Native American (102 individuals).

Jap: South Japan (91 individuals).

3. METHODS OF ANALYSIS

The Penrose Size and Shape Statistic (Penrose 1954) provides a simple way of measuring overall similarity without resorting to complex multivariate procedures which include assumptions about the equality of variance–covariance matrices between different samples of populations or individual crania. An overall Penrose distance between any two samples is derived from the sum of the squared differences between the standardized means of each variable, divided by the number of variables. Standardization of means is necessary to prevent large measurements having an undue effect and is usually achieved by dividing by the overall standard deviation, but here I have preferred to standardize by logarithmic transformation, as this allows flexibility in sample composition without extensive recomputations, and provides very comparable results to standardizing by standard deviation. (See, for example, Stringer (1979).)

The size component is the square of the mean difference in size, and this can be subtracted from the overall Penrose distance described above to provide the shape component, which represents the variance among the measurement differences. The following discussions will be based primarily on the shape distances.

One of the potential problems with the Penrose Size and Shape Statistic concerns the fact that (unlike methods such as the Generalized Distance Statistic of Mahalanobis) correlations between the variables are not taken into account. So in these analyses the potential number of variables (38) has been reduced by both practical considerations (missing values) in important specimens such as Jebel Irhoud and Dali, and by the removal of one of each pair of the remaining most highly correlated variables (e.g. glabello-occipital length, GOL, which is highly correlated with nasio-occipital length NOL, and biorbital breadth, EKB, which is highly correlated with frontomalare breadth, FMB). The remaining variables to be analysed are shown in table 1, and will be referred to by their abbreviations for the rest of this paper.

4. Shape Analysis

A matrix of shape distances between the samples is shown in table 2, and it is immediately apparent that the four left hand columns generally display large shape distances compared with the columns to the right and especially with those between the recent samples. This is consistent with the inferred grade differences between the 'archaic' groups and the *Homo sapiens* samples because the archaic groups have another archaic group as first or second nearest neighbour (except for DaMa, where SQ is second nearest), while conversely all the anatomically modern groups have 'modern' nearest neighbours. If we first examine shape relationships between the archaic groups, EuNea and AsNea are similar to each other, comparable with shape distances obtained between the recent samples, while AflmP and DaMa are somewhat further apart, but still closely related. Although the first result was completely predictable, the second was (to me at least) unexpected, and I will return to its possible significance later. Distances between members of these two sets are larger, especially DaMa/EuNea and DaMa/AsNea. So whereas the four archaic groups seem at first glance to

Table 1. *Measurements and abbreviations used (Howells 1973, 1989)*

(Measurements marked with asterisk were used in the size and shape analyses.)

GOL	glabello-occipital length
NOL	nasio-occipital length*
BNL	basion-nasion length*
BBH	basion-bregma height*
XCB	maximum cranial breadth*
XFB	maximum frontal breadth*
AUB	biauricular breadth*
ASB	biasterionic breadth
BPL	basion-prosthion length
NPH	nasion-prosthion height
NLH	nasal height
OBH	orbit height*
OBB	orbit breadth*
NLB	nasal breadth*
MAB	palate breadth, external*
MDH	mastoid length
ZMB	bimaxillary breadth*
SSS	bimaxillary subtense*
FMB	bifrontal breadth*
NAS	nasio-frontal subtense*
EKB	biorbital breadth
DKB	interorbital breadth*
FRC	nasion-bregma chord* (frontal chord)
FRS	nasion-bregma subtense*
FRF	nasion-subtense fraction*
PAC	bregma-lambda chord* (parietal chord)
PAS	bregma-lambda subtense*
PAF	bregma-subtense fraction*
OCC	lambda-opisthion chord* (occipital chord)
OCS	lambda-opisthion subtense*
OCF	lambda-subtense fraction*
NAR	nasion radius
SSR	subspinale radius
PRR	prosthion radius
ZMR	zygomaxillare radius
AVR	molar alveolus radius
BRR	bregma radius*
LAR	lambda radius

represent a common evolutionary grade when compared with *Homo sapiens*, they show internal diversity and an apparent separation into two subgroups.

When we move on to consider archaic–modern comparisons, the two archaic subgroups differ markedly in their relationships. Except for the AsNea/RAus and AsNea/UC comparisons, the relative ordering of rela-

Table 2. *Shape distances* ($\times 10^4$): 25 log vars

	DaMa	AflmP	EuNea	AsNea	SQ	UP	AfTaf	RAus	Keil	Wad	UC	No	Zu	Aus	SCr
AflmP	9														
EuNea	23	14													
AsNea	29	18	6												
SQ	20	15	37	29											
UP	36	33	58	51	11										
AfTaf	34	29	59	48	7	5									
RAus	54	40	56	36	18	23	18								
Keil	36	26	43	32	11	13	13	19							
Wad	26	22	45	35	5	13	6	18	16						
UC	27	23	36	27	8	9	9	18	7	11					
No	35	32	51	42	11	5	6	23	14	9	5				
Zu	34	31	54	46	8	7	5	26	17	9	9	5			
Aus	25	24	41	34	8	7	7	22	17	8	5	3	3		
SCr	24	21	35	30	8	8	10	23	13	10	7	3	10	6	
Jap	40	38	64	54	11	6	5	26	17	14	11	5	4	7	7

tionships to all the modern samples is (i) AflmP, (ii) DaMa, (iii) AsNea and (iv) EuNea, often with a substantial increase in shape distance when considering AsNea–modern and EuNea–modern comparisons. The nearest modern neighbours for the two Neanderthal groups are SCr and UC (EuNea) and UC and SQ (AsNea), but the shape distances are substantially smaller between DaMa, AflmP and these modern samples except in the case of UC where AsNea and DaMa have equivalent distances. There is no evidence here of the shape correspondence sometimes claimed between European Neanderthals and both Upper Palaeolithic specimens and recent Europeans. Because of the lack of any specific EuNea or AsNea shape similarities which would support a general multiregional model, I will now concentrate on the DaMa–modern and AflmP–modern relationships.

In a multiregional model we might expect the closest shape relationship between the archaic–recent groups to lie between AflmP and Zu, and between DaMa and Jap. However, the shape distance to Jap is actually the largest recent comparison, both for AflmP and DaMa. The AflmP–Zu distance is much smaller, but the smallest comparison is actually AflmP–SCr. If we compare the distance AflmP–Zu with the mean AflmP distance to the other recent groups, and we also compare the mean DaMa–Jap/SCr value (as possible clade members) with the other DaMa–recent comparisons, in each case the supposed regional clade distance is larger than the mean of the other corresponding shape distances. The shape relationships thus do not show any special archaic–recent regional correspondence, but reveal an overall ordering of shape similarity of (i) AflmP; (ii) slightly more distant, DaMa; (iii) more distant, AsNea; and (iv) over 50% more distant than AflmP, EuNea.

Turning now to the early modern specimens, SQ occupies a unique position in relation to the archaic and recent groups. Although SQ is closer to all the modern groups than it is to the archaic groups (with the exception of AflmP at a distance of 15 and RAus at 18), its relative proximity to the archaic groups means that it usually provides a shorter route for archaic–recent shape change than by the archaic–recent shape distance direct. Thus AflmP–Jap = a distance of 38, AflmP–SQ–Jap = 26. Wadjak, which is the nearest shape neighbour to SQ, does not have this effect, because it is more distant from the archaic samples.

Moving on to consider specific early modern–recent shape comparisons, we will now examine possible regional relationships for Europe (UP–No), East Asia (UC–Jap/SCr), Australia (RAus/Keilor/Wad–Aus) and Africa (Af Taf–Zu). The shape distance UP–No is favoured compared with the mean UP shape distance to the other recent populations, as is RAus–Aus, and Wad–Aus in their own regional comparisons. However, the UC–Jap/SCr mean distance is greater than the mean UC distance to the other recent samples, as is Keil–Aus compared with the rest. In the case of Keil and RAus, all the shape distances are relatively large, particularly so for RAus. For the latter sample, this result is comparable with that obtained for the Cohuna cranium alone in a previous study (Stringer 1974). Part of this distinctiveness might be due to artificial deformation of the cranium, as noted for parts of the early Australian sample (Brown, this symposium). In addition to the shape distinctiveness evident in early modern–Aus comparisons, there are also large size differences (see below).

The shape distances show, firstly, a predominance of grade over clade in comparing archaic and recent samples. This might have been expected using a phenetic technique, but it is surprising that even between the *Homo sapiens* groups there is such a poor signal of regionality when comparing such crania as Upper Cave and recent Japanese or Native Americans, or Keilor and recent Native Australians. Given the dating of the Upper Cave crania to 20–25 ka and Keilor to about 12 ka ago, these specimens are separated from the recent samples by less than 5 per cent of the total time proposed for the existence of their regional clades by Wolpoff (1989). When combined with the separate analysis of regionality given below, a major retrodiction of the general multiregional model is therefore falsified, and a retrodiction of the recent African model is supported: modern regionality is apparently a product of the late Pleistocene. However, as will also be seen below, the retrodiction of the recent African origin model that the archaic African sample would be uniquely placed as closest to *Homo sapiens* is supported, but not as clearly as might have been expected. DaMa closely follows AflmP in shape distance for some comparisons (e.g. with UP, No, Aus, Jap).

So far I have been discussing Penrose shape distances only. However, it is instructive to compare size distances as well. Table 3 shows a comparison of some archaic and early *Homo sapiens* groups with recent samples for the 25 measurement analyses. Although shape distance generally predominates over size, it is evident that there have been major cranial size reductions in the evolution of some recent populations, especially in the SCr, Jap and Aus samples. Perhaps the most striking comparison is in Australasia, where there has been considerable Holocene size reduction, for reasons which are still not fully understood (Brown, this symposium). However, for the RAus comparison, in particular, sexual dimorphism is an important factor, because the sample consists of two large male individuals only. Whereas comparisons between the modern samples generally show a reasonable balance between size and shape distances, those between archaic and anatomically modern groups consistently show a predominance of shape differences over those of size. However, comparing the samples with the largest and smallest cranial dimensions in the whole analysis does give an exception to this generalization (AsNea and SCr have Size distance 36, Shape distance 30).

Table 3. Size and shape comparisons

comparison	EuNea No	AflmP Zu	DaMa SCr	DaMa Jap	UP No	UP Jap	AfTaf Zu	AfTaf Jap	UC SCr	UC Jap	RAus Aus	Keil Aus	Wad Aus
size (all+)	9	8	11	7	2	3	3	5	10	7	14	13	20
shape	51	31	24	40	5	6	5	5	7	11	22	17	8

187

5. Row Standardized Cranial Data

Unlike methods of analysis such as Principal Components, Canonical Variates and Mahalanobis' Generalized Distance, the Penrose Size and Shape Statistic provide no straightforward method for determining the relative contributions of the different measurements used to the shape distances generated. However, an independent means of examining the most important contributors to shape difference comes from row standardization (Corruccini 1987). Here, cranial data are standardised through division by a mean (size) measure calculated from the individual row of measurements for each cranium or sample. After standardization, the measurements have been compared with a similarly standardised overall mean value for recent *Homo sapiens* (Howells 1989) to give the index 100 (standardized sample mean/standardized recent mean).

Table 4 shows a comparison for four archaic and two *Homo sapiens* groups. It is interesting that row standardization minimizes what have traditionally been considered as some of the most distinctive Neanderthal features (e.g. long skull: GOL, NOL; broad skull: XCB; high orbits: OBH), but others are very much accentuated (e.g. high face and nose: NPH, NLH; prominent mid-face: SSS, NAS, AVR). DaMa, in particular, looks primitive in the low vault, broad at the base, with prominent occiput (BBH, BRR, AUB and OCS values). SQ and UP more closely approximate the modern values in most respects (BBH, NPH, NLH, FRS, PAC, PAS, OCC, OCF, PRR, AUR and BRR) but remain distinctive in the low OBH, and apparently primitive in total prognathism (higher BPL, PRR flatter frontal (FRF) and small mastoid (MDH)). The AflmP sample is generally archaic but has a distinctively low NLH, MDH, and high MAB, EKB, DKB (broader palate and upper face breadths). DaMa and AflmP are closer to *Homo sapiens* than are the Neanderthals in the lower SSS, NAS and higher FRC, FRS and PAC values. The former characters of transverse facial flattening are probably primitive retentions, whereas the latter (longer frontal and parietal, higher frontal) may reflect real synapomorphies in frontal and parietal shape.

We can estimate the divergence of these groups from the recent human mean by several different methods. One is to calculate the standard deviation for each data set in table 4. Although each one has a mean value close to 100 (reassuringly, because size standardization has been carried out), the standard deviations show considerable variation. SQ and UP have low values, EuNea a high value, and the three others are intermediate. AflmP is narrowly the least divergent archaic sample, but the closely comparable DaMa standard deviation may well be atypically low because a number of measurements were not available for inclusion, some of which can be estimated to be very different from the modern mean. For example the apparent low facial height of Dali is certainly misleading because vertical crush-

Table 4. Size standardized cranial data. All comparisons are overall group means

	GOL	NOL	BNL	BBH	XCB	XFB	AUB	ASB	BPL	NPH
EuNea/mod	100.4	101.8	104.0	88.7	99.8	97.9	100.8	103.0	109.7	115.1
AsNea/mod	100.0	102.1	102.6	89.7	97.9	97.6	102.7	102.2	104.1	118.5
ImPA/mod	102.6	100.2	98.4	89.4	98.0	96.8	104.8	104.7		105.3
DaMa/mod	108.2	106.2	107.2	85.0	103.6	94.4	112.6			
SQ/mod	98.9	98.2	98.0	93.5	100.3	97.4	101.5	103.1	107.2	104.8
UP/mod	102.4	103.4	97.0	96.4	98.3	102.2	100.9	99.6	102.0	96.9

	NLH	OBH	OBB	NLB	MAB	MDH	ZMB	SSS	FMB	NAS
EuNea/mod	110.5	99.5	101.3	112.0	106.2	67.6	106.4	146.8	103.4	127.1
AsNea/mod	113.7	95.5	101.6	113.5	103.7	83.9	103.9	141.1	103.3	128.5
ImPA/mod	87.7	96.4	104.4	110.3	111.2	63.3	104.6	116.1	109.6	102.9
DaMa/mod		96.6	102.4	119.3	109.4		109.7	102.6	106.7	97.1
SQ/mod	99.7	91.6	104.8	111.1	105.4	82.1	107.0	102.4	110.5	100.2
UP/mod	96.8	84.6	99.5	89.0	95.6	78.2	97.2	97.7	99.8	94.0

	EKB	DKB	FRC	FRS	FRF	PAC	PAS	PAF	OCC	OCS
EuNea/mod	99.5	113.4	93.8	75.0	106.3	88.1	67.7	85.2	87.3	110.1
AsNea/mod	102.3	111.7	92.9	66.4	108.8	90.4	81.3	89.6	92.4	104.3
ImPA/mod	111.0	132.6	97.7	86.1	111.2	96.0	68.7	94.4	90.8	108.7
DaMa/mod	104.6	117.9	97.9	93.3	102.9	92.9	70.8	87.7	87.2	119.4
SQ/mod	108.6	114.9	95.3	95.2	104.3	100.1	90.8	94.1	95.7	100.0
UP/mod	99.2	98.3	101.3	106.6	107.4	102.5	94.2	100.0	98.3	105.2

	OCF	NAR	SSR	PRR	ZMB	AVR	BRR	LAR	mean	s.d.
EuNea/mod	77.8	108.0	108.5	108.4	95.7	113.2	90.0	90.8	100.6	15.1
AsNea/mod	85.4	101.0	105.4	104.0	94.4	107.5	89.3	100.0	100.9	12.9
ImPA/mod	86.4	106.2	101.9	105.4	99.4	103.8	93.0	94.2	99.8	12.2
DaMa/mod	80.0						81.8		99.9	12.3
SQ/mod	106.8	96.6	97.5	101.1	93.4	97.6	96.1	96.3	100.0	6.4
UP/mod	101.4	104.2	102.7	101.6	106.9	100.2	99.3	96.3	98.9	5.7

189

ing has considerably reduced the real NLH and NPH values. Values for both facial height and lower facial projection will have to be considerably increased if and when this fossil is reconstructed.

6. The Description and Interpretation of Regional Features

A fundamental problem in the study of supposed regional clade characters is that the characters used may be poorly defined or standardized. Although this is a serious issue, it is not one which I will address here. Another problem with many studies of 'regionality' used to support the multiregional model is that often only one region is examined at a time, with lists compiled of the characters in common between the archaic and recent representatives of the supposed local clade (see, for example, Wolpoff *et al.* (1984); Wolpoff (1989)). Moreover, the comparisons are often highly selective and ignore or minimise conflicting data. As a parallel example I could refer to metrical comparisons I have made between the Upper Cave and recent Japanese crania in 38 cranial measurements. If I selected the ten measurements where they were similar to each other I could provide support for regionality. However, this would mean ignoring the 28 other measurements in which European early Upper Palaeolithic mean values were actually more similar than Upper Cave to those of recent Japanese crania! When proper interregional comparisons of supposed clade characters are made, the results are much more equivocal (see, for example, Groves (1989); Habgood (1989, 1992); Stringer (1992)). In such cases many of the characters either show inconsistency through variation within regions or even a higher frequency outside the supposed clade area.

Using cranial metrics rather than morphological characters provides an alternative method of looking at past and present regionality. This approach has been used descriptively with great success by Howells (1973, 1989). Suites of measurements in which certain regional populations are distinctive can be recognized, and individual crania can then be tested to see to which region they appear to be best assigned on the basis of their craniometric characteristics. For research still in progress, I have used size standardized data to test individual fossil crania, and their most probable regional affiliation using Howells' recent regional criteria are shown in the middle column of table 5. This approach is closest to a cladistic one, where distinctive regional characteristics are being selected albeit, in some cases, probable distinctive primitive retentions).

A completely separate method of investigating regionality (this time phenetically based) is provided by Richard Wright's CRANID package which uses Howells' cranial database to test the affinities of individual crania on the basis of 33 cranial measurements. Principal Components analysis is used to relate the samples in multivariate space and to provide the 50

Table 5. *Primary regional affiliations of individual crania*
(Am = Native   American,   Eu = European/Egyptian,
As = East Asian/Inuit, Aus = Australian/New Guinea,
Af = Subsaharan African.)

	Row standardized: Howells variables sets	CRANID: 50 nearest neighbours
La Ferrassie 1	Aus	Af[a]
Jebel Irhoud 1	Aus/Am	Af[a]
DaMa	Aus	—
Qafzeh 6	Am	Aus
Qafzeh 9	Aus	Af
Skhul 5	Am	—
Mladeč 1	Aus	Eur
Predmostí 3	Aus	Aus
Predmostí 4	Aus	Eur
Cro-Magnon 1	Af	Aus
Grotte des Enfants 6	Aus	Eur
Abri Pataud	Aus	As
Afalou 9	As	Eu
Afalou 29	Af	Eu
Taforalt 11	Af	Af
Taforalt 17	Aus	Aus
Coobol Creek	Aus	Aus
Upper Cave 101	Aus	Aus
Upper Cave 103	Aus	Af
Wadjak	Aus	Af
Keilor	Aus	Af

[a] CRANID provided a warning in these cases that the crania were unusual by comparison with Howells' database. They were more than three standard deviations from the mean nearest-neighbour distance and from the mean distance from the overall centroid.

nearest neighbour crania (of whatever population) using Euclidean distances. I have analysed most of the same crania listed in table 5 using CRANID, and have summarized the primary regional affiliation of the 50 nearest neighbours obtained, in the right hand column of the table. As can be seen if we omit the Skhul–Qafzeh specimens, of the 35 regional affiliations determined in table 5, only 11 could be considered as geographically appropriate. This shows the weak signals of modern regionality given out by these Pleistocene crania. Of the five possible regional affiliations, two predominate: Australian (19) and African (9). This is probably because the regional shape characters of low NPH (Australia and Africa), NLH (Australia), OBH (Australia), BRR (Australia) and sss (Africa) are common in the Pleistocene samples.

7. CONCLUDING REMARKS: ANCESTORS AND REGIONALITY

Returning to the tests of the multiregional and recent African origin models mentioned in the Introduction, can one or more archaic populations be identified as 'best shape ancestors' for *Homo sapiens*? From the phenetic shape analyses, the Neanderthal samples of Europe and Asia make unlikely ancestors for any of the modern cranial samples. Overall shape distances are too large, and the Neanderthal samples lose out in most comparisons with AflmP and DaMa (figure 1). From the row standardized data, the Neanderthals are no more distinct from the modern mean than AflmP and DaMa on a number of measurements, but where the Neanderthals do diverge (e.g. on NLH, sss), they do so markedly. Comparing AflmP and DaMa in the shape analyses shows that AflmP is closer to every one of the other groups (modern or Neanderthal) than is DaMa. However for some of the modern groups (e.g. Aus, Jap) the differences are small. Bearing in mind the motley composition of the African sample, and the limitations of the Dali data (none of it obtained by me on the original fossil, which is not yet available for general study), we should remain somewhat cautious about the results (although the combination of Dali and Maba data seems to have little effect on the results). What the results do show, surprisingly for me, is that AflmP and DaMa share more similarities with each other in metrical data and shape than either share similarities with the Neanderthals or moderns (figure 1). So I conclude the 'best shape ancestor' test with a relatively confident statement that the two Neanderthals samples should be eliminated from consideration, but a less confident statement that the late archaic African sample remains the exclusive best ancestor for early and later *Homo sapiens*. If we can turn away from a universal multiregional model for modern human origins, we cannot so easily exclude a dual African and East Asian ancestry model (see, for example, Habgood (1988)). But in such a case the DaMa sample appears most closely related to recent Australians (or Native Americans) rather than East Asians. However, if we do propose something like a special Dali–Australian relationship, it would still be necessary to infer the existence of an East Asian or Australasian intermediate population comparable to the Skhul–Qafzeh sample. It remains true that the most economical single route for shape changes from archaic–recent groups is via AflmP and SQ. Given recent age estimates for the Skhul–Qafzeh sample of 80–120 ka, these specimens may well lie close to the origin of all later *Homo sapiens*.

For the second test, that of regional affiliations, the results from tables 2, 3 and 5 are very clear. Archaic–modern regional affiliations are not reflected in these phenetic cranial shape analyses. Regionality appears to develop in

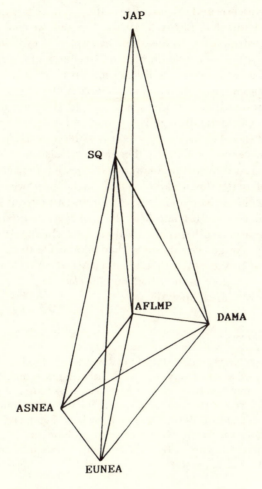

Figure 1. A two-dimensional approximation of shape distances between the four archaic samples (late Asian Neanderthals, late European Neanderthals, late archaic Africans, and Dali–Maba), Skhul–Qafzeh, and a recent sample (Japanese). The Skhul–Qafzeh sample is relatively closer to both the archaic and recent groups than can be shown in two dimensions.

the late Pleistocene, and a sample like the Skhul–Qafzeh crania seems a reasonable primitive modern template to which later regionality could be added. Samples of present day East Asians (e.g. Japanese) suggest that these populations are highly derived away from any archaic or early modern ancestors. In contrast, the Australian sample (and to a lesser extent

SCr) bears a closer overall resemblance to the Pleistocene material, perhaps because as Macintosh & Larnach (1976) proposed 'we could postulate the Aboriginal Australians as the earliest examples of evolving generalised modern *Homo sapiens* to arrive in their ultimate area of migration'.

Thus a model of universal multiregionalism is not supported by these analyses. If *Homo sapiens* originated in one region, that region was probably Africa, as represented here by the AflmP sample. However, if we take figure 1 and rotate it clockwise through 90°, we can obtain a different perspective on the AflmP–DaMa relationship. Is it possible that DaMa represents a more primitive version of AflmP, either an ancestral form or a relict population of an ancestral form? To answer that question depends on both the availability of better fossil samples and on an improved chronological framework for the African and Asian material. However, it seems unlikely to me that Dali represents a late Asian form of *Homo heidelbergensis*, as other analyses (not discussed here) show African (e.g. Bodo, Broken Hill) and European (e.g. Arago, Petralona) earlier middle Pleistocene fossils to be more similar to Neanderthals than to either AflmP or DaMa. Neither does Dali appear to be close to the Zhoukoudian *Homo erectus* sample in shape, from other more limited analyses.

Acknowledgments

I thank my coorganisers and the staff of the Royal Society for their roles in organising and running what was a very successful Discussion Meeting. I also thank the staff of the numerous institutes where I have been allowed to study relevant fossil material, as well as Bill Howells for providing me with continuing inspiration. I would also like to thank the Royal Society and the Boise Fund, Oxford, for supporting my research work in China. My colleague Robert Kruszynski drafted the figure, and Mrs Irene Baxter has tirelessly retyped numerous versions of this manuscript: I thank them both.

References

Corruccini, R.S. 1987 Shape in morphometrics: comparative analyses. *Am. J. Phys. Anthrop.* **73**, 289–303.

Groves, C.P. 1989 A regional approach to the problem of the origin of modern humans in Australasia. In *The human revolution: behavioural and biological perspectives on the origins of modern humans*, vol. I (ed. P. Mellars & C. B. Stringer), pp. 274–285. Edinburgh University Press.

Habgood, P.J. 1988 A morphometric investigation into the origin(s) of anatomically modern humans. Ph.D. thesis, University of Sydney.

Habgood, P.J. 1989 The origin of anatomically modern humans in Australasia. In *The human revolution: behavioural and biological perspectives on the origins of modern humans*, vol. I (ed. P. Mellars & C. B. Stringer), pp. 245–273. Edinburgh University Press.

Howells, W.W. 1973 *Cranial variation in Man.* Cambridge, Massachusetts: Peabody Museum.

Howells, W.W. 1989 *Skull shapes and the map.* Cambridge, Massachusetts: Peabody Museum.

de Lumley, H. & Sonakia, A. 1985 Premiere découverte d'un *Homo erectus* sur le continent indien á Hathnora, dans la moyenne vallée de la Narmada. *Anthropologie* **89**, 13–61.

Macintosh, N.W.G. & Larnach, S.L. 1976 Aboriginal affinities looked at in world context. In *The Origin of the Australians* (ed. R. L. Kirk & A. G. Thorne), pp. 113–126. Canberra: Australian Institute of Aboriginal Studies.

Penrose, L.S. 1954 Distance, size and shape. *Ann. Eugenics* **18**, 337–343.

Stringer, C.B. 1974 Population relationships of later Pleistocene hominids; a multivariate study of available crania. *J. archaeol. Sci.* **1**, 317–342.

Stringer, C.B. 1979 A reevaluation of the fossil human calvaria from Singa, Sudan. *Bull. Br. Mus. nat. Hist. (Geol.)* **32**, 77–83.

Stringer, C.B. 1992 Replacement, continuity, and the origin of *Homo sapiens.* In *Continuity or replacement: controversies in Homo sapiens evolution.* (ed. G. Bräuer & F. H. Smith), pp. 9–24. Rotterdam: Balkema.

Stringer, C.B. & Andrews, P., 1988 Genetic and fossil evidence for the origin of modern humans. *Science, Wash.* **239**, 1263–1268.

Trinkaus, E. 1983 *The Shanidar Neanderthals.* New York: Academic Press.

Wolpoff, M.H. 1989 Multiregional evolution: the fossil alternative to Eden. In *The human revolution: behavioural and biological perspectives on the origins of modern humans,* Vol. I (ed. P. Mellars & C. B. Stringer), pp. 62–108. Edinburgh University Press.

Wolpoff, M.H., Wu, Z. & Thorne, A.G. 1984 Modern *Homo sapiens* origins: a general theory of hominid evolution involving the fossil evidence from east Asia. In *The origins of modern humans* (ed. F. H. Smith & F. Spencer), pp. 411–83. New York, Liss.

Wu, X.Z. 1981 A well preserved cranium of an archaic type of early *Homo sapiens* from Dali, China. *Scientia Sin.* **24**, 530–539.

Archaeology and the Population-Dispersal Hypothesis of Modern Human Origins in Europe

P. A. Mellars[1]

SUMMARY

The transition from anatomically 'archaic' to 'modern' populations would seem to have occurred in most regions of Europe broadly between *ca.* 40 and 30 ka ago: much later than in most other areas of the world. The archaeological evidence supports the view that this transition was associated with the dispersal of new human populations into Europe, equipped with a new technology ('Aurignacian') and a range of radical behavioural and cultural innovations which collectively define the 'Middle-Upper Palaeolithic transition'. In several regions of Europe there is archaeological evidence for a chronological overlap between these populations and the final Neanderthal populations and, apparently, for various forms of contact, interaction and, apparently, 'acculturation' between these two populations. The fundamental behavioural adaptations implicit in the 'Upper Palaeolithic Revolution' (possibly including language) are thought to have been responsible for this rapid dispersal of human populations over the ecologically demanding environments of last-glacial Europe.

1. INTRODUCTION

Archaeology is concerned—by its nature and by definition—with the evidence for the behaviour of early human populations, rather than with their biology or genetic history. Archaeological evidence can however have a very direct and relevant bearing on the demographic structure and organization of prehistoric groups, and on their potential ancestry and relationships with other groups. The aim of the present paper is to examine the bearing of the available archaeological evidence from the European continent on two of the most central and currently controversial issues posed by the present symposium.

1. How far—if at all—does the archaeological evidence support the hypothesis of a rapid dispersal of new human populations into Europe associated with the first appearance of 'anatomically modern' anatomy? Conversely, can this evidence be accounted for equally if not more economically in terms of the alternative scenario of essentially continuous biological and

[1] Department of Archaeology, University of Cambridge, Downing Street, Cambridge CB2 3DZ, U.K.

demographic development over the period of the archaic-to-modern human transition?

2. If we accept the implications of the current 'population dispersal' scenarios of modern human origins, how far can we recognize any patterns of coexistence, contact or interaction between the hypothetically intrusive populations of anatomically modern humans and the indigenous populations of anatomically archaic (i.e. 'Neanderthal') hominids in the different regions of Europe?

One of the central assumptions underlying this paper is that the archaeological evidence is no less relevant to addressing these issues about the relationships between archaic and modern populations than is that provided by the more 'direct' evidence of the skeletal remains themselves. The obvious limitation of the skeletal evidence, of course, lies in the sheer incompleteness of this record: the relatively small number of specimens available, the highly fragmentary state of many of the remains and (in many cases) the degree of ambiguity surrounding the chronology and precise associations of the different finds. By any standards of comparison, the archaeological evidence provides a record of human development over the period of the archaic-to-modern human transition which is not only much more detailed and complete than that of the skeletal material, but also much better documented and more fine-grained in chronological terms.

2. THE ISSUE OF POPULATION REPLACEMENT VERSUS POPULATION CONTINUITY

The issue of population continuity versus population replacement has of course formed the core of the debate over the transition from anatomically archaic to anatomically modern populations in Europe throughout virtually the whole of the present century: effectively since the initial publication of the famous Neanderthal skeleton from La-Chapelle-aux-Saints by Marcellin Boule in 1909. Although there are no doubt a range of essentially intermediate positions which could potentially be taken on this issue (involving varying degrees of gene flow, interbreeding, acculturation, small scale population shifts, etc. between adjacent regions: cf. Smith *et al.* (1989); Smith (1991)) the interpretations of the recent DNA studies of modern human populations have tended to present this issue as an opposition between two fairly stark alternatives: either a fairly rapid, abrupt and effectively total replacement of one population by another (e.g. Cann *et al.* 1987; Stoneking & Cann 1989); or alternatively a largely continuous process of demographic and evolutionary development, in which episodes of population dispersal, migration and ultimately replacement were, at best, on a relatively localized and demographically minor scale (e.g. Wolpoff 1989; Thorne & Wolpoff 1992; Clark & Lindly 1989; Clark 1992). In terms of the theme of the present symposium, therefore, it is appropriate to examine the implications of the archaeological evidence from Europe primarily in terms of these two, sharply dichotomized points of view.

Reviewing the literature which has appeared on this topic over the past ten years, it is probably fair to say that a clear majority of archaeological opinion in Europe is now in favour of the population dispersal scenario of modern human origins, even if a significant and vociferous minority would still argue for the population continuity hypothesis (cf. Allsworth–Jones 1986, 1990; Kozlowski 1988, 1990; Demars & Hublin 1989; Demars 1990; Hublin 1990; Harrold 1989; Mellars 1989a, 1991; Mussi 1990; Goia 1990; Farizy 1990; Bischoff et al. 1990; versus Clark & Lindly 1989; Clark 1992). The central component in these arguments rests fairly critically and pivotally on one basic correlation: namely the assumption that all of the earliest, typical and securely documented occurrences of fully anatomically modern hominids within the different regions of Europe are associated with one specific archaeological entity: namely with the grouping of so-called Aurignacian industries. Totally explicit associations of this kind are perhaps not quite as abundant or unambiguous as one might hope, once allowance has been made for the limitations of earlier excavation techniques, and the uncertainties of some of the associated stratigraphic and dating evidence. Nevertheless there is at present little dispute that essentially clear and well documented associations of this kind can be recognized in at least four or five separate localities in different regions of Europe, notably at Vogelherd in Germany, Mladeč in Czechoslovakia, Velika Pečina in Yugoslavia, and Les Rois in France, with highly probable associations of the same kind at a range of other sites (Cro-Magnon, Le Crouzade, Fontéchevade, Isturitz, etc.) (Smith 1984, 1991; Stringer et al. 1984; Howell 1984; Gambier 1989; Hublin 1990). Certainly, no well documented claim has ever been made for an association between distinctively Aurignacian assemblages and characteristically Neanderthal skeletal morphology in Europe. Clearly, to clinch this particular argument there is an urgent need for direct absolute dating of the relevant skeletal remains, presumably based on direct accelerator mass spectrometry (AMS) dating of small samples from the skeletal remains themselves.

If this critical association between culturally 'Aurignacian' assemblages and anatomically 'modern' skeletal morphology is accepted, then of course the whole of the archaeological aspect of this debate hinges essentially on the evidence for the specific origins and mutual interrelationships of the Aurignacian industries within the different regions of Europe. Specifically, do these industries appear to reflect the dispersal of a demographically 'new' population over the different parts of the continent, or do they reflect simply a diversity of essentially local patterns of technological and cultural development, deriving directly from the immediately preceding Middle

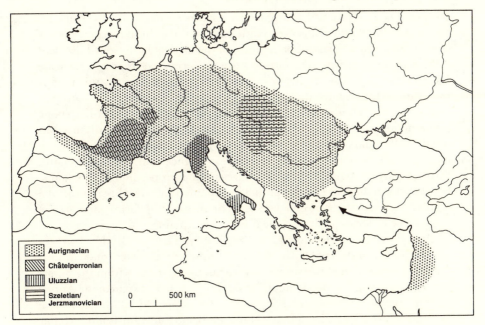

Figure 1. Geographical distribution of Aurignacian industries in Europe and the Middle East, compared with the distribution of Châtelperronian, Szeletian and Uluzzian industries. Based on Kozlowski (1992) and other sources. In addition to the distribution shown, further occurrences of apparently Aurignacian industries have been reported from Portugal, Britain, Sicily, southern Russia and Afghanistan.

Palaeolithic/Neanderthal populations within each region? As noted above, most of the recent reviews of the archaeological evidence have opted fairly strongly in favour of the former (population dispersal) hypothesis, based essentially on the following range of observations.

1. Archaeologically, one of the most striking features is the remarkable uniformity of Aurignacian technology, extending from the extreme western fringes of Europe (i.e. Cantabria and western France) through effectively all areas of central, eastern and southern Europe, and reaching into at least the northern parts of the Middle East (northern Israel and Lebanon), in all a span of almost 4000 km (see figure 1). As Bordes (e.g. 1968, p. 200) and several other workers have pointed out, many of the typically 'Aurignacian' industries from sites such as El Wad and Hayonim in Israel are virtually indistinguishable in general typological and technological terms from those recovered from many of the 'classic' Aurignacian sites in southwest France or northern Spain. This is reflected not only in a range of highly distinctive stone tool types (i.e. various forms of steeply-retouched nosed and 'carinate'

scrapers, edge-retouched Aurignacian blades, and small, inversely retouched Dufour and Font-Yves bladelets), but also by the occurrence of even more esoteric forms of bone tools, in the form of both 'split-base' and 'biconical' bone points (the former recently recovered from two separate Israeli sites: Bar-Yosef & Belfer-Cohen (1988)). Significantly, this uniformity can be documented during at least two separate stages of the Aurignacian sequence. Thus a basic chronological succession from split-base bone points to simpler lozangic and biconical forms (both apparently used as functionally similar missile heads) can now be documented in areas ranging from extreme western Europe (southwest France and northern Spain), through various parts of central and eastern Europe, into the Balkans. Similar chronological trends can be documented in several regions in the relative frequencies of nosed versus carinate scraper forms, and in the occurrence of forms such as typical Font-Yves points and edge-retouched Aurignacian blades (Kozlowski & Otte 1984). These and other features point strongly to the conclusion that some kind of close social and cultural links were maintained between Aurignacian populations within the different regions of Europe throughout, apparently, the whole span of the Aurignacian development. At no other point in the Upper Palaeolithic sequence can one demonstrate such a remarkable uniformity in culture and technology extending over such a wide diversity of contrasting topographic and ecological zones. Whether or not this uniformity would have been possible without some corresponding uniformity in language patterns across this broad region remains, no doubt, an intriguing point for speculation.

What makes this geographical uniformity of Aurignacian technology especially impressive is the sharp contrast with the highly varied patterns of technology documented over the same areas of Europe during the immediately preceding stages of the Middle Palaeolithic sequence. As Kozlowski (1992) has recently emphasized, it is now clear that the final stages of the Middle Palaeolithic in the different regions of Europe were characterized by a range of sharply contrasting technologies, ranging from the classic 'Mousterian of Acheulian tradition' industries of western Europe, through various forms of 'Micoquian', 'Eastern Charentian' and 'leaf-point' industries of central and eastern Europe, 'Denticulate' industries (apparently) in Italy and northeastern Spain, to the much more Levallois (especially Levallois point) dominated technologies of southeastern Europe and the Middle East. As discussed further below, it is this striking diversity of technological patterns documented during the final stages of the Middle Palaeolithic sequence which makes it particularly difficult to visualize the Aurignacian as a purely indigenous development within the different regions of Europe, emerging directly from the immediately preceding Mousterian technologies in the same regions.

2. The difficulties of identifying convincing local origins for Aurignacian

technology have been emphasized by a range of different authors for almost all the individual regions in Europe: by Kozlowski (1982, 1988, 1992), Allsworth-Jones (1986, 1990) and others for the industries of central and eastern Europe; by de Sonneville-Bordes (1960), Bordes (1968), Demars (1990) and others for western France; by Hahn (1977) and Otte (1990) for north–central Europe; by Mussi (1990) and Goia (1990) for the Italian industries; and by Bischoff *et al.* (1990) for northern Spain. In all these regions the earliest Aurignacian industries seem to appear as a relatively sudden and abrupt break in the local patterns of technological development, without any clear or convincing technological antecedents within the immediately preceding Middle Palaeolithic industries: a pattern reflected not only in the basic 'technology' and 'typology' of the industries, but also (in many cases) in the specific geological sources exploited for raw materials (Kozlowski 1988, 1990). Only very rarely have arguments been advanced for a potentially local origin of Aurignacian technology, as for example by Valoch (1983) for some of the industries in Czechoslovakia, and by Cabrera Valdes and Bernaldo de Quiros (1990) for the succession at El Castillo in northern Spain. These suggestions however have been contested by other workers, and hardly take full account of the more general patterns of Aurignacian technology documented over Europe as a whole. As noted above, the most obvious obstacle to any notion of an essentially independent of Aurignacian technology within the different regions of Europe is posed by the sheer diversity of the technological patterns documented within these regions during the final stages of the Middle Palaeolithic/Mousterian succession. How such a remarkably uniform technology could emerge—rapidly, consistently, and over such an immense area—from such a diversity of technological roots remains, as yet, to be explained. At present the most plausible origin for Aurignacian technology would seem to be provided by a number of sites in the Middle East, most notably by the long succession at Ksar Akil in the Lebanon, which appears to show a gradually evolving sequence of Aurignacian and Proto-Aurignacian industries extending over a total time span of at least 8–10 ka (Copeland 1976; Marks & Ferring 1988; Ohnuma & Bergman 1990; Mellars & Tixier 1989).

3. The relative and absolute chronology of the earliest stages of the Aurignacian in different regions of Europe is clearly crucial to any notion of population dispersal, and is of course central to the specific theme of the present symposium. At this point we inevitably encounter all of the problems of the inherent 'credentials' of radiocarbon dating in the 30+ ka time range (i.e. the problems of contamination effects, large standard deviations, the inter-comparability of radiocarbon with other dating methods, etc.) which have been discussed in other papers in this volume (e.g. Miller; Schwarcz; Aitken & Valladas). What can be said with some confidence however is that there is now fairly explicit evidence that early forms of

essentially 'Aurignacian' or 'Proto-Aurignacian' technology were already established in most regions of Europe by between 35 and 40 ka BP, and in certain areas were apparently present substantially before this date. The most significant dates in this context are those obtained for early Aurignacian levels at El Castillo and l'Arbreda in northern Spain, at Willendorf, das Geissenklösterle and Krems-Hundsteig in the Rhineland, Istállóskö in Hungary, and Bacho Kiro and Temnata in Bulgaria (see figure 2). Whether or not one can speak of an overall 'cline' of dates running progressively from east to west across Europe is no doubt too early to say. However, there seems no reason to doubt the date of more than 43 ka BP obtained by the Groningen laboratory on a large charcoal sample from the earliest Aurignacian levels at Bacho Kiro in Bulgaria, the date of 44 330±1900 BP for a level with abundant split-base bone points at Istállóskö in Hungary, or the recently obtained thermoluminescence (TL) dates of 45 000 ± 7000 and 46 000 ± 8000 (though with large standard deviations) for the early Aurignacian levels at Temnata in Bulgaria (Kozlowski 1982, 1992, personal communication; Allsworth-Jones 1986, 1990). All of these dates are at present substantially earlier than any of the dates so far secured for early Aurignacian horizons in western Europe. In the Middle East there is at least a possibility that the initial stages of the Aurignacian sequence go back to a similar if not even earlier date, as for example in levels XII-XIII at Ksar Akil in Lebanon, tentatively dated to around 42–44 ka BP (Mellars & Tixier 1989; Ohnuma & Bergman 1990). If this pattern of dates is accepted at face value, it would clearly accord well with the hypothesis of a gradual dispersal of Aurignacian technology—and potentially of the associated human populations—progressively from east to west across Europe. Curiously—and potentially most significant of all—this technology seems to have penetrated into the most 'classic' region of western Europe (i.e. the Perigord and immediately adjacent areas of southwest France) only at a substantially later date of around 34–35 ka BP (figure 2).

4. Finally, it is now generally recognized that the Aurignacian (and specifically the earlier stages of the Aurignacian) shows the earliest well documented occurrence of most if not all of the distinctive technological, 'symbolic' and other cultural innovations which are generally regarded as the diagnostic behavioural hallmarks of fully 'Upper Palaeolithic' culture. The details of these behavioural innovations have been discussed more fully elsewhere (e.g. Mellars 1989a,b, 1991; Kozlowski 1990), but it can be said that they include not only the earliest manifestations of fully developed 'punch' blade technology and an associated range of characteristically Upper Palaeolithic tool forms (i.e. typical end scrapers, new forms of burins, small retouched bladelet forms etc.) but also the earliest examples of extensively shaped (and highly complex) bone, antler and ivory artefacts, the earliest occurrences of explicit personal ornaments (in the form of perforated animal teeth, sea shells, and carefully shaped bead forms, deliberately

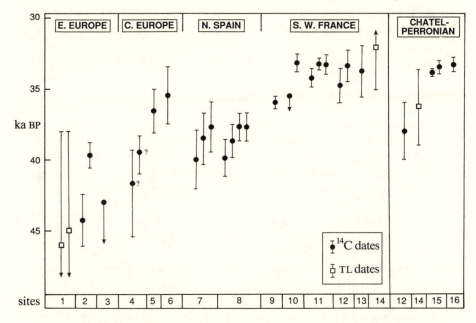

Figure 2. Absolute age measurements for early Aurignacian industries in eastern, central and western Europe, and for Châtelperronian industries in France. For the radiocarbon dates (indicated by circles) the graph includes only the oldest dates available from each region, on the assumption that these are likely to show patterns least affected by problems of residual contamination with more recent, intrusive carbon. Thermoluminescence dates are indicated by square symbols. Vertical bars indicate one standard deviation. Vertical arrows indicate 'greater than' ages. The sites shown are: 1, Temnata (Bulgaria); 2, Istállóskö (Hungary); 3, Bacho Kiro (Bulgaria); 4, Willendorf (Austria); 5, Geissenklösterle (Germany); 6, Krems (Austria); 7, Castillo (N.W. Spain); 8, L'Arbreda (N.E. Spain); 9, La Rochette (France); 10, La Ferrassie (France); 11, Abri Pataud (France); 12, Roc de Combe (France); 13, Le Flageolet (France); 14, Saint-Césaire (France); 15, Arcy-sur-Cure (France); 16, Les Cottés (France). The dates are taken from the following sources: Allsworth-Jones (1986); Bischoff *et al.* (1989); Cabrera-Valdes & Bischoff (1989); Delibrias & Fontugne (1990); Haesaerts (1990); Kozlowski (1982, 1992); Leroi–Gourhan (1964); Mellars (1990a); Mellars *et al.* (1987); Mercier *et al.* (1991); Movius (1975). Note that radiocarbon dates in this age range are likely to be systematically younger than those produced by other dating techniques, perhaps by *ca.* 3000 years (Bard *et al.* 1990). The precise taxonomy of the industries from Willendorf remains to be clarified.

manufactured from stone, bone and ivory), expanded networks in the procurement and distribution of high-quality flint and other raw materials, far-travelled marine shells, and the earliest examples of complex and remarkably sophisticated naturalistic art and geometrical decoration (Kozlowski 1988, 1990; Hahn 1972, 1977; Delluc & Delluc 1978; Mellars 1973, 1989a,b,

1991; White 1989; Bosinski 1990). As the evidence stands at present, it would seem that all of these cultural innovations make their first well documented appearance specifically in early Aurignacian contexts in the different regions of Europe and (with a number of very rare and highly debatable exceptions: cf. Marshack (1972, 1990), versus Chase & Dibble (1987)) are conspicuously lacking from earlier, Middle Palaeolithic contexts in the same areas. In at least certain regions there are indications that the earlier stages of the Aurignacian also witnessed a substantial increase in human population densities (marked by a sharp increase in the total numbers of occupied sites), the formation of larger and perhaps more permanent social groupings, and the appearance of more highly specialized patterns of faunal exploitation focused on the intensive hunting of a single, migratory herd species (Mellars 1973, 1989a).

Exactly what these innovations signify in more general behavioural and cultural terms is of course still a matter of lively debate. Few prehistorians however would question either the scale and complexity of the behavioural changes involved (extending apparently into almost all spheres of human activity) or the evidence for a dramatic 'explosion' in various forms of explicitly symbolic behaviour (e.g. White 1989). Most workers agree that these changes would be inconceivable in the absence of some form of relatively complex, highly structured language among the early Aurignacian groups. Needless to say, radical and wide-ranging behavioural innovations of this kind cannot be taken as an automatic reflection of population dispersal or replacement in the archaeological record, since it is clear that in certain contexts episodes of rapid behavioural and cultural change can occur either through processes of simple cultural diffusion, or indeed through rapid and multivariate patterns of purely internal cultural change. Nevertheless, the point hardly needs labouring that the close association of all these radical and wide-ranging behavioural innovations with the first appearance of Aurignacian technology within the different regions of Europe—and apparently with the earliest occurrences of fully modern skeletal anatomy—is at least consistent with the hypothesis of an actual population dispersal at this point in the archaeological sequence, even if the archaeological evidence cannot be held—in isolation—to conclusively demonstrate this.

On the basis of the various lines of evidence outlined above it could be argued that the total spectrum of the archaeological evidence for the Aurignacian phenomenon within the different regions of Europe coincides closely, if not precisely, with the pattern that one would reasonably predict from the implications of the current population dispersal scenarios of modern human origins. Whether the same body of data could be held to be equally consistent with the population continuity or 'multiregional evolution' hypothesis is much more open to debate. How in this case would one account for the striking uniformity of Aurignacian technology over such a vast area of Europe and the Middle East, superimposed on so much diversity in the technology of the immediately preceding Middle Palaeolithic populations in the same regions? How would one explain the very sudden and apparently abrupt way in which this technology appears in so many different regions without, apparently, any clear or convincing technological origins or antecedents in the preceding technologies in the same areas? Or indeed the sheer range, diversity and magnitude of the various cultural and behavioural innovations involved? In the classic region of western France at least there can no longer be any serious dispute that the appearance of the Aurignacian reflects the intrusion of an essentially new human population, reflected not only in the totally sudden and abrupt appearance of this technology (clearly later than its appearance in the immediately neighbouring areas of northern Spain and the Mediterranean coast) but also in the explicit evidence that the earliest Aurignacian communities in this area clearly persisted (and apparently coexisted) for some time alongside the latest Mousterian/Neanderthal populations in the same region (as discussed further below; cf. Mellars (1989a); Demars & Hublin (1989)). If we accept this kind of population intrusion within the fully documented region of southwest France, we should presumably be prepared to give the same hypothesis equal consideration in the other regions of Europe, where the overall spectrum and character of the archaeological evidence appears to show a broadly similar pattern.

3. POPULATION INTERACTION

One element which is of course implicit and ultimately inescapable in the current 'population dispersal' models for the appearance of anatomically modern populations is that there must, inevitably, have been some period of chronological overlap, and presumably certain forms of contact and potential interaction, between the earliest (hypothetically intrusive) populations of anatomically modern humans within the different regions of Europe and the latest populations of anatomically archaic hominids. However these population dispersal–replacement models are visualized or expressed, this is clearly an inherent and ultimately inescapable prediction for the archaeological and biological record, if this particular scenario is to be upheld. The issue, in archaeological terms, is how far we can identify any evidence for this kind of situation within the archaeological record itself.

Over the past decade, evidence for this kind of chronological overlap, contact and apparent 'interaction' between the final archaic and earliest anatomically modern populations has indeed been claimed from several different regions of Europe (e.g. Allsworth-Jones 1986, 1990; Kozlowski 1988, 1990; Harrold 1989; Otte 1990; Mussi 1990; Goia 1990; Valoch 1990;

Demars 1990; Demars & Hublin 1989; Hublin 1990; Mellars 1989*a*, 1991). By far the strongest and best documented evidence in this context comes from the extreme western fringes of Europe, centred on the Perigord and adjacent provinces of southwest France. The evidence resides essentially in the demonstrable contemporaneity in this region of two quite distinct and sharply contrasting technological patterns, represented on the one hand by the classic 'Aurignacian' industries (discussed in the preceding section), and on the other hand by those of the so-called 'Châtelperronian' or 'Lower Perigordian' group. Briefly, the relevant observations in this context may be summarized as follows.

1. On the basis of simple technological and geographical criteria alone, there can be no serious doubt that the Aurignacian and Châtelperronian industries were the products of distinct human populations within the southwestern French sites. The distinctive 'type fossils' which define the two industrial groups (i.e. Châtelperron points in the case of the Châtelperronian, versus several forms of nosed and carinate scrapers, Aurignacian blades, Dufour and Font Yves bladelets, split-base bone points, etc. in the Aurignacian) seem to have mutually exclusive distributions (at least in material from the most recently excavated sites) and there is also evidence that both the basic techniques of flake and blade production and the specific sources exploited for lithic raw materials in the two variants were markedly different (de Sonneville-Bordes 1960; Harrold 1989; Demars 1990; Demars & Hublin 1989; Pelegrin 1990). Perhaps most significant, the overall geographical distributions of the two industries are radically different: whereas (as noted above) the Aurignacian has a distribution extending over effectively the whole of western, central and eastern Europe, the Châtelperronian is restricted to a relatively small zone confined entirely to the western and central parts of France (to the west of the Rhône valley) and penetrating for a short distance into the adjacent areas of the Pyrenees and northern Spain (see figure 1).

2. The existence of a substantial period of overlap between the Aurignacian and Châtelperronian industries can now be demonstrated from several different aspects of the chronological data. In addition to correlations based on the detailed climatic and vegetational sequences recorded in individual sites (Saint-Césaire, Quinçay, Trou de la Chèvre, Roc de Combe, Les Cottés, les Tambourets, Arcy-sur-Cure, etc.: cf. Leroyer & Leroi-Gourhan (1983); Leroyer (1988)) there are now at least three sites known in southern France and northern Spain where discrete levels of Châtelperronian and Aurignacian industries have been found clearly interstratified within the same stratigraphic sequences: notably at Roc de Combe and le Piage in southwest France, and Cueva Morín in northwest Spain (Harrold 1989; Demars 1990). The direct evidence from radiocarbon dating admittedly remains rather sparse, and potentially ambiguous, at least for the south-

west French sites (see figure 2). From the immediately adjacent areas of both northwest and northeast Spain however there is now clear radiocarbon evidence that typically Aurignacian industries were present (as noted earlier) by at least 38–40 ka BP: i.e. clearly preceding by at least 4000–5000 years the dates for the occurrence of equally typical Châtelperronian industries at sites such as Les Cottés (Vienne) and Grotte de Renne (Arcy-sur-Cure, Yonne) (Bischoff *et al.* 1989; Cabrera Valdes & Bischoff 1989; Harrold 1989; Farizy 1990). Combining all of the available palaeoclimatic, stratigraphic and radiocarbon evidence, there can be no doubt that the time ranges of the Aurignacian and Châtelperronian industries must have overlapped within these extreme western zones of Europe over a period of at least several thousand years.

3. The critical importance of this demonstrable chronological overlap of the Aurignacian and Châtelperronian industries in western Europe lies in the fact that there is now strong, if not conclusive, evidence that these two technologies were the product of sharply contrasting biological populations within this region. As discussed earlier, all of the current skeletal evidence (from both France itself and other regions of Europe) suggests that the Aurignacian industries were the product of fully anatomically modern populations (Howell 1984; Stringer *et al.* 1984; Smith 1984; Gambier 1989; Demars & Hublin 1989; Hublin 1990). By contrast, there is now explicit evidence from the skeletal remains recovered from Saint-Césaire (as well as from the series of human teeth recovered from the earlier excavations at Arcy-sur-Cure) that the populations responsible for the Châtelperronian industries were of distinctively archaic, essentially 'classic' Neanderthal type (Lévêque & Vandermeersch 1980; Stringer *et al.* 1984; Leroi-Gourhan 1958). If this evidence is accepted at face value, then we would seem to have direct and explicit evidence for the effective coexistence of these two biologically contrasting populations within these extreme western fringes of Europe, over a very substantial span of time.

What has not always been so clearly recognized in the earlier literature is that these specifically archaic, Neanderthal associations of the Châtelperronian industries had already been effectively predicted—several decades before the discovery of the Saint-Césaire hominid—purely on the basis of the technology of these industries. As long ago as 1954 Bordes argued that several of the distinctive technological features of the Châtelperronian industries (such as the character of the steeply backed 'Châtelperron points', as well as the occurrence in these industries of typical side scrapers, denticulates, and even small, bifacial hand-axe forms) showed obvious links with the preceding Mousterian industries of the same region especially with those of the Mousterian of Acheulian tradition ('MTA') group (Bordes 1954–55, 1958, 1968, 1972). In a later paper, I added a number of further components to these arguments, by pointing to the closely similar geographical distributions of the Châtelperronian and MTA industries (both confined strictly to areas to the west of the Rhône valley in France, and both extending into the adjacent areas of northern Spain) and arguing that the MTA industries represented the final stages of the local Mousterian sequence in southwest France, immediately preceding the emergence of the Châtelperronian industries (Mellars 1973). As pointed out elsewhere (Mellars 1989a) these arguments for a purely local origin for the Châtelperronian could no doubt be summed up most succinctly by observing that since the geographical distribution of the Châtelperronian is effectively restricted to these extreme, western fringes of Europe, it would be bordering on the perverse to seek an origin outside this region. In short, the arguments for believing that the Châtelperronian industries are the product of entirely indigenous (i.e. Neanderthal) populations within western Europe can be supported equally strongly on the basis of both the direct skeletal associations of the industries (at Saint-Césaire and Arcy-sur-Cure) and the basic technology, chronology and spatial distribution of the archaeological material itself.

4. The final point to be emphasized here is that this period of overlap between the Aurignacian and Châtelperronian populations in western Europe would appear to be reflected in various forms of interaction or 'acculturation' between the two populations. As discussed in more detail elsewhere (e.g. Harrold 1989; Mellars 1973, 1989a, 1991; Farizy 1990) it is now clear that while the basic technological roots of the Châtelperronian industries seem to lie clearly within the immediately preceding Mousterian industries (as discussed above), many of the more specific features of these industries are of clearly Upper Palaeolithic type. This applies not only to the relatively strong component of typically blade technology documented in the majority of the Châtelperronian assemblages, but also to the presence of highly typical and relatively abundant forms of both end scrapers and burins and—in at least some sites—a range of simple but extensively shaped bone and antler tools, and even 'personal ornaments', in the form of carefully perforated animal teeth (Harrold 1989; Farizy 1990; Leroi-Gourhan & Leroi-Gourhan 1964). The most important point to recognize in this context is that all of these specifically Upper Palaeolithic elements in the Châtelperronian would appear to have developed at a chronologically late stage: certainly long after the initial appearance of fully Aurignacian industries in northern Spain, and most probably while Aurignacian populations were already present in at least the southeastern parts of France (Leroyer & Leroi–Gourhan 1983; Leroyer 1988; Cabrera Valdes & Bischoff 1989). Exactly how these processes of interaction and apparent 'acculturation' between the final Neanderthal and earliest anatomically modern populations should be visualized remains, perhaps, one of the most enigmatic and intriguing issues in recent human evolution (see Graves (1991) and

associated comments for further discussion of this point). But there seems little doubt that this emergence of typically Upper Palaeolithic technological features amongst the final Neanderthal populations of western Europe can be explained much more economically by the action of various contact and acculturation processes of some kind than by a purely spontaneous 'invention' of Upper Palaeolithic technology on the part of the final Neanderthal communities themselves.

How far similar interaction and acculturation patterns between the final Neanderthal and earliest anatomically modern populations can be identified in other regions of Europe still remains a matter for lively debate. Allsworth-Jones (1986, 1990), Kozlowski (1988, 1990), Valoch (1990) and several others have put forward precisely this argument for the emergence of the Szeletian and related Jerzmanowician and Bohunician industries of central and eastern Europe, arguing once again that the time range occupied by these industries almost certainly overlaps with that of the (apparently intrusive) Aurignacian industries within the same regions, and that the existence of strictly local roots for these distinctive forms of 'leaf-point' industries can be documented very clearly from the technology—and spatial distribution—of the archaeological industries themselves. Mussi (1990), Goia (1990) and others have presented similar arguments for the emergence of the 'Uluzzian' industries within the Italian peninsula—again almost certainly contemporaneous with the presence of typically Aurignacian industries within the adjacent areas of the Mediterranean coast, and again showing a tightly restricted geographical distribution within the Italian sites (figure 1). Further to the east, similar patterns may be reflected in the dichotomy between the Streletska and Spitsinskaya industries of the south Russian Plain (Soffer 1985, Hoffecker 1988).

To summarize, recent research into the earliest stages of the Upper Palaeolithic now seems to be revealing a broadly similar pattern within the different regions of Europe. In each area there is evidence for the presence of apparently intrusive, characteristically 'Aurignacian'-type industries, apparently associated with fully anatomically modern hominids, and appearing in most regions between *ca.* 43 and 35 ka BP. Closely alongside these industries—and apparently at a broadly similar date—there is evidence for the emergence of a range of sharply contrasting forms of early Upper Palaeolithic technology, each restricted to a relatively limited and sharply prescribed geographical range (see figure 1), and each showing a number of strong and obvious links with the latest Middle Palaeolithic/Mousterian technologies in the same regions. As yet it is only in western Europe that these 'local' technologies have been found in association with substantial and well documented human skeletal remains, but in this particular case (i.e. the Châtelperronian) the skeletal remains are of explicitly archaic, Neanderthal form. Proponents of the population dispersal hypothesis would argue that this pattern coincides closely, if not precisely, with the situation that one would predict from the scenario of a rapid dispersal of entirely new populations over the different regions of Europe, combined with varying degrees of chronological overlap, contact, and eventually 'acculturation' with the local, indigenous population of 'archaic' humans within the different regions.

4. Colonization Scenarios

The final question of how and why a major episode of population dispersal should have occurred at this particular point in the Upper Pleistocene has been discussed in more detail elsewhere (Mellars 1989a, Zubrow 1989). From the results of the recent dating of the skeletal remains from Skhul and Qafzeh in Israel it is now clear that populations of essentially anatomically modern type had become established in the Middle Eastern zone by at least 100 ka, and must therefore have coexisted (in a broad geographical sense) alongside the Neanderthal populations in the immediately adjacent areas of Europe over a period of at least 50–60 ka (Bar-Yosef, this symposium). The potential reasons for the prolonged coexistence of these two populations may not be difficult to discern. If—as most scenarios still suggest—the anatomically modern populations had evolved initially in the tropical and subtropical environments of southern Africa, then they could hardly be expected to possess the necessary range of either biological or cultural adaptations to allow the rapid colonization of the sharply contrasting range of glacial and perigacial environments which made up the greater part of Europe during Upper Pleistocene times. By contrast, the Neanderthal populations had evolved, and evidently flourished, in these particular environments over a period of at least 100 ka if not 200 ka (Stringer et al. 1984; Hublin 1990). As I have argued elsewhere (Mellars 1989a), it was almost certainly the range of technological and other cultural innovations which took place in the Middle Eastern region around 45–50 ka BP—the so-called 'Upper Palaeolithic Revolution'—which eventually gave some strong adaptive advantage to the anatomically modern populations in this region, and equipped them not only to colonize a complex range of entirely new glacial environments, but also to compete effectively with the local Neanderthal populations in these regions. Although inevitably speculative, the possibility that the development of highly structured, fully syntactic language played some crucial role in this event (with its attendant consequences for almost all spheres of human behaviour and organization) demands serious consideration (Mellars 1989a, 1991; Clark, this symposium).

Regardless of the initial stimulus, the actual process of population expansion may well have been at least partially facilitated by the pattern of climatic and ecological events around the middle of the last glaciation. It is now clear that the period centred on *ca*. 50–30 ka BP (i.e. the later part of stage 3 of the oxygen-isotope sequence) was marked by a series of major climatic oscillations, during which average temperatures in many regions rose by at least 5–6°C, and allowed the expansion of temperate woodland into many areas of Europe which had previously been dominated by peri-glacial tundra or steppe (Guiot *et al*. 1989). To groups who were ecologically adapted—both biologically and culturally—to the temperate environments of the east Mediterranean zone, these ecological changes would inevitably have made a process of population expansion into areas lying to the north and west easier to achieve—especially if (as the present archaeological evidence suggests) this process of population expansion extended initially along the north Mediterranean littoral zone, from the Balkans, through northern Italy, to northern Spain. It could no doubt be argued that the same ecological changes might well have served to destabilize some of the specific ecological and cultural adaptations of the local Neanderthal popu-lations in these regions, leading either to significant shifts in the geographi-cal ranges occupied by individual groups, or perhaps even to major epi-sodes of population decline. Zubrow (1989) has recently argued that it would require little more than a relatively minor shift in relative birth and death rates between the two populations (i.e. Neanderthal on the one hand, versus anatomically modern on the other) to lead to a process of effective population replacement of one population by the other within specific re-gions of Europe within a span of at most 1000 years.

Whether or not such a process of total demographic and biological re-placement did in fact occur—in Europe or any other part of the world—remains, of course, the most centred and controversial element in the cur-rent debates. It is now clear however that such a process of population replacement is by no means inconceivable in either cultural or demographic terms, and could well have been achieved without any of the more dramatic scenarios of 'confrontation'—let alone mass genocide—which have been envisaged in some of the more fanciful recent discussions of the origins and dispersal of modern humans.

ACKNOWLEDGMENTS

I am greatly indebted to Janusz K. Kozlowski for discussion of points raised in this paper, and for providing information on his current excavations in the Temnata Cave.

REFERENCES

Allsworth-Jones, P. 1986 *The Szeletian and the transition from Middle to Upper Palaeo-lithic in Central Europe*. Oxford University Press.

Allsworth-Jones, P. 1990 The Szeletian and the stratigraphic succession in Central Europe and adjacent areas: main trends, recent results, and problems for solution. In Mellars (ed.) 1990*b*, pp. 160–243.

Bard, E., Hamelin, B., Fairbanks, R.G. & Zindler, A. 1990 Calibration of the ^{14}C timescale over the past 30,000 years using mass spectrometric U-Th Ages from Barbados corals. *Nature, Lond.* **345**, 405–410.

Bar-Yosef, O. & Belfer Cohen, A. 1988 The early Upper Palaeolithic in the Levantine Caves. In *The early Upper Palaeolithic: evidence from Europe and the Near East* (ed. J. F. Hoffecker & C. A. Wolf), pp. 23–42. Oxford: British Archaeological Reports International Series 437.

Bischoff, J.L., Soler, N., Maroto, J. & Julia, R. 1989 Abrupt Mousterian/Aurignacian boundary at c. 40 ka bp: accelerator 14C dates from l'Arbreda Cave (Catalunya, Spain). *J. archaeol. Sci.* **16**, 563–576.

Bordes, F. 1954–55 Les gisements du Pech de l'Azé (Dordogne). I. Le Moustérien de tradition Acheuléenne. *Anthropologie* **58**, 401–432; **59**, 1–38.

Bordes, F. 1958 Le passage du Paléolithique moyen au Paléolithique supérieur. In *Hundert Yahre Neanderthaler* (ed. G. H. R. von Koenigswald), pp. 175–181. Utrecht: Kemink en Zoon.

Bordes, F. 1968 *The Old Stone Age*. London: Weidenfeld & Nicolson.

Bordes, F. 1972 Du Paléolithique moyen au Paléolithique supérieur: continuité ou discontinuité? In *The origin of Homo sapiens* (ed. F. Bordes), pp. 211–218. Paris: UNESCO.

Bosinski, G. 1990 *Homo Sapiens*. Paris: Editions Errance.

Boule, M. 1909 L'Homme fossile de la Chapelle-aux-Saints (Corrèze). *Anthropologie* **25**, 257–271.

Cabrera Valdes, V. & Bernaldo de Quiros, F. 1990 Données sur la transition entre le Paléolithique moyen et Paléolithique supérieur dans la région cantabrique: révision critique. In Farizy (ed.) 1990, pp. 185–188.

Cabrera Valdes, V. & Bischoff, J.L. 1989 Accelerator ^{14}C dates for early Upper Palaeolithic (basal Aurignacian) at El Castillo Cave (Spain). *J. archaeol. Sci.* **16**, 577–584.

Cann, R.L., Stoneking, M. & Wilson, A.C. 1987 Mitochondrial DNA and human evolution. *Nature, Lond.* **325**, 31–36.

Chase, P.G. & Dibble, H.L. 1987 Middle Palaeolithic symbolism: a review of current evidence and interpretations. *J. anthrop. Archaeol.* **6**, 263–293.

Clark, G.A. 1992 Continuity or replacement? Putting modern human origins in an evolutionary context. In *The Middle Palaeolithic: adaptation, behavior and variability* (ed. H. L. Dibble & P. Mellars), pp. 183–205. Philadelphia: University Museum of Pennsylvania Press.

Clark, G.A. & Lindly, J.M. 1989 The case for continuity: observations on the biocultural transition in Europe and Western Asia. In Mellars & Stringer (eds) 1989, pp. 626–676.

Copeland, L. 1976 Terminological correlations in the early Upper Palaeolithic of Lebanon and Palestine. In *Deuxième Colloque sur la Terminologie de la Préhistoire du Proche Orient* (ed. F. Wendorf), pp. 35–48. Nice: International Union of Prehistoric and Proto-historic Sciences.

Delibrias, G. & Fontugne, M. 1990 Datations des gisements de l'Aurignacien et du Moustérien en France. In Farizy (ed.) 1990, pp. 39–42.

Delluc, B. & Delluc, C. 1978 Les manifestations graphiques aurignaciennes sur support rocheux des environs des Eyzies (Dordogne). *Gallia Préhistoire* **21**, 213–438.

Demars, P.Y. 1990 Les interstratifications entre Aurignacien et Châtelperronien a Roc de Combe et au Piage (Lot): approvisionnement en matières premières et position chronologique. In Farizy (ed.) 1990, pp. 235–240.

Demars, P.Y. & Hublin, J.-J. 1989 La transition Néandertaliens/Hommes de type moderne en Europe occidentale: aspects paléontologiques et culturels. In *L'Homme de Néandertal*, vol. 7 (*L'extinction*) (ed. M. Otte), pp. 23–27. Liege: Etudes et Recherches Archéologiques de l'Université de Liège 34.

Farizy, C. 1990 Du Moustérien au Châtelperronien a Arcy-sur-Cure: un état de la question. In Farizy (ed.) 1990, pp. 281–290.

Farizy, C. (ed.) 1990 *Paléolithique Moyen Récent et Paléolithique Supérieur Ancien en Europe* Nemours: Mémoires du Musée de Préhistoire d'Ile de France 3.

Gambier, D. 1989 Fossil hominids from the early Upper Palaeolithic (Aurignacian) of France. In Mellars & Stringer (eds) 1989, pp. 194–211.

Goia, P. 1990 La transition Paléolithique moyen/Paléolithique supérieur en Italie et la question de l'Uluzzien. In Farizy (ed.) 1990, pp. 241–250.

Graves, P. 1991 New models and metaphors for the Neanderthal debate. *Curr. Anthrop.* **32**, 513–541.

Guiot, J., Pons, A., de Beaulieu, J.L. & Reille, M. 1989 A 140,000-year continental climate reconstruction from two European pollen records, *Nature, Lond.* **388**, 309–313.

Haesaerts, P. 1990 Nouvelles recherches au gisement de Willendorf (Basse Autriche). *Bull. Inst. R. Sci. Nat. Belgique* (Sciences de la Terre) **60**, 203–218.

Hahn, J. 1972 Aurignacian signs, pendants, and art objects in Central and Eastern Europe. *World Archaeology* **3**, 252–266.

Hahn, J. 1977 *Aurignacien: Das Altere Jungpaláolithikum in Mittel- und Osteuropa*. Koln: Fundamenta Series A9.

Harrold, F.B. 1989 Mousterian, Châtelperronian, and Early Aurignacian in Western Europe: continuity or discontinuity? In Mellars & Stringer (eds) 1989, pp. 677–713.

Hoffecker, J.F. 1988 Early Upper Paleolithic sites of the European USSR. In *The early Upper Paleolithic: evidence from Europe and the Near East* (ed. J. F. Hoffecker & C. A. Wolf), pp. 237–272. Oxford: British Archaeological Reports International Series 437.

Howell, F.C. 1984 Introduction. In *The origins of modern humans: a world survey of the fossil evidence* (ed. F. H. Smith & F. Spencer), pp. xiii–xxii. New York: Alan R. Liss.

Hublin, J.-J. 1990 Les peuplements paléolithiques de l'Europe: un point de vue géographique. In Farizy (ed.) 1990, pp. 29–37.

Kozlowski, J.K. 1982 *Excavation in the Bacho Kiro Cave (Bulgaria): Final Report*. Warsaw: Panstwowe Wydawnictwo Naukowe.

Kozlowski, J.K. 1988 Transition from the Middle to the early Upper Paleolithic in Central Europe and the Balkans. In *The early Upper Paleolithic: evidence from Europe and the Near East* (ed. J. F. Hoffecker & C. A. Wolf), pp. 193–236. Oxford: British Archaeological Reports International Series 437.

Kozlowski, J.K. 1990 A multi-aspectual approach to the origins of the Upper Palaeolithic in Europe. In Mellars (ed.) 1990*b*, pp. 419–437.

Kozlowski, J.K. 1992 The Balkans in the Middle and Upper Palaeolithic: the gateway to Europe of a cul de sac? *Proc. Prehist. Soc.* (In the press.)

Kozlowski, J.K. & Otte, M. 1984 L'Aurignacien en Europe centrale, orientale et balkanique (travaux recents 1976–1981). In *Aurignacien et Gravettien en Europe*, vol. 3 (ed. J. K. Kozlowski & R. Désbrosses), pp. 61–72. Liège: Etudes et Recherches Archéologiques de l'Université de Liège 13.

Leroi-Gourhan, A. 1958 Etude des restes humains fossiles provenant des grottes d'Arcy-sur-Cure. *Ann. Paléontol. (Vertébrés)* **44**, 97–140.

Leroi-Gourhan, A. & Leroi-Gourhan, A. 1964 Chronologie des grottes d'Arcy-sur-Cure (Yonne). *Gallia Préhistoire* **7**, 1–64.

Leroyer, C. 1988 Des occupations castelperroniennes et aurignaciennes dans leur cadre chrono-climatique. In *L'Homme de Néandertal*, vol. 8 (*La Mutation*) (ed. M. Otte), pp. 103–108. Liège: Etudes et Recherches Archéologiques de l'Université de Liège 35.

Leroyer, C. & Leroi-Gourhan, A. 1983 Problèmes de chronologie: le castelperronien et l'aurignacien. *Bull. Soc. préhist. fr.* **80**, 41–44.

Lévêque, F. & Vandermeersch, B. 1980 Découverte de restes humains dans un niveau castelperronien à Saint-Césaire (Charente-Maritime). *C. R. Acad. Sci. Paris*, series 2, **291**, 187–189.

Marks, A.E. & Ferring, C.R. 1988 The early Upper Paleolithic of the Levant. In *The early Upper Paleolithic: evidence from Europe and the Near East* (ed. J. F. Hoffecker & C. A. Wolf), pp. 43–72. Oxford: British Archaeological Reports International Series 437.

Marshack, A. 1972 *The roots of civilization*. New York: McGraw-Hill.

Marshack, A. 1990 Early hominid symbols and evolution of the human capacity. In Mellars (ed.) 1990*b*, pp. 457–498.

Mellars, P.A. 1973 The character of the Middle-Upper Palaeolithic transition in southwest France. In *The explanation of culture change* (ed. C. Renfrew), pp. 255–276. London: Duckworth.

Mellars, P.A. 1989*a* Major issues in the emergence of modern humans. *Curr. Anthrop.* **30**, 349–385.

Mellars, P.A. 1989*b* Technological changes across the Middle-Upper Paleolithic transition: technological, social, and cognitive perspectives. In Mellars & Stringer (eds) 1989, pp. 338–365.

Mellars, P.A. 1990*a* Comment on radiocarbon-accelerator dating of Roc de Combe samples. *Archaeometry* **32**, 101–102.

Mellars, P.A. (ed.) 1990*b* *The emergence of modern humans: an archaeological perspective*. Edinburgh University Press.

Mellars, P.A. 1991 Cognitive changes and the emergence of modern humans in Europe. *Cambr. Archaeol. J.* **1**, 63–76.

Mellars, P.A., Bricker, H.M., Gowlett, J.A.J. & Hedges, R.E.M. 1987 Radiocarbon accelerator dating of French Upper Palaeolithic sites. *Curr. Anthrop.* **28**, 128–133.

Mellars, P.A. & Stringer, C.B. (eds) 1989 *The human revolution: behavioural and biological perspectives on the origins of modern humans*. Edinburgh University Press.

Mellars, P.A. & Tixier, J. 1989 Radiocarbon-accelerator dating of Ksar 'Aqil (Lebanon) and the chronology of the Upper Palaeolithic sequence in the Middle East. *Antiquity* **63**, 761–768.

Mercier, N., Valladas, H., Joron, J.L., Reyss, J.L., Lévêque, F. & Vandermeersch, B. 1991 Thermoluminescence dating of the late Neanderthal remains from Saint-Césaire. *Nature, Lond.* **351**, 737–739.

Movius, H.L. Jr 1975 Summary of the stratigraphic sequence. In *Excavation of the Abri Pataud, Les Eyzies (Dordogne)* (ed. H. L. Movius), pp. 7–18. Cambridge, Massachusetts: Peabody Museum of Archaeology and Ethnology.

Mussi, M. 1990 Le peuplement de l'Italie à la fin du Paléolithique moyen et au début du Paléolithique supérieur. In Farizy (ed.) 1990, pp. 251–262.

Ohnuma, K. & Bergman, C.A. 1990 A technological analysis of the Upper Palaeolithic levels (XXV–VI) of Ksar Akil, Lebanon. In Mellars (ed.) 1990*b*, pp. 56–80.

Otte, M. 1990 From the Middle to the Upper Palaeolithic: the nature of the transition. In Mellars (ed.) 1990, pp. 438–456.

Pelegrin, J. 1990 Observations technologiques sur quelques séries du Châtelperronien et du MTA B du sud-ouest de la France: une hypothèse d'évolution. In Farizy (ed.) 1990, pp. 195–201.

Smith, F.H. 1984 Fossil hominids from the Upper Pleistocene of Central Europe and the origin of modern Europeans. In *The origins of modern humans: a world survey of the fossil evidence* (ed. F. H. Smith & F. Spencer), pp. 137–210. New York: Alan R. Liss.

Smith, F.H. 1991 The Neandertals: evolutionary dead ends or ancestors of modern people? *J. anthrop. Res.* **47**, 219–238.

Smith, F.H., Simek, J.F. & Harrill, M.S. 1989 Geographic variation in supraorbital torus reduction during the later Pleistocene (c. 80,000–15,000 BP). In Mellars & Stringer (eds) 1989, pp. 172–193.

Soffer, O. 1985 *The Upper Paleolithic of the Central Russian Plain.* Orlando, Academic Press.

Sonneville-Bordes, D. de 1960 *Le Paléolithique Supérieur en Périgord.* Bordeaux: Delmas.

Stoneking, M. & Cann, R.L. 1989 African origin of human mitochrondrial DNA. In Mellars & Stringer (eds) 1989, pp. 17–30.

Stringer, C.B. & Andrews, P. 1988 Genetic and fossil evidence for the origin of modern humans. *Science, Wash.* **239**, 1263–1268.

Stringer, C.B., Hublin, J.-J. & Vandermeersch, B. 1984 The origin of anatomically modern humans in Western Europe in *The origins of modern humans: a world survey of the fossil evidence* (ed. F. H. Smith & F. Spencer), pp. 51–135. New York: Alan R. Liss.

Thorne, A.G. & Wolpoff, M.H. 1992 The multiregional evolution of humans. *Scient. Am.* **266**, 28–33.

Valoch, K. 1983 L'origine des différents technocomplexes du Paléolithique supérieur en Morave. In *Aurignacien et Gravettien en Europe*, vol. 2 (ed. L. Banesz & J. K. Kozlowski), pp. 371–378. Liège: Etudes et Recherches Archéologiques de l'Université de Liège 13.

Valoch, K. 1990 La Morave il y a 40 000 ans. In Farizy (ed.) 1990, pp. 115–124.

White, R. 1989 Production complexity and standardization in early Aurignacian bead and pendant manufacture: evolutionary implications. In Mellars & Stringer (eds) 1989, pp. 366–390.

Wolpoff, M.H. 1989 Multiregional evolution: the fossil alternative to Eden. In Mellars & Stringer (eds) 1989, pp. 62–108.

Zubrow, E. 1989 The demographic modelling of Neanderthal extinction. In Mellars & Stringer (eds) 1989, pp. 212–231.

Recent Human Evolution in East Asia and Australasia

Peter Brown[1]

SUMMARY

In both East Asia and Australasia arguments for evolutionary continuity between middle-late Pleistocene hominid populations and modern *Homo sapiens* are of long standing. In both regions, however, problems of chronological distribution, dating and preservation of hominid skeletal materials provide an effective barrier to extending regional sequences back to 'archaic' *Homo sapiens* or *Homo erectus*. The earliest securely dated modern *Homo sapiens* in East Asia are currently represented by Zhoukoudian Upper Cave at a minimum of 29 ka BP. In Australia skeletal remains of modern *Homo sapiens* have been dated to 26 ka BP, with archaeological materials at 38 to 50 ka BP. Late Pleistocene human skeletons from sites like Coobool Creek are morphologically and metrically outside the range of recent Australian Aboriginal populations. Similarly Liujiang and the Upper Cave crania can be distinguished from recent East Asian 'Mongoloids'. Evolutionary change within the Holocene needs to be taken into consideration when the evidence for regional evolutionary continuity is considered.

1. INTRODUCTION

Over the past 30 years the recent, late Pleistocene to mid-Holocene evolution of our species has been documented in increasing detail. In Australasia and East Asia osteological and dental research has focused on three separate, although interrelated, aspects of human evolution. These are the diversity of modern *Homo sapiens* populations (Pietrusewsky 1984; Wang 1986; Brown 1987; Li *et al.* 1991), the evolutionary relationships between these *H. sapiens* and earlier hominids from within, and outside, Asia (Weidenreich 1939a; Thorne & Wolpoff 1981; Wolpoff *et al.* 1984; Kaminga & Wright 1988; Wu 1988a, b) and change in skeletal and dental form during the Holocene (Zhang *et al.* 1982; Brace *et al.* 1984; Wu & Zhang 1985; Wang 1986; Brown 1987, 1989). Although the documentation of modern human variation is a continuing process, and there is general agreement as to the direction of post-Pleistocene evolution in both China and Australia, the

---

[1] Department of Archaeology, University of New England, Armidale, New South Wales, Australia

origins and diversity of the first modern human populations is a topic of continued debate.

Evolutionary continuity between Pleistocene and recent human populations within China was first argued in detail by Weidenreich (1939*b*, 1943) and later developed, although with varying emphasis, by Coon (1962) and Wolpoff *et al.* (1984). Weidenreich's argument for evolutionary continuity rested on the identification of 'Mongoloid' skeletal characteristics in the Zhoukoudian *Homo erectus* remains and in modern northern Chinese. A persistent obstacle to expanding Weidenreich's 'Mongoloid' lineage has been the distribution, dating and preservation of the east Asian hominid skeletal remains. Although *H. erectus* and early *H. sapiens* (Dali, Maba, Jinniushan and Xujiayao) are reasonably well represented there are still substantial gaps in the Chinese hominid sequence (Chen & Zhang 1991). In particular the earliest examples of modern *H. sapiens* in China, Zhoukoudian Upper Cave, may only date to 10–13 ka BP (Wu & Zhang 1985; Hedges *et al.* 1988; Chen *et al.* 1989). There is also some debate over the 'Mongoloid' affinities of the crania from this locality (Weidenreich 1939*a*; Wolpoff *et al.* 1984; Wu & Zhang 1985; Kaminga & Wright 1988) which could undermine the east Asian regional evolutionary model.

For reasons of geographic proximity, rather than unequivocal archaeological or skeletal evidence, most researchers have focused on a possible Asian origin for the Australian Aborigines (Weidenreich 1945; Macintosh 1963; Birdsell 1967; Thorne 1977). The first person to have raised the possibility of a specific regional connection between fossil hominid skeletal material from Asia, Javan *Pithecanthropus*, and Australian Aborigines was Hermann Klaatsch (1908). This regional evolutionary sequence linking Indonesia and Australia was then further developed by Weidenreich (1946), Coon (1962) and Thorne & Wolpoff (1981). The argument for an Australasian evolutionary sequence also depends upon the identification of morphological and metrical osteological traits, which in combination, occur in the highest frequency in *Homo erectus* crania from Indonesia and terminal Pleistocene and recent Australians. Problems of temporal clustering of sites, inadequate chronological control, and poor preservation which occur in East Asia are also a feature of the Australasian sequence. The major differences between these two regions are that terminal Pleistocene *H. sapiens* are relatively common in Australasia (Thorne & Macumber 1972; Bowler *et al.* 1972; Bowler & Thorne 1976; Brown 1989), while if the Ngandong crania are considered to be *H. erectus* (Santa Luca 1980) then early *H. sapiens* comparable to Dali (Wu 1981) are not represented.

In both East Asia and Australasia the strength of the evolutionary continuity model rests on the interpretation of several key skeletons. In China, while the 'Mongoloid' morphology of the mid-Holocene skeletal materials from Huaxian, Baoji, Hemudu and Banpo is clear (Wu & Zhang 1985;

Wang 1986), the same cannot be said for the single reliably dated terminal Pleistocene locality, Zhoukoudian Upper Cave. Weidenreich (1939a), although committed to a regional evolutionary sequence, did not think that the Upper Cave skeletons were morphologically Chinese. This raises the possibility that 'Mongoloid' osteological traits, as represented in modern East Asians, were a Holocene development or that morphologically 'Mongoloid' people only moved into northern China during the Holocene. Recently a uranium-series date of 67 ka has been reported for the Liujiang skeleton from Guangxi in southeastern China (Wu 1988a, 1990). If the dated material and skeleton from Liujiang are contemporary then this provides the earliest evidence of modern *H. sapiens* in East Asia. Such an early date for a skeleton with 'Mongoloid' skeletal characteristics would also strengthen arguments for evolutionary continuity within southern China.

In Australasia it is the terminal Pleistocene collections from the southeastern Australian sites of Coobool Creek and Nacurrie (Brown 1989, 1992a), Kow Swamp (Thorne & Macumber 1972; Thorne 1976), Willandra Lakes (Bowler *et al.* 1972; Bowler & Thorne 1976; Thorne 1984; Wolpoff 1991) and Keilor (Wunderly 1943; Brown 1987) which are crucial to the regional continuity argument. It is these sites in combination which are important, as there has been continued debate over the significance of morphological and metrical variation in terminal Pleistocene Australia (Thorne 1977; Habgood 1986; Brown 1987; Webb 1989; Pardoe 1991). Most recently the literature has contained references to an as yet undated and undescribed cranial vault, WLH-50 (Flood 1983; Thorne 1984), which has been directly connected with the Indonesian Ngandong crania (Stringer & Andrews 1988; Wolpoff 1991).

2. REGIONAL CHRONOLOGY OF MODERN *H. SAPIENS*

(a) Australasia

The earliest, widely accepted, evidence for human occupation in Australia is a radiocarbon date of 39 500 ± 2300–1800 BP (SUA-1500) for charcoal associated with stone artifacts from the Upper Swan in Western Australia (Pearce & Barbetti 1981). More recently Roberts *et al.* (1990a) have argued on the basis of themoluminescence dates from the Malakunanja II rockshelter that human occupation in Australia may predate 50 ka. However, Hiscock (1990) has expressed concern over the extent of the discrepancy between the radiocarbon and TL dates, and stratigraphic association of the artifacts. Roberts *et al.* (1990b) have defended their original assessment of the age of Malakunanja II.

Although there are an increasing number of archaeological sites which are older than 30 ka BP, few radiometrically dated late Pleistocene human skeletal remains have been recovered from Australia. The oldest positively dated human skeleton is the Lake Mungo 1 cremation dated to 24 700 ± 1270 BP (ANU-618A) (Bowler *et al.* 1970; Bowler *et al.* 1972). Bowler & Thorne (1976) have argued, on the basis of geomorphological criteria and stratigraphic association with Lake Mungo 1, that the extended burial Lake Mungo 3 may be in the order of 28–32 ka BP in age. Morphological comparisons have suggested to some people (Flood 1983; Thorne 1984; Wolpoff 1991) that at least one of the undated Willandra Lakes specimens, WLH-50, is considerably older than Lake Mungo 1. Kow Swamp (Thorne & Macumber 1972; Thorne 1976) is bracketed by radiocarbon dates on shell from the grave of KS5 of 13 000 ± 280 BP (ANU-1236) and on bone apatite from KS9 to 9590 ± 130 BP (ANU-532) (Thorne 1975). Morphologically and metrically similar skeletons to those from Kow Swamp were collected from the nearby sites of Coobool Creek and Nacurrie (Brown 1989, 1992*a*). Unfortunately the skeletons from both of these locations are without archaeological provenance and have proved difficult to date due to contamination from a gelatin based preservative. A $^{234}U/^{230}Th$ date of 14 300 ± 1000 (LLO-416) has been obtained for bone from Coobool Creek 65 (Brown 1989) and uncontaminated bone from Nacurrie 1 has recently been AMS dated to 11 440 ± 160 BP (NZA-1069) (Brown 1992*a*). The Keilor skeleton (Brown 1987) is dated to 13 000 ± 100 BP (NZ-1327).

Skeletal materials from southeast Asia with some claim to being examples of early modern *H. sapiens* are the deep skull from Niah Cave in Borneo (Brothwell 1960; Kennedy 1977), Wadjak I and II from Java (Dubois 1922) and Tabon from the Philipines (Fox 1970). The Niah cave juvenile cranium, which is poorly preserved, has been radiocarbon dated on the basis of charcoal associated with the cranium at 39 820 ± 1012 BP (GrN-1339) (Oakley *et al.* 1975). Wolpoff (1980) is sceptical of the contemporaneity of the dated material and human skull, but an earlier review of the excavation reports by Kennedy (1977) supports the original date. The Wadjak cave crania, although undated, have on the basis of perceived morphological similarities with prehistoric Australian Aboriginal crania been considered to be of late Pleistocene age (Dubois 1922; Weidenreich 1945). This is not upheld by an analysis of the associated fauna which contains few extinct species and is considered to be broadly recent in age (Theunissen *et al.* 1990). The Tabon frontal and mandible are poorly preserved (Macintosh 1978), but are radiocarbon dated by association to 23 ka BP (Fox 1970).

(*b*) *East Asia*

Two recent articles (Wu & Wang 1985; Chen & Zhang 1991) have presented detailed reviews of the dating and distribution of the major Middle and late Pleistocene hominid localities in China. Although a consensus is being reached on the age of *H. erectus* and early *H. sapiens* in east Asia, the first appearance of modern *H. sapiens* continues to be problematic. Fossilized remains of modern *H. sapiens* have been recovered from relatively few late Pleistocene contexts in China (Wu & Zhang 1985). Specimens which combine a reasonable state of preservation, with information on provenance, and claims of a Pleistocene antiquity are Liujiang (Wu 1959) and Zhoukoudian Upper Cave 101, 102 and 103 (Weidenreich 1939; Wu 1960, 1961; Kaminga & Wright 1988). The Liujiang skeleton, consisting of a cranium and limited postcranial material was discovered in a cave at Tongtianyan, Guangxi, in 1958 by people collecting fertilizer. Liujiang was initially described by Wu (1959) with Wu & Zhang (1985) providing additional comparative anatomical information. The *Ailuropoda–Stegodon* fauna found in association with Liujiang were interpreted as being of Middle Pleistocene age but the contemporaneity of the fauna and the human skeletal materials has not been established. Wu (1959) did not support a Middle Pleistocene age for the human skeletal materials arguing that the morphology of the cranium suggested a more recent date. Recently a Uranium series date of $67\,000^{+6000}_{-5000}$ has been reported for Liujiang (Wu 1988*a*; Wu 1990). However, the stratigraphic relationship of the dated stalactite layer and the human skeletal materials can not be confirmed (Chen & Zhang 1991).

A stronger claim for terminal Pleistocene antiquity can be established for the Upper Cave at Zhoukoudian. The Zhoukoudian Upper Cave skeletons were excavated in 1933 and 1934, with the archaeological assemblage discussed by Pei (1935, 1939) and the human skeletal materials briefly described by Weidenreich (1939). The fauna recovered from the lower chamber of the cave suggested to Pei that the deposits were of late Pleistocene age and this was subsequently confirmed by a series of radiocarbon dates (Wu & Zhang 1985). Conventional ^{14}C dates on non-human bone provided dates of $10\,175 \pm 360$ BP (ZK-136-0-4) for the upper part of the cave and $18\,340 \pm 410$ BP (ZK-136-0-2) for the basal layers. Wu & Wang (1985) argue that the older date is for a layer well below the human occupation and the archaeological deposits are closer to 10 ka. More recent AMS dates, again on non-human bone, range in age from $10\,100 \pm 160$ BP (OXA-891) to $30\,100 \pm 2000$ BP (OXA-190) (Hedges *et al.* 1988, 1992; Chen *et al.* 1989), with a suggested age of 29–24 ka BP for the cultural layers. Unfortunately, the published accounts of the excavation contain insufficient information to be certain of the stratigraphic relationships between the human burials and the dated faunal material. It is unclear whether the burials are contemporaneous with the deposition of layer 4 or had been interred from a higher layer. In contrast to the uncertainties surrounding Chinese terminal Pleistocene skeletons, collections of mid-Holocene skeletal material are extensive. Wu & Zhang (1985) provide a list of the major Neolithic sites which range in age from 7000 to 3000 years BP and a discussion of geographic variation and diachronic change in skeletal morphology.

3. RECENT HUMAN EVOLUTION

(a) *Australasia*

Morphological and metrical comparison of terminal Pleistocene, mid-Holocene and recent Australian Aboriginal crania and dentitions have highlighted the distinctiveness of the Pleistocene materials from Kow Swamp, Coobool Creek and Nacurrie (Thorne & Macumber 1972; Pietrusewsky 1979; Brown 1987, 1989). At a general level terminal Pleistocene crania can be distinguished by greater overall size, with significantly larger endocranial volumes than recent crania from the same region (table 1). This size distinction also extends to the orofacial skeleton, post cranial skeleton, and to a lesser degree, tooth dimensions (Brown 1992*b*). More detailed consideration of morphological differences between terminal Pleistocene and recent crania is complicated by the presence of artificially deformed crania at Coobool Creek, Kow Swamp and Nacurrie (Brothwell 1975; Brown 1981, 1989). Fortunately most of the crania from these locations have not been deformed and the deformation process does not appear to have significantly influenced facial dimensions (Brown 1989). The terminal Pleistocene cranial vaults can be distinguished by their greater length, height and breadth dimensions, thicker vault bone, more receding frontal squama and greater supraorbital breadth (table 1).

Morphological features associated with general robusticity, including the median sagittal ridge, supramastoid and mastoid crests, occipital torus and supraorbital region are generally more prominent. Although true supraorbital tori are present in low numbers (Brown 1989), the supraorbital trigones reduce laterally and are distinct from those in Ngandong. Terminal Pleistocene Australian facial skeletons are dominated by the functional requirements of a large dentition (Brown 1992*b*). Mean orofacial dimensions in terminal Pleistocene males are significantly greater than those in the Holocene (table 1 and figure 1), with the only exceptions being for the height and breadth of the orbit. Facial prognathism, particularly subnasally, is greater with increased facial height and palate length dimensions influencing the angles of the facial triangle (figure 1). By the middle of the Holocene a reduction in tooth size, and associated alveolar support, results in a significantly shorter and less prognathic face.

Although the terminal Pleistocene average is for larger overall size and morphological robustness, there is considerable variation, both metrically and morphologically, in the undeformed male and female crania. Areas of the cranium which are particularly variable include the angle and curvature of the frontal bone, development of median ridge and prebregmatic

Table 1. *Comparison of orofacial and cranial dimensions in the terminal Pleistocene Australian Aboriginal male sample with those in the two Holocene male Aboriginal groups using Student's t-test (mm)*

	terminal-Pleist.[a]			mid-Holocene[b]			late-Holocene[c]		
	n	x̄	s.d.	n	x̄	s.d.	n	x̄	s.d.
cranial length[d]	23	195.8	7.57	11	191.7[e]	7.10	29	190.3[e]	5.60
cranial height[d]	18	140.7	5.07	7	136.1[e]	3.76	28	129.8[e]	4.93
endocranial volume/ml	19	1404.9	96.96	—	—	—	23	1271.5[e]	92.95
supraorbital breadth	31	117.2	4.98	9	107.8[e]	2.48	29	110.2[e]	2.94
thickness at bregma[d]	21	10.7	2.32	4	10.7	1.70	24	7.8[e]	1.09
frontal angle/deg.[d]	17	140.3	3.75	7	136.4[e]	3.89	26	137.1[e]	3.42
occipital angle/deg.[d]	14	118.6	3.63	3	115.3	9.61	24	117.6	5.05
bi-zygion	9	144.1	4.85	9	136.3[e]	5.26	24	136.5[e]	2.93
nasion-nasospinale	22	54.5	3.18	10	50.8[e]	2.65	29	51.7[e]	2.56
nasospinale-prosthion	23	20.8	3.40	10	18.8	3.36	28	16.5[e]	2.42
nasal breadth	26	29.3	1.82	11	27.9[e]	2.25	25	26.4[e]	1.35
orbital height	26	31.2	2.49	10	33.3[f]	2.86	29	34.1[f]	2.33
orbital breadth	26	43.4	3.46	9	44.4	2.65	25	43.9	1.18
alveolar length	22	64.9	2.42	10	61.8[e]	4.31	29	61.5[e]	3.15
symphyseal height	25	39.2	2.94	8	34.2[e]	4.16	15	32.3[e]	2.87

[a] Coobool Creek, Nacurrie, Keilor, Cohuna, Lake Mungo and Kow Swamp.
[b] Barham, Roonka and Keera Station.
[c] Swanport.
[d] Crania which previous research indicates are artificially deformed are excluded from sample.
[e] Mean value significantly less than terminal Pleistocene mean, $p < 0.05$.
[f] Mean value which is significantly greater than terminal Pleistocene mean, $p < 0.05$.

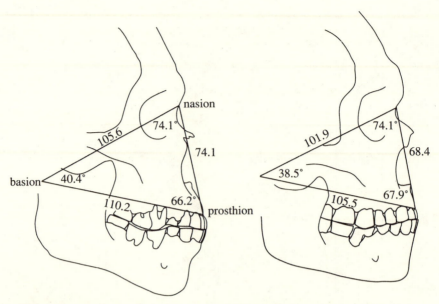

Figure 1. Comparison of mean facial dimensions (mm) in male terminal Pleisto-cene (left) and late Holocene Australian Aboriginal crania (right).

eminence, facial prognathism, supraorbital morphology which ranges in males from a true torus to minimal development of the lateral trigone and superciliary components, the angle and curvature of the occipital bone, morphology of the occipital torus and lambdoidal region and cranial vault thickness (Brown 1987, 1989). This variation has implications for the re-gional evolutionary continuity model as it effects many of the clade features cited by Thorne and Wolpoff (1981).

Groves (1989) and Bräuer (1989) have emphasized that many of Thorne & Wolpoff's (1981) traits occur singly, and in combination, in hominids outside the Australasian region, with the parietal breadth, frontal flatness, prebregmatic eminence and prognathism characters best considered as primitive retentions. Several of the traits are sexually dimorphic in Austra-lian Aboriginal crania (frontal flatness, prognathism, tooth size, prebreg-matic eminence, location of minimum frontal breadth, location of parietal breadth and malar eversion) and some have undergone significant change in the early Holocene (prognathism, tooth size, frontal flatness, frontal and parietal breadths). Pronounced prognathism and large posterior tooth size, which are functionally related, appears to be a particularly poor regional characteristic as people in most parts of the world had large teeth and relatively prognathic faces during the late Pleistocene (Brace & Mahler 1971; Carlson 1976; Frayer 1977, 1984; Smith 1982; Calcagno 1986; Smith et al. 1986; Brown 1987, 1992b).

Most surprisingly, Thorne & Wolpoff (1980) seem to assume that terminal Pleistocene Australians were a fairly homogenous group and are suitably represented by Kow Swamp (Thorne & Macumber 1972) and the undated Cohuna cranium. This runs contrary to a series of earlier publications by Thorne (1976, 1977) in which he argued the complete opposite. Variation in Pleistocene Australia was interpreted as being so great that it could most readily be explained by the migration of two morphologically distinct founder populations. On the evidence so far published the earliest group of immigrants, and those temporally less removed from the Indonesian hominids, are represented by the Lake Mungo 1 and 3 skeletons (Bowler et al. 1970; Bowler et al. 1972; Bowler & Thorne 1976). The Lake Mungo materials, along with Keilor, were excluded from Thorne & Wolpoff's (1981) regional comparison. In retrospect this may have been because the morphology of these crania did little to support their chosen hypothesis. Their characteristics include the following: facial skeletons relatively orthognathic, dentitions of moderate size, frontal bones very curved, bregmatic eminence not present, and maximum parietal breadths not located in an inferior position.

The undated WLH-50 calvaria (Flood 1983; Thorne 1984; Stringer & Andrews 1988; Wolpoff 1991), recovered from a deflating land surface in the Garnpung/Laghur Lake region, has been argued to be morphologically intermediate between middle Pleistocene Indonesian hominids and late Pleistocene Australians (Stringer & Andrews 1988; Wolpoff 1991). Features cited in support of this include the thickness of the vault, morphology of the frontal, inion prominence, occipital torus morphology and position of maximum cranial breadth. Vault thickness in WLH-50 does not comply with the pattern in Asian *H. erectus* or early *H. sapiens*. In these middle-late Pleistocene hominids the vaults are preferentially thickened at the parietal eminence and asterion but not particularly thick elsewhere (Brown 1992c). WLH-50 is uniformly thick (Brown 1989), with extremely thin tabular bone and greatly expanded diploë, and without preferential thickening basally or at the parietal eminence. Both Brown (1989) and Webb (1990) have suggested that vault thickness in WLH-50 is pathological. Other unusual aspects of WLH-50 are its extreme size and parietal curvature, with maximum cranial breadth in a basal position. Overall cranial shape has little in common with Ngandong. The vault is long, but also extremely high and supraorbital development is minimal for an Aboriginal cranium of this size. The morphology of the inion, lambdoid and occipital torus regions are not unusual for an Aboriginal male cranium and are unlike Ngandong.

(b) East Asia

The Zhoukoudian Upper Cave crania were briefly described by Weidenreich (1939) prior to being lost, along with the Locality 1 *Homo erectus* materials, in 1941. Fortunately good quality casts were made of the originals and these have been widely studied ever since (Kaminga & Wright 1988). Weidenreich's description of the Upper Cave crania, 101, 102 and 103, concentrated on determining their racial affinities. The male cranium 101 was argued to have European Upper Palaeolithic features, the female 102 supposedly resembled an artificially deformed Melanesian, and the female 103 an Eskimo. Weidenreich's (1939) interpretation of the racial affinities of the Upper Cave crania was challenged by Wu (1960, 1961) who, after correcting Weidenreich's assignment of the 104 mandible to the 102 cranium, could find no reason to exclude them from the 'Mongoloids'.

More recently a principal components analysis involving 33 dimensions and a comparative sample of 26 recent human populations concluded that there is 'nothing especially Mongoloid about the 101 cranium in terms of its shape' (Kaminga & Wright 1988: 751). Interpretation of the principal components indicated that Upper Cave 101 did not have the Mongoloid characteristics of relatively great cranial height, cheek height and orbital height, as well as having a vault which was too long and a frontal which was too broad (table 2). The distinctions they draw are correct but rather than indicating that 101 is not a 'Mongoloid' it just indicates that 101 is not a modern 'Mongoloid'. The metrical and morphological features which distinguish 101 from mid-Holocene and recent Chinese crania are similar to those which distinguish terminal Pleistocene and mid-Holocene crania in other parts of the world. Terminal Pleistocene crania tend to be longer, with great supraorbital breadth, low rectangular orbits, deeper facial skeletons which are generally more prognathic and have larger dentitions than their mid-Holocene counterparts (tables 1 and 2, Figures 1 and 2). The remarkable thing about Upper Cave 101 is that it goes against the normal terminal Pleistocene pattern with facial prognathism, and presumably palate and tooth dimensions, which are close to the modern Chinese mean (figure 2). Whatever has been selecting for 'Mongoloid' facial characteristics appears to have been doing so for a long period of time.

The remaining East Asian specimen to be considered is Liujiang (Wu 1959; Wu & Zhang 1985). Liujiang has been described as having a mixture of 'Mongoloid' and 'Australoid' characters, with 'Australoid' perhaps best interpreted as a synonym for greater than average robusticity. Compared with modern southern Chinese male crania Liujiang has a vault which is long and low, a short and broad face with low rectangular orbits and a low frontal angle (table 2). Alveolar dimensions, tooth size, nasal breadth and vault thickness dimensions all fall close to the modern male mean. The supraorbital region has a glabella and superciliary ridges which are prominent relative to modern Chinese and there is a pronounced occipital bun. 'Mongoloid characteristics' include a shovel shaped central incisor, shallow prenasal fossa, congenitally absent third molars and an anterolateral surface of the frontal process which is rotated forwards (Wu and Zhang 1985).

Table 2. *Comparison of orofacial and cranial dimensions of male modern southern and northern Chinese using Student's t-test and values for Upper Cave 101, Liujiang and a combined mid-Holocene sample (mm)*

	South China[a]			North China[b]			101	Liujiang	Mid-Holocene[c]
	n	x̄	s.d.	n	x̄	s.d.			x̄
cranial length	38	181.7	7.5	37	175.5[d]	5.7	204	191	181.6
cranial height	38	141.1	5.0	37	136.2[d]	3.9	136	135	142.1
endocranial volume/ml	37	1499.7	130.5	37	1369.7[d]	94.9	1500	1540	1510.0
supraorbital breadth	39	104.6	4.0	37	102.4[d]	3.5	108	106	—
thickness at bregma	38	7.6	1.4	37	6.4[d]	1.3	—	7	—
frontal angle/deg.	38	137.1	4.9	37	136.4	4.6	—	129	—
occipital angle/deg.	39	117.4	3.6	36	119.2	9.6	109	122	—
bi-zygion	38	133.4	4.9	36	131.8	4.8	143	(134)	135.6
nasion-nasospinale	39	54.0	3.4	37	55.1	2.7	58	46	53.8
nasospinale-prosthion	35	19.4	2.4	35	18.7	2.2	18	20	19.0
nasal breadth	38	26.1	2.1	37	25.2	2.1	32	25	27.4
orbital height	39	33.7	2.1	37	36.2[e]	1.9	34	27	33.2
orbital breadth	39	40.3	1.9	37	40.3	1.7	45	41	42.5
alveolar length	34	53.2	2.9	34	51.4[d]	3.2	57	54	—
symphyseal height	36	35.1	3.1	34	33.7[d]	2.6	—	—	34.4

[a] Collection of Department of Anatomy, University of Hong Kong.
[b] Collection of I.V.P.P., Beijing.
[c] Mid-Holocene mean calculated from Neolithic data in Wu & Zhang (1985) with deformed crania excluded.
[d] Mean value significantly less than southern Chinese mean, $p < 0.05$.
[e] Mean value which is significantly greater than South China mean, $p < 0.05$.

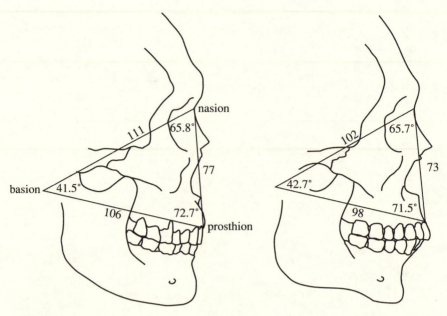

Figure 2. Comparison of facial dimensions (mm) in Upper Cave 101 (left) with the modern southern Chinese male mean.

The major area of uncertainty surrounding Liujiang is not its 'Mongoloid' morphology, which seems fairly uncontroversial, but its age. Multivariate comparisons (direct discriminant analysis and cluster analysis) of Liujiang with modern northern and southern Chinese males, Neolithic males and Upper Cave 101 will, depending upon which variables are selected, link Liujiang most closely with the southern Chinese or Neolithic samples. Upper Cave 101 is invariably at a greater distance from the modern and Neolithic samples than Liujiang. Features which suggest an early Holocene, or terminal Pleistocene, age for Liujiang are the relatively great length of the cranium, prominent occipital bun, low cranial height relative to cranial length, and low and rectangular orbits. Features which appear inconsistent with a date of 67 ka BP, particularly if Liujiang is a male, are the relatively small facial height, minimal alveolar and tooth dimensions, low orbits, and a supraorbital and occipital torus development which would be slight for a late Pleistocene female.

4. CONCLUSION

In both East Asia and Australasia the skeletal remains of terminal Pleistocene *H. sapiens* have morphological and metrical features which leave little doubt that they are ancestral to people living in the same regions during the mid to late Holocene. In other words there is clear evolutionary continuity during the Holocene. The available skeletal materials from both East Asia and Australia are, however, too limited to extend this evolutionary continuity back to the middle Pleistocene. There are a common set of features which distinguish terminal Pleistocene *H. sapiens* from their mid-Holocene counterparts in most parts of the world. These features are not as evident in the East Asian terminal Pleistocene remains, but the sample is extremely small. Post-Pleistocene reductions in dental and skeletal mass, and associated changes in craniofacial morphology, should be taken into consideration when the evidence for regional evolutionary continuity is examined. The earliest directly dated example of modern *Homo sapiens* from the East Asian and Australasian regions, which has not been the subject of dispute, is Lake Mungo I dated to 24 000 ka BP.

ACKNOWLEDGMENTS

I would like to thank Dr C. Stringer and the Royal Society for inviting me to contribute to the Discussion Meeting on the origin of modern humans and the impact of chronometric dating. The following individuals and institutions granted me access to human skeletal materials in their care. Dr N. Jablonski, formerly Department of Anatomy, University of Hong Kong; Mr G. Pretty, South Australian Museum; Mr P. Gordon, Australian Museum; Dr R. Vanderwal, Museum of Victoria; Dr A. Thorne, Australian National University; the late Professor L. Ray, Professor G. Ryan and Dr G. Kenny of the Department of Anatomy, University of Melbourne and Professor Wu Xinzhi, Associate Professor Dong Xingren and Associate Professor Wu Maolin of the Institute of Vertebrate Paleontology and Paleoanthropology, Academia Sinica. Without their help this research would not have been possible.

REFERENCES

Birdsell, J.B. 1967 Preliminary data on the trihybrid origin of the Australian Aborigines. *Arch. Phys. Anthropol. Oceania* **2**, 100–155.

Bowler, J.M., Jones, R., Allen, H. & Thorne, A.G. 1970 Pleistocene human remains from Australia: a living site and human cremation from Lake Mungo, western New South Wales. *World Archaeol.* **2**, 39–60.

Bowler, J.M. & Thorne, A.G. 1976 Human remains from Lake Mungo: Discovery and excavation of Lake Mungo III. In *The Origin of the Australians* (ed. R. L. Kirk & A. G. Thorne), pp. 127–138. Canberra: Australian Institute of Aboriginal Studies.

Bowler, J.M., Thorne, A.G. & Polach, H. 1972 Pleistocene man in Australia: age and significance of the Mungo skeleton. *Nature, Lond.* **240**, 48–50.

Brace, C.L. & Mahler, P.E. 1971 Post-Pleistocene changes in the human dentition. *Am. J. phys. Anthrop.* **34**, 191–204.

230 • P. Brown

Brace, C.L., Shae, X.-Q. & Zhang, Z.-B. 1984 Prehistoric and modern tooth size in China. In *The origins of modern humans* (ed. F. H. Smith & F. Spencer), pp. 485–516. New York: Alan R. Liss.

Bräuer, G. 1989 The evolution of modern humans: a comparison of the African and non-African evidence. In *The human revolution: behavioural and biological perspectives on the origins of modern humans* (ed. P. Mellars & C. Stringer), pp. 123–155. Princeton University Press.

Brothwell, D. 1975 Possible evidence of a cultural practise affecting head growth in some late Pleistocene East Asian and Australasian populations. *J. archeol. Sci.* **2**, 75–77.

Brothwell, D.R. 1960 Upper Pleistocene Human Skull from Niah Caves. *Sarawak Mus. J.* **9**, 323–349.

Brown, P. 1981 Artificial cranial deformation: a component in the variation in Pleistocene Australian Aboriginal crania. *Archaeol. Oceania* **16**, 156–167.

Brown, P. 1987 Pleistocene homogeneity and Holocene size reduction: the Australian human skeletal evidence. *Archaeol. Oceania* **22**, 41–71.

Brown, P. 1989 *Coobool Creek: A morphological and metrical analysis of the crania, mandibles and dentitions of a prehistoric Australian human population.* Terra Australis 13. Canberra: Department of Prehistory, Australian National University.

Brown, P. 1992a Human skeletons. In *The Encyclopedia of Aboriginal Australia* (ed. D. Horton). Canberra: Australian Aboriginal Studies Press. (In the Press.)

Brown, P. 1992b Post-Pleistocene change in Australian Aboriginal tooth size: dental reduction or relative expansion? In *Human craniofacial variation in the Pacific* (ed. T. Brown & S. Molnar), pp. 33–52. Adelaide: University of Adelaide.

Brown, P. 1992c Cranial vault thickness in Asian *Homo erectus* and modern *Homo sapiens. Courier Forschungsinstitut Senckenberg.* (In the Press.)

Calcagno, J.M. 1986 Dental reduction in Post-Pleistocene Nubia. *Am. J. phys. Anthrop.* **70**, 349–363.

Carlson, D.S. 1976 Temporal variation in prehistoric Nubian crania. *Am. J. phys. Anthrop.* **45**, 467–484.

Chen, T., Hedges, R.E.M. & Yuan, Z. 1989 Accelerator radiocarbon dating for the Upper Cave of Zhoukoudian. *Acta Anthrop. Sin.* **8**, 216–221.

Chen, T. & Zhang, Y. 1991 Palaeolithic chronology and possible coexistance of *Homo erectus* and *Homo sapiens* in China. *World Archaeol.* **23**, 147–154.

Coon, C.S. 1962 *The origin of races.* New York: Knopf.

Dubois, E. 1922 The proto-Australian fossil man of Wadjak, Java. *Koninklijke Akademie van Wetenschappen te Amsterdam.* **B23**, 1013–1051.

Flood, J. 1983 *Archaeology of the dreamtime.* Sydney: Collins.

Fox, R. 1970 *The Tabon Caves. Archaeological explorations and excavations on Palawan Island, Philippines.* Manila: National Museum of the Philippines.

Frayer, D.W. 1977 Metric dental changes in the European Upper Paleolithic and Mesolithic. *Am. J. phys. Anthrop.* **46**, 109–120.

Frayer, D.W. 1984 Biological and cultural change in the European late Pleistocene and early Holocene. In *The origin of modern humans* (ed. F. H. Smith & F. Spencer), pp. 211–250. New York: Alan R. Liss.

Groves, C.P. 1989 A regional approach to the problem of the origin of modern humans in Australasia. In *The human revolution* (ed. P. Mellars & C. Stringer), pp. 274–285. Princeton University Press.

Habgood, P.J. 1986 The origin of the Australians: a multivariate approach. *Archaeol. Oceania* **21**, 130–137.

Hedges, R.E.M., Housley, R.A., Law, I.A., Perry, C. & Hendy, E. 1988 Radiocarbon Dates from the Oxford AMS System: *Archaeometry* Datelist 8. *Archaeometry* **30**, 291–305.

Hedges, R.E.M., Housley, R.A., Bronk, C.R. & Van Klinken 1992 Radiocarbon dates from the Oxford AMS system: *Archaeometry* Datelist 14. *Archaeometry* **34**, 141–159.

Hiscock, P. 1990 How old are the artefacts in Malakunanja II? *Archaeol. Oceania* **25**, 122–124.

Kaminga, J. & Wright, R.V.S. 1988 The Upper Cave at Zhoukoudian and the origins of the Mongoloids. *J. hum. Evol.* **17**, 739–767.

Kennedy, K.A.R. 1977 The deep skull of Niah: An assessment of twenty years of speculation concerning its evolutionary significance. *Asian Perspect.* **20**, 32–50.

Klaatsch, H. 1908 The skull of the Australian Aboriginal. *Rep. Path. Lab. Lunacy Dept., New South Wales* **1**, 43–167.

Li, Y., Brace, C.L., Gao, Q. & Tracer, D.P. 1991 Dimensions of Face in Asia in the Perspective of Geography and Prehistory. *Am. J. phys. Anthrop.* **85**, 269–279.

Macintosh, N.W.G. 1963 Origin and physical differentiation of the Australian Aborigines. *Aust. Nat. Hist.* **14**, 248–252.

Macintosh, N.W.G. 1978 The Tabon Cave mandible. *Arch Phys. Anthrop. Oceania.* **13**, 143–159.

Oakley, K.P., Campbell, B.G. & Molleson, T.I. 1975 *Catalogue of fossil hominids.* London: British Museum of Natural History.

Pardoe, C. 1991 Competing paradigms and ancient human remains: the state of the discipline. *Archaeol. Oceania* **26**, 79–85.

Pearce, R.H. & Barbetti, M. 1981 A 38,000-year-old archaeological site at Upper Swan, Western Australia. *Archaeol. Oceania* **16**, 173–78.

Pei, W. 1935 A preliminary report on the Late Palaeolithic Cave of Choukoutien. *Bull. Geol. Soc. China* **13**, 327–358.

Pei, W. 1939 On the Upper Cave Industry. *Palaeont. Sin* **D9**, 1–141.

Pietrusewsky, M. 1984 Metric and non-metric cranial variation in Australian Aboriginal populations compared with populations from the Pacific and Asia. *Occ. Papers Hum. Biol.* **3**, 1–113.

Roberts, R.G., Jones, R. & Smith, M.A. 1990a Thermoluminesence dating of 50,000 year-old human occupation site in northern Australia. *Nature, Lond.* **345**, 153–156.

Roberts, R.G., Jones, R. & Smith, M.A. 1990b Stratigraphy and statistics at Malakunanja II: reply to Hiscock. *Archaeol. Oceania* **25**, 125–129.

Santa Luca, A.P. 1980 *The Ngandong fossil hominids.* New Haven: Department of Anthropology Yale University.

Smith, P. 1982 Dental reduction: Selection or drift? In *Teeth: form, function, and evolution* (ed. B. Kurten), pp. 366–379. New York: Columbia University Press.

Smith, P., Wax, Y., Adler, F., Silberman, D. & Heinic, G. 1986 Post-Pleistocene changes in tooth root and jaw relationships. *Am. J. phys. Anthrop.* **70**, 339–348.

Stringer, C.B. & Andrews, P. 1988 Genetic and fossil evidence for the origin of modern humans. *Science, Wash.* **239**, 1263–1268.

Theunissen, B., De Vos, J., Sondaar, P.Y. & Aziz, F. 1990 The establishment of a chronological framework for the hominid-bearing deposits of Java; A historical survey. In *Establishment of a geologic framework for paleoanthropology* (ed. L. F. Laporte), pp. 39–54. Boulder: Geological Society of America.

Thorne, A.G. 1975 Kow Swamp and Lake Mingo. Ph.D. thesis, University of Sydney.

Thorne, A.G. 1976 *Morphological contrasts in Pleistocene Australians*. Canberra: Australian Institute of Aboriginal Studies.

Thorne, A.G. 1977 Separation or reconciliation? Biological clues to the development of Australian society. In *Sunda and Sahul* (ed. J. Allen, J. Golson & R. Jones), pp. 187–204. London: Academic Press.

Thorne, A.G. 1984 Australias human origins—how many sources? *Am. J. phys. Anthrop.* **63,** 227.

Thorne, A.G. & Macumber, P.G. 1972 Discoveries of Late Pleistocene man at Kow Swamp. *Nature, Lond.* **238**, 316–319.

Thorne, A.G. & Wolpoff, M.H. 1981 Regional continuity in Australasian Pleistocene hominid evolution. *Am. J. phys. Anthrop.* **55**, 337–349.

Wang, L. 1986 Secular change and geographic variation in Chinese Neolithic and modern inhabitants: a statistical study of cranial metric traits. *Acta Anthrop. Sin.* **5**, 243–258.

Webb, S. 1989 *The Willandra Lakes Hominids*. Canberra: Department of Prehistory, Australian National University.

Webb, S. 1990 Cranial thickening in an Australian hominid as a possible palaeo-epidemiological indicator. *Am. J. phys. Anthrop.* **82**, 403–412.

Weidenreich, F. 1939a On the earliest representatives of modern mankind recovered on the soil of East Asia. *Bull. Nat. Hist. Soc. Peking.* **13**, 161–174.

Weidenreich, F. 1939b Six lectures on Sinanthropus and related problems. *Bull. Geol. Soc. China.* **19**, 1–110.

Weidenreich, F. 1943 The skull of *Sinanthropus pekinensis*: a comparative study of a primitive hominid skull. *Palaeont. Sin.* **D10**, 1–485.

Weidenreich, F. 1945 The Keilor skull: a Wadjak type from south-east Australia. *Am. J. phys. Anthrop.* **3**, 225–236.

Weidenreich, F. 1946 *Apes, giants, and man*. Chicago University Press.

Wolpoff, M.H. 1980 *Paleoanthropology.* New York: Alfred A. Knopf.

Wolpoff, M.H. 1991 Theories of Modern Human Origins. In *Continuity or replacement? Controversies in Homo sapiens evolution* (ed. G. Bräuer & F. H. Smith), Rotterdam: A. A. Balkema.

Wolpoff, M.H., Wu, X.-Z. & Thorne, A.G. 1984 Modern *Homo sapiens* origins: a general theory of hominid evolution involving the fossil evidence from east Asia. In *The origins of modern humans* (ed. F. H. Smith & F. Spencer), pp. 411–484. New York: Alan R. Liss.

Wu, R. 1959 Human fossils found in Liukiang, Kwangsi, China. *Gu Jizhuidongwu yu Gu Renlei* **1**, 97–104.

Wu, X. 1960 On the racial type of Upper Cave Man of Choukoutien. *Gu Jizhuidongwu yu Gu Renlei* **2**, 141–149.

Wu, X. 1961 Study of the Upper Cave Man of Choukoutien. *Verteb. Palasiat.* **3**, 181–211.

Wu, X. 1981 A well-preserved cranium of an archaic type of early *Homo sapiens* from Dali, China. *Scientia Sin.* **24**, 530–539.

Wu, X. 1988a The relationship between upper Palaeolithic human fossils of China and Japan. *Acta Anthrop. Sin.* **7**, 235–238.

Wu, X. 1988b Comparative study of early *Homo sapiens* from China and Europe. *Acta Anthrop. Sin.* **7**, 292–299.

Wu, X. 1990 The evolution of humankind in China. *Acta Anthrop. Sin.* **9**, 312–322.

Wu, X. & Wang, L. 1985 Chronology in Chinese Palaeoanthropology. In *Palaeoanthropology and palaeolithic archaeology in the People's Republic of China* (ed. R. Wu & J. W. Olsen), pp. 29–68. London: Academic Press.

Wu, X. & Zhang, Z. 1985 *Homo sapiens* remains from Late Palaeolithic and Neolithic China. In *Palaeoanthropology and palaeolithic archaeology in the People's Republic of China* (ed. R. Wu & J. W. Olsen), pp. 107–133. London: Academic Press.

Wunderly, J. 1943 The Kilor fossil skull: anatomical description. *Mem. Nat. Mus. Victoria.* **13**, 57–69.

Zhang, Z., Wang, L. & Ouyang, L. 1982 Physical patterns of Neolithic skulls in China in view of cluster analysis. *Verteb. Palasiat.* **20**, 72–80.

Models and Realities in Modern Human Origins:
The African Fossil Evidence

Fred H. Smith[1]

SUMMARY

The recent application of such chronometric techniques as electron spin resonance (ESR), thermoluminescence (TL), and uranium series dating has had a significant impact on perceptions of modern human origins. Claims for the presence of anatomically modern humans in Africa prior to 100 ka and for the transition leading to modern Africans at an even earlier date have been made, partly based on results of these techniques. However, a careful examination of the pertinent record shows that these claims are not unequivocally supported by the available fossil and chronological evidence.

1. INTRODUCTION

The concept of a recent African origin for all modern people represents nothing less than a revolution in our perception of late Pleistocene human evolution and the pattern of modern human origins. A scant 30 years ago, Coon (1962) was able to argue that Africa south of the Sahara (southern Africa) was one of the final regions of the Old World to witness the emergence of modern people from their indigenous archaic forerunners. The basic reason Coon could support such a claim was an erroneous chronological framework for the southern African Middle Stone Age (MSA), which placed the emergence of the MSA from the Final Acheulean (or 'First Intermediate') at roughly 40 ka BP (Clark 1970). Consequently, relatively primitive and somewhat *Homo erectus*-like hominids, such as Kabwe 1 (Broken Hill), which derived from late or Final Acheulean cultural contexts, appeared to inhabit southern Africa long after similar hominids disappeared in Eurasia. As recently as 1970, implications arising from these factors also led the eminent Africanist J. Desmond Clark to suggest that archaic humans in southern Africa were suddenly and relatively recently replaced by invading modern humans who had emerged in some other region of the Old World (Clark 1970).

The African revolution began not with new human fossil or archaeological discoveries, but rather with chronometric dating evidence supporting a greater antiquity for the MSA. In 1969, a uranium–thorium date of 130 ka was derived from *Etheria* shell associated with a partial human skeleton

[1] Department of Anthropology, Northern Illinois University, DeKalb, Illinois, 60115, U.S.A.

(Omo 1) from the KHS site in the Kibish Formation at Omo (Butzer *et al.* 1969). Only 3 years later, publication of a series of conventional radiocarbon dates from a number of key South African sites, including Border Cave and Die Kelders, indicated that the MSA ended, not began, about 30–40 ka BP (Vogel & Beaumont 1972). By the mid-1970s, amino acid racemization provided a date of 125 ka for the MSA at the Klasies River Mouth Caves (Klein 1973), and potassium–argon dates from the Gademotta Formation in Ethiopia indicated that MSA components could be as old as *ca.* 180 ka (Wendorf *et al.* 1975). In addition, Butzer argued that MSA components from several South African sites could be correlated to oxygen isotope stage 6, dated to between 127 ka and 195 ka ago (Butzer *et al.* 1978). Therefore, because modern human remains were presumably associated with MSA deposits, particularly at the sites of Border Cave and Omo KHS, initial arguments began to surface in the late 1970s postulating that the earliest appearance of modern humans was in southern Africa.

Compared to these initial attempts, present-day palaeontological models supporting an African origin of modern humans are based on much more accurate assessments of the fossil record (Bräuer 1984, 1989, 1992; Rightmire 1984, 1986, 1989; Rightmire & Deacon 1991; Stringer 1989, 1990; Stringer & Andrews 1988). However, there is nothing inherent in the pertinent African fossil record itself which identifies Africa as the source for all modern people. There are no unequivocal regional or clade features which demonstrate in a cladistic sense an African influence on early modern Eurasians (Smith 1992; Wolpoff 1989, 1992). The similarity of early Europeans or Asians to early modern Africans is a phenetic one, involving overall cranial form, facial and dental reduction, and changes in postcranial robusticity (Howells 1989; Smith et al. 1989). Thus the key to demonstrating palaeontological accuracy of African origin models is still the chronology. Africa must be shown to have the earliest evidence of a transition in the direction of the modern human anatomical pattern and, ideally, the earliest evidence of the appearance of that pattern. As Deacon (1989, p. 547) has so clearly stated: 'The plausibility of the interpretation of an African centre of origin for anatomically modern peoples . . . rests on the precision with which the archaeological evidence can be dated and with which the context of the finds can be established.' Thus the catalyst and core of this African revolution has always been a chronological revolution based on results of the application of 'science-based dating' to the palaeoanthropological record, rather than major new insights into the record itself.

2. THE EVIDENCE FOR AN AFRICAN TRANSITION: A CRITICAL ASSESSMENT

Documenting an African transition to modern humans depends, first of all, on the identification of a hominid sample intermediate in both morphology and date between archaic specimens such as Kabwe, Bodo, or Ndutu (hereafter referred to as the Kabwe group) and unequivocally modern Africans. Many palaeoanthropologists recognize the specimens listed in table 1 as fulfilling both these criteria, and I agree that the morphological pattern of these specimens is commensurate with this interpretation. There are, however, some limitations inherent in this sample. First, it should be noted that these few sites and specimens are extremely widely dispersed in Africa (from Morocco to South Africa). Consequently, there are no respectable samples sizes for any sub-region of Africa, and the possible effects of regional variability or sexual dimorphism cannot be effectively evaluated. Second, the material is rather fragmentary and incomplete. For example, except for the juvenile Jebel Irhoud mandible and humerus (Hublin *et al.* 1987; Hublin & Tillier 1981), there are no mandibles or postcranial remains known for this sample. Furthermore, two of the four specimens with faces (Florisbad and Ngaloba) have at best limited contact between their facial and neurocranial portions, making assessment of craniofacial relationships (e.g. prognathism) very difficult. Additionally, much of the facial structure of both Ngaloba and Florisbad must be reconstructed, and no informative teeth are known for any of these specimens (except for the Jebel Irhoud 3 mandible).

Third and finally, contextual problems are present at four of the five sites. Eliye Springs (Kenya) and Omo 2 (from site PHS in the Kibish Formation) may fit morphologically into this group, but both are surface finds and lack primary geological contexts. Omo 2 is probably from member 1 of the Kibish Formation, but its exact stratigraphic context cannot be determined with certainty (Butzer 1969). Of the Jebel Irhoud specimens, only the juvenile humerus (Jebel Irhoud 4) was recovered in an accurate stratigraphical and archaeological context (Hublin *et al.* 1987). The other specimens were found close to the cave floor, in association with Mousterian artifacts. Although it is not unreasonable to believe that Jebel Irhoud 1–3 probably derive from the same deposit as the humerus, this cannot be conclusively demonstrated at the present time. The Florisbad specimen was recovered from the eye of an old spring, at the level of an organic deposit known as Peat 1, associated with MSA artifacts and fauna (Clarke 1985). However, as the specimen was found in a debris-cone of the spring eye, it may be derived from a stratigraphically higher, and younger, level than Peat 1 (but see Kuman 1989).

In contrast, the Ngaloba (Laetoli hominid 18) specimen was excavated in direct association with MSA artifacts and fauna. The deposits from which the cranium comes are dated to 129 ± 4 ka and 108 ± 30 ka by uranium–thorium analysis applied to a giraffe vertebra (Hay 1987) and to 120 ± 30 ka based on a geological correlation to the Ndutu Beds at Olduvai (Magori & Day 1983). Grün & Stringer (1991) have suggested that the Jebel Irhoud 1–

Table 1. *The African transitional group*

site (country)	archaeological association	age estimate	basis of estimate	hominid specimens
Jebel Irhoud (Morocco)[a]	Mousterian	130–190 ka	ESR	two crania (one with face), juvenile mandible, juvenile humerus
Eliye Springs (Kenya)[a]	—	—	—	cranium with damaged face
Florisbad (South Africa)[a]	Middle Stone Age	> 100 ka	uranium series	anterior cranium with fragmentary face
Ngaloba (Tanzania)	Middle Stone Age	129 + 4 ka 108 + 30 ka	uranium–thorium	cranium with face
Omo (Ethiopia)[a]	—	—	—	cranium (no face)

[a] Indicates contextual uncertainty. Eliye Springs and Omo are surface finds. The stratigraphic positions of Jebel Irhoud and Florisbad are not certain. See text for further discussion.

3 specimens might belong to oxygen isotope stage 6 (130–190 ka), based on extrapolation from a series of ESR dates. Also, Clarke (1985) has argued that preliminary uranium series results from Florisbad support an age of more than 100 ka for Peat 1 (see also Kuman & Clarke 1986).

If Florisbad does come from Peat 1 and the Jebel Irhoud specimens are from oxygen isotope stage 6, they could be considered to date between roughly 100 ka and 200 ka. The same may be true for Ngoloba, which would appear to be the most securely dated specimen since it is associated with uranium series dates. Unfortunately, uranium–thorium dates on bone can be unreliable due to problems of diagenesis (Parkes 1986; Aitken 1990). Thus, whereas discussions of this African transitional group often imply that dating of the specimens in the sample solidly establishes an age of 100 ka to 200 ka for them, the fact is that all of these age estimates are problematic to some extent. All of the specimens in this sample could be either younger or older than this time span.

Because of its secure contextual position and associations, the Ngaloba cranium is particularly critical to the validation of an African transitional group. Compared with Kabwe, Ngaloba certainly exhibits considerable facial size reduction. For example, if the estimated upper facial height of Ngaloba is scaled to minimum frontal breadth (UFH/MFB × 100), the resulting value of 80 is 11.6% lower than the 90.5 value for Kabwe and 12.6% lower than the 91.5 value for Bodo. Ngaloba also exhibits a rather horizontal inferior zygomaxillary margin, which almost forms a right angle with the lateral aspect of the alveolar process. A canine fossa is also present. In all of these morphological attributes, Ngaloba is more similar to the modern human pattern than are the more complete faces of the Kabwe group. However, the more fragmentary (possibly female) faces of Kabwe 2 and Ndutu may also exhibit these 'transitional' features.

Other aspects of Ngaloba are more archaic. For example, the specimen preserves a well-developed, continuous supraorbital torus; and despite the fact that torus dimensions are markedly reduced compared to Kabwe or Bodo, the supraorbital morphology is clearly archaic. Furthermore, the cranial vault of Ngaloba is rather low, with a frontal bone far more similar to Kabwe than to more modern Africans according to multivariate analyses by Bräuer (1984) and Simmons & Smith (1991). According to Bräuer's studies (1984), however, the form of Ngaloba's parietals and occipital are more modern like. The mosaic of features exhibited by this specimen, as well as its possible date, make it an excellent transitional specimen between more primitive and more modern African hominids (Bräuer 1984, 1989; Rightmire 1984, 1989; Smith 1985; Smith et al. 1989).

Both Florisbad and Jebel Irhoud I share facial morphology and a pattern of facial reduction similar to Ngaloba. For example, the upper facial index (UFH/MFB × 100) for Jebel Irhoud I is 69 and for Florisbad (reconstructed) is 67. Size of the supraorbital torus also reduces in the Florisbad and Jebel Irhoud specimens compared to the Kabwe group, but both specimens retain a true supraorbital torus. The pattern of reduction in Florisbad is rather even across the torus, a pattern characteristic of African hominids, however Jebel Irhoud 1 and 2 exhibit a torus shape more like that documented in Europe (Smith 1992). The cranial vaults of Florisbad and Jebel Irhoud 1 are also relatively more archaic than the face, mirroring the mosaic pattern in Ngoloba. Given the morphological pattern of Ngaloba, Florisbad and Jebel Irhoud and the possibility of ages on the order of 100 ka or more for them, I have tended to accept them as *bona fide* members of an African transitional group (Smith 1985, 1992; Smith *et al.* 1989). However, the uncertainties regarding their geological ages are cause for considerable caution.

For Africa to be considered the anatomical point of origin for all modern people, the African transition must be documented to have occurred before any possible indications of transition from other regions of the Old World. Evidence of transitional samples between *Homo erectus* or archaic *Homo sapiens* on the one hand and modern humans on the other has been presented for Central Europe, Australasia, western Asia, and East Asia (Kramer 1991; Pope 1988, 1991; Smith 1985, 1992; Smith *et al.* 1989; Wolpoff 1989, 1992; Wolpoff *et al.* 1984). In Central Europe, the transitional late Neanderthals would appear to post-date the African transitional group by several tens-of-thousands of years (Smith *et al.* 1989). The Skhul–Qafzeh sample from the Near East is about 100 ka old, assuming the recent ESR and TL dating of the western Asian sites is accurate (Grün & Stringer 1991). These hominids do exhibit some features that can be interpreted as transitional (Corrucini 1992; Kidder *et al.* 1992; Simmons *et al.* 1991; Wolpoff 1989), but their total morphological pattern is commensurate with what one would expect in early modern populations. However, the absence of a West Asian morphologically transitional sample, comparable to the African one, makes it difficult to establish whether the Skhul–Qafzeh people are derived from West Asian archaic humans or from archaic humans from some other region (*cf.* Stringer 1988*a,b*).

In East Asia and Australasia, the relatively meager published fossil record of archaic and early modern *Homo sapiens* and the lack of precise dating for the Chinese post-*erectus* specimens and key Australasian specimens (Willandra Lakes, Ngandong) makes it very difficult to construct a clear picture of the details of modern human origins in these regions (*cf.* Smith *et al.* 1989). Although there is reasonable evidence of morphological continuity extending from *Homo erectus* through archaic (when available) to modern *Homo sapiens* in both regions (Habgood 1989*a,b*, 1992; Kramer 1991; Pope 1988, 1991; Wolpoff 1992; Wolpoff *et al.* 1984), gaps in the fossil record and uncertain dating make it difficult to establish a precise age framework for the transition in either of these regions. In China, however, specimens such as Dali exhibit a pattern of facial morphology and reduction that is quite similar to the African transitional group and may date to approximately the same time span (*cf.* Pope 1991, Wolpoff 1992, Wu & Wu 1985).

It would appear that the transition in Africa was under way while Neanderthals still inhabited Europe and western Asia. But if a pattern similar to that in Africa is also occuring in China during the same time frame, the palaeontological argument for a uniquely African derivation of the modern human anatomical pattern would be severely compromised. Furthermore, the uncertainties in the dating of the members of the African Transitional group preclude dogmatic assertions regarding precisely when the the transition was in full swing in that part of the world. Such secure assertions must await sounder, probably direct, dating of the specimens listed in table 1 or the recovery of additional data.

3. The Earliest Modern Africans: Some Problems

Arguments for considerable antiquity of the modern human anatomical pattern have a long history in palaeoanthropology (*cf.* Bräuer 1984). The modern versions of these arguments began to develop in the 1970s, based primarily on claims that the human remains from Omo Kibish site KHS and Border Cave were very old and fundamentally modern. The Omo 1 and Border Cave 1 crania are fragmentary but do seemingly conform to a modern human morphological pattern, as do the three mandibles and postcranial fragments from these sites (Beaumont *et al.* 1978; Bräuer 1984, 1989, 1992; Day & Stringer 1982; Howell 1978; Rightmire 1979, 1984, 1989; Smith 1985; Smith *et al.* 1989; Stringer 1988*b*, 1989; Stringer & Andrews 1988). These specimens also exhibit some archaic-reminiscent features in terms of their overall cranial metric pattern (Corruccini 1992, Van Vark *et al.* 1989) and brow ridge morphology (Smith 1992), but such reflections of their pre-modern ancestry are to be expected in early representatives of modern people.

Unfortunately, although the morphology of these remains is not open to serious question, the geological ages claimed for the adult remains from both sites are very questionable. The Omo 1 skeleton was found partially *in situ* in number 1 of the Kibish formation. This level was dated to 130 ka ago by uranium–thorium applied to mollusc shell (Day & Stringer 1982). However, shell-derived uranium–thorium dates are generally considered dubious (H. P. Schwarcz, personal communication). Errors usually involve underestimates of age because of uranium uptake into the shell (Aitken 1990) but it may be also possible that leaching might produce erroneously older ages (as is the case with bone). The associated fauna and a greater than 37 ka conventional radiocarbon date for the overlying member 3 deposits in the Kibish formation (Day & Stringer 1982) do indicate some antiquity for Omo 1, but it is impossible to confidently determine the precise antiquity of this specimen at the present time. Also, whereas the dating of the Border Cave archaeological stratigraphy is apparently reliable (Beaumont *et al.* 1978; Grün & Stringer 1991), the stratigraphic context of the Border Cave 1 cranium and Border Cave 2 mandible is uncertain as they were not recovered by controlled excavations. Even the Border Cave 5 mandible, apparently excavated *in situ*, appears to represent an intrusive element into its claimed level of origin, based on aspects of bone preservation (Klein 1983).

The stratigraphic context of the Klasies River Mouth (KRM) hominid fossils is not at issue. These specimens were recovered during controlled excavations, and the stratigraphic correlation between cave 1 and shelters 1a and 1b now seems clear (Deacon & Geleijnse 1988). All of the MSA associated hominids, except for two maxillary fragments, are from the SAS member (Rightmire & Deacon 1991). The SAS member is maximally 98–110 ka, based on uranium disequilibrium dating of the top of the immediately underlying LBS member (Deacon 1989). This is supported by linear uptake ESR dates of 94 ka and 88 ka for the base of the SAS member (Grün & Stringer 1991). The minimum age for the SAS member and KRM hominids is geologically determined to be *ca.* 60 ka (Deacon & Geleijnse 1988).

The hominid fossils from KRM consistently have been described as totally modern in morphology (Bräuer 1984, 1989, 1992; Rightmire 1984, 1989; Rightmire & Deacon 1991) except for the LAS maxillae, which will not be considered here. However, this impression may be misleading, as it would appear that interpretation of the KRM specimens has been strongly influenced by their supposed contemporaneity with the Border Cave and Omo 1 specimens. I, for one, have certainly been influenced in my assessments of the KRM specimens by lumping them with Border Cave and Omo 1 (Smith *et al.* 1989; see also Stringer 1988*b*). Thus, it is worthwhile to see how well the KRM sample, the only supposedly modern sample firmly dated to around 100 ka, conforms to a modern human pattern without the influence of the possibly younger Omo and Border Cave specimens.

The first important point is that the KRM material is very fragmentary, and sample size for most elements stands at one. There is a reasonable sample of mandibles ($n = 5$), four of which preserve symphyses. Upper facial morphology is revealed in only two specimens: a glabellar fragment of a frontal bone, also preserving the medial portion of the right supraorbital region (KRM 16425) and a massive left zygomatic (KRM 16651). A few isolated teeth, fragmentary postcranial elements, and cranial vault fragments complete the sample. A complete catalogue of the KRM hominids, except for teeth, is given by Rightmire & Deacon (1991, p. 137).

The KRM mandibles differ in several ways from the Vindija and Shan-

idar Neanderthals (Rightmire & Deacon 1991), which is certainly not surprising given the geographic distance between these samples. The KRM
mandibles are smaller overall; but when one excludes the aberrantly small
KRM 16424 specimen, the size difference between the KRM and Vindija
sample is not impressive. Based on their symphyseal region, I would argue
that the KRM sample is more primitive than Border Cave 2 and 5 or more
recent Africans. Of the four KRM mandibles preserving the symphysis,
only one (KRM 41815) exhibits distinct mental eminence development;
and the damage to the alveolar process in the symphyseal region might
accentuate this development more than it would have been without the
damage. The KRM mandibles 13400, 14695 and 21776, as well as 41815,
are described an exhibiting moderate to clearly visible mental trigones and
eminences. Except for 41815, I would argue that both of these features are
at best only slightly more developed than in Vindija Neanderthal mandibles 206 and 231. Furthermore, I am not convinced that any recent African
samples would have 75% of their mandibles exhibiting the relatively
weakly developed mental eminences and mental trigones that characterize
the KRM sample. It would indeed be interesting to compare these mandibles to mandibles from the African transitional sample, for example from
specimens like Florisbad or Ngaloba. Unfortunately no mandibles are
known for these specimens, and this makes assessment of the KRM specimens more difficult. Clearly, the KRM mandibles are not Neanderthals.
Still, one wonders if the KRM mandibles are really very much more 'modern' in an African context than Vindija is in a European one.

The KRM zygomatic (16651) is an extremely interesting specimen. It
exhibits a rather horizontal inferior (zygomatico–alveolar) margin, which
differs from the more oblique margin in Neanderthals. However, this feature is also characteristic of the African transitional sample and thus is not
unique to modern Africans. Furthermore, this specimen's vertical cheek
height is virtually identical to Kabwe's and larger than Ngaloba's or Florisbad's. The KRM value lies 2.6 and more than 5 standard deviations above a
sample of definitely Holocene South Africans and a sample of Asian In-
dians respectively (table 2). Finally, the frontal process, which forms much
of the lateral orbital margin, is columnar-like (see figure 1). This is a condition typical for Neanderthals but rare in more recent humans (Smith 1976).
Indeed an examination of a large series of modern Asian Indian zygomatics
($n = 51$) failed to yield a single example comparable to the KRM specimens.

The frontal fragment (KRM 16425) certainly does not exhibit the level of
supraorbital projection of earlier African specimens, including Florisbad or
Ngaloba. Just medial to the supraorbital notch, the Klasies specimen measures 14 mm compared to 20 mm for Florisbad. However, there is an important question regarding KRM 16425 that has yet to be answered ade-

Table 2. *Horizontal height of the zygomatic (Martin no. 48 (3a)) in Pleistocene and Holocene Africans*

(Data courtesy of R. Caspari and M. Wolpoff.)

specimen or sample	M 48 (3a)
Klasies River Mouth 16651	> 30
Border Cave 1	20.5
Florisbad	24.1
Ngaloba	27.6
Holocene Cape Africans	
$(x, \sigma)^a$	22.5 (2.87)
Range (n)	15.9–28.2 (33)
Asian Indians	
$(x, \sigma)^b$	20.3 (1.97)
Range (n)	17.1–24.3 (51)

[a] These specimens are Cape Africans with secure context, dated to more than 4 ka BP.

[b] These specimens are located in the osteological collection of Northern Illinois University and were measured by the author.

quately (see also Stringer 1988*b*). Could KRM 16425 be an adolescent? This is important because adolescent Neanderthals, such as Le Moustier 1 or Vindija 224, do not exhibit the well-developed supraorbital tori of adult Neanderthals but their supraorbital morphology is clearly the ontogenetic precursor of the adult pattern. If KRM 16425 is an adolescent, then an adult of its population might have had more impressive supraorbital super-structures. KRM 16425 does appear to have respectable frontal sinus devel-opment, which might suggest adult status, but so too do the VI 224 and VI 279 adolescent Neanderthals. The point is that to date, a careful study demonstrating that the KRM frontal is definitely an adult has yet to be published. Even if it is adult, one could argue that KRM 16425 is a small, gracile female and that a male supraorbital might be considerably more robust.

Based on this assessment, it can be argued that the 100–60 ka KRM specimens are not demonstrably fully anatomically modern, as they have often been described. Rather, they may actually be closer morphologically to the African transitional group discussed previously. In reality the KRM sample by itself is too small and fragmentary to make any secure taxonomic assessment. Thus until such time that more complete specimens exhibiting a modern human pattern can be conclusively dated to this time span, dogmatic assertions that anatomically modern people are definitely found in southern Africa 100 ka ago are not palaeontologically supportable.

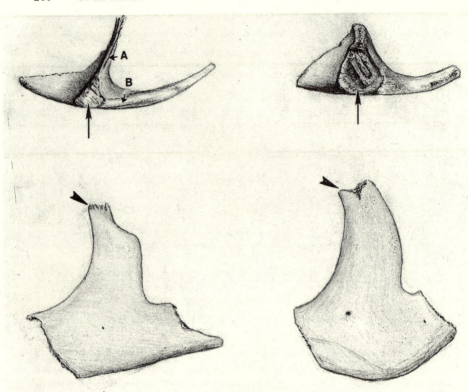

Figure 1. Facial and superior views of the KRM 16651 zygomatic (right) from Klasies River, compared with a recent human. The zygomatico-frontal suture, located at the top of the frontal process of the zygomatic, is indicated by the arrows in both the facial (below) and superior views of each specimen. In the recent human, note the smaller area of contact surface with the frontal and the presence of distinct orbital (A) and facial (B) plates converging at the contact surface. In the Klasies specimen, these plates are not apparent because of the expansion of the contact surface into a columnar lateral orbital margin. See text for further discussion.

4. A CONCLUDING PERSPECTIVE

It is not my claim in this paper that the human palaeontological evidence refutes an African origin model for the modern human morphological pattern. In fact, from a strictly morphological perspective, I regard the African transitional sample as providing the most impressive phenetic evidence available of the morphological shift between unequivocally archaic *Homo sapiens* and modern people. The chronological framework for this transition may not extend back as far as is often implied, but this does not detract from the elegance of the morphological picture. However, the argument that modern humans *senso stricto* appear earliest in Africa is equivocal given the available palaeontological evidence. At this point, we have no reliable chronological evidence that establishes exactly when anatomically modern people first appear in southern Africa.

Interestingly, if recent chronological data, based on ESR and TL determinations are accurate, the earliest definite evidence of early modern humans is the Skhul–Qafzeh sample from western Asia (Grün & Stringer 1991; Stringer 1988a). The lack of a convincing morphological sequence in western Asia may mean the Skhul–Qafzeh people do indeed represent migrants, possibly from Africa (cf. Stringer 1988b). To date, however, no studies have demonstrated any cladistic connection between Skhul–Qafzeh and African archaic or modern samples. Until this is done, it is unwise to simply assume an African origin for Skhul–Qafzeh, no matter how attractively this fits into any particular models. The phenetic similarity of Skhul–Qafzeh and possible early modern Africans (e.g. Border Cave 1 or Omo 1) cannot be used as proof of the former's African origin unless future work establishes unequivocally that this anatomical pattern appears earlier in Africa than in western Asia.

The pressure to make the African transition and appearance of earliest modern Africans as ancient as possible stems, in large part, from the desire to see the palaeontological data and some interpretations of recent human genetic variation as unequivocally mutually supporting an African origin for all modern people. This has led to a tendency to be less critical about the adequacy of the pertinent African fossil record to make this case than is probably prudent. Technically, of course, genetic arguments for an African origin of modern people do not require that the last common African ancestor of modern Eurasians be modern itself. An origin of the Skhul–Qafzeh people and other modern Eurasians from the African transitional sample would not run counter to the genetic African origin model, but such a connection has yet to be cladistically demonstrated. Still the desire to have a 'neat' genetic-fossil package has put considerable pressure on interpretation of the palaeontological record. Continued debate over the available African record is unlikely to resolve existing problems, at least not without some new chronological data. It is my hope that we will see both renewed efforts to directly date some of the critical specimens already known to science (e.g. Border Cave, Omo 1, Florisbad, Jebel Irhoud) and more attempts to recover and date additional specimens in reliable contexts (like those from Ngaloba and KRM). Until this happens, we need to be more cautious than we have been about the palaeontological basis of the African origins model.

ACKNOWLEDGMENTS

I thank the Royal Society for sponsoring this meeting; M. J. Aitken, P. A. Mellars, and especially C. B. Stringer for inviting me to participate in it. I am grateful to the

Royal Society and Northern Illinois University for the financial support that allowed me to participate. Finally, I am indebted to J. C. Ahern, R. Caspari, L. J. Shirley, C. B. Stringer, M. O. Smith, and M. H. Wolpoff for various forms of assistance with the preparation of this manuscript.

REFERENCES

Aitken, M.J. 1990 *Science-based dating in archaeology.* London: Longman.

Beaumont, P.B., DeVilliers, H. & Vogel, J.C. 1978 Modern man in sub-Saharan Africa prior to 49000 years BP: A review and evaluation with particular reference to Border Cave. *S. Afr. J. Sci.* **74**, 409–419.

Bräuer, G. 1984 A craniological approach to the origin of anatomically modern *Homo sapiens* in Africa and implications for the appearance of modern Europeans. In *The origins of modern humans.* (ed. F. H. Smith & F. Spencer), pp. 327–410. New York: Alan Liss.

Bräuer, G. 1989 The evolution of modern humans: A comparison of the African and non-African evidence. In *The human revolution.* (ed. P. Mellars & C. B. Stringer), pp. 123–154. Edinburgh University Press.

Bräuer, G. 1992 Africa's place in the evolution of *Homo sapiens.* In *Continuity or replacement; controversies in Homo sapiens evolution.* (ed. G. Bräuer & F. H. Smith), pp. 83–98. Rotterdam: Balkema.

Butzer, K. 1969 Geological interpretation of two Pleistocene hominid sites in the lower Omo Basin. *Nature, Lond.* **222**, 1133–1135.

Butzer, K., Beaumont, P.B. & Vogel, J.C. 1978 Lithostratigraphy of Border Cave, Kwa Zulu, South Africa: A Middle Stone Age sequence beginning *ca.* 195,000. B.P. *J. archaeol. Sci.* **5**, 317–341.

Butzer, K., Brown, F. & Thurber, D. 1969 Horizontal sediments of the lower Omo Valley: Kibish Formation. *Quaternaria* **110**, 15–29.

Clark, J.D. 1970 *The prehistory of Africa.* New York: Praeger.

Clarke, R.J. 1985 A new reconstruction of the Florisbad cranium, with notes on the site. In *Ancestors: the hard evidence.* (ed. E. Delson), pp. 301–305. New York: Alan Liss.

Coon, C. 1962 *The origin of races.* New York: A. A. Knopf.

Corruccini, R. 1992 Metrical reconsideration of Skhul crania IV and IX and Border Cave 1 in the context of modern human origins. *Am. J. phys. Anthropol.* **87**, 433–445.

Day, M. & Stringer, C.B. 1982 A reconsideration of the Omo-Kibish remains and the erectus-sapiens transition. In *Homo erectus et la place de l'homme de Tantavel parmi les hominides fossiles.* Nice: Louis-Jean Scientific and Literary Publication **2**, 814–846.

Deacon, H.J. 1989 Late Pleistocene paleoecology and Archaeology in the Southern Cape, South Africa. In *The human revolution.* (ed. P. Mellars & C. Stringer), pp. 547–564. Edinburgh University Press.

Deacon, H.J. & Geleijnse, V. 1988 The stratigraphy and sedimentology of the main site sequence, Klasies River, South Africa. *S. Afr. Arch. Bull.* **43**, 5–15.

Grün, R. & Stringer, C.B. 1991 Electron spin resonance dating and the evolution of modern humans. *Archaeometry* **33**, 153–199.

Habgood, P. 1989*a* The origin of anatomically modern humans in Australasia. In *The human revolution*. (ed. P. Mellars & C. B. Stringer), pp. 245–273. Edinburgh University Press.

Habgood, P. 1989*b* An examination of regional features on Middle and early Late Pleistocene sub-Saharan African hominids. *S. Afr. Arch. Bull.* **44**, 17–22.

Habgood, P. 1992 The origin of anatomically modern humans in East Asia. In *Continuity or replacement: controversies in Homo sapiens evolution.* (eds. G. Bräuer & F. H. Smith), pp. 273–288. Rotterdam: Balkema.

Hay, R. 1987 Geology of the Laetoli area. In *Results of the Laetoli Expeditions 1975– 1981.* (ed. M. D. Leakey & J. M. Harris), pp. 23–47. Oxford University Press.

Howell, F.C. 1978 Hominidae. In *Evolution of Africa mammals.* (ed. V. Maglio & H. Cooke). pp. 154–248. Cambridge: Harvard University Press.

Howells, W.W. 1989 Skull Shapes and the Map. *Peabody Mus. Archaeol. Anthrop.* **79**, 1–189.

Hublin, J.J. & Tillier, A.M. 1981 The Mousterian juvenile mandible from Irhoud (Morocco): A phylogenetic interpretation. In *Aspects of human evolution.* (ed. C. B. Stringer), pp. 167–185. London: Taylor and Francis.

Hublin, J.J., Tillier, A.M. & Tixier, J. 1987 L'humérus d'enfant Moustérien (Homo 4) de Jebel Irhoud (Maroc) dans son contexte archéologique. *Bull. Mém. Soc. Anthrop., Paris* **2**, 115–142.

Kidder, J., Jantz, R.L. & Smith, F.H. 1992 Defining modern humans: A multivariate approach. In *Continuity or replacement: controversies in Homo sapiens evolution.* (ed. G. Bräuer & F. H. Smith), pp. 157–177. Rotterdam: Balkema.

Klein, R. 1973 Geological antiquity of Rhodesian man. *Nature, Lond.* **244**, 311–312.

Klein, R. 1983 The Stone Age prehistory of southern Africa. *A. Rev. Anthrop.* **12**, 25–48.

Kramer, A. 1991 Modern human origins in Australasia: Replacement or evolution? *Am. J. Phy. Anthrop.* **86**, 455–473.

Kuman, K. 1989 Florisbad and #Gi.: the contribution of open air sites to the study of the Middle Stone Age in Southern Africa. Ph.D. thesis, University of Pennsylvania.

Kuman, K. & Clarke, R.J. 1986 Florisbad—New investigations at a Middle Stone Age hominid site in South Africa. *Geoarchaeology* **1**, 103–128.

Magori, C. & Day, M. 1983 Laetoli hominid 18: an early *Homo sapiens* skull. *J. hum. Evol.* **12**, 747–753.

Parkes, P.A. 1986 *Current scientific techniques in archaeology.* London: Croom Helm.

Pope, G. 1988 Recent Advances in Far Eastern paleoanthropology. *An. Rev. Anthrop.* **17**, 43–77.

Pope, G. 1991 Evolution of the zygomaticomaxillary region in the genus *Homo* and its relevance to the origin of modern humans. *J. hum. Evol.* **21**, 189–213.

Rightmire, G.P. 1979 Implications of the Border Cave skeletal remains for later Pleistocene human evolution. *Curr. Anthrop.* **48**, 23–35.

Rightmire, G.P. 1984 *Homo sapiens* in sub-Saharan Africa. In *The origins of modern humans.* (ed. F. H. Smith & F. Spencer), pp. 295–325. New York: Alan Liss.

Rightmire, G.P. 1986 Africa and the origins of modern humans. In *Variation, culture and evolution in African populations: papers in honor of Dr Hertha de Villiers.* (ed. R. Singer & J. K. Lundy), pp. 209–220. Johannesburg: Witwatersrand University Press.

Rightmire, G.P. 1989 Middle Stone Age humans from eastern and southern Africa. In *The human revolution.* (ed. P. Mellars & C. B. Stringer), pp. 109–122. Edinburgh University Press.

Rightmire, G.P. & Deacon, H.J. 1991 Comparative Studies of late Pleistocene human remains from Klasies River Mouth, South Africa. *J. hum. Evol.* **20**, 131–156.

Simmons, T. & Smith, F.H. 1991 Human population relationships in the late Pleistocene. *Curr. Anthrop.* **32**, 623–627.

Simmons, T., Falsetti, A.B. & Smith, F.H. 1991 Frontal bone morphometrics of southwest Asian Pleistocene hominids. *J. hum. Evol.* **20**, 249–269.

Smith, F.H. 1976 The Neanderthal Remains from Krapina: A Descriptive and Comparative Study. *Univ. Tennessee Dept. Anthrop. Rep. Invest.* **15**, 1–376.

Smith, F.H. 1985 Continuity and change in the origin of modern Homo sapiens. *Z. Morphol. Anthropol.* **75**, 197–222.

Smith, F.H. 1992 The role of continuity in modern human origins. In *Continuity or replacement: controversies in Homo sapiens evolution.* (ed. G. Bräuer & F. H. Smith), pp. 145–156. Rotterdam: Balkema.

Smith, F.H., Falsetti, A.B. & Donnelly, S. 1989 Modern human origins. *Yb. Phys. Anthrop.* **32**, 35–68.

Stringer, C.B. 1988*a* The dates of Eden. *Nature, Lond.* **331**, 565–566.

Stringer, C.B. 1988*b* Archaic *Homo sapiens* and Archaic Moderns. In *Encyclopedia of human evolution and prehistory.* (ed. I. Tattersall, E. Delson & J. Van Couvering), pp. 49–56. New York: Gerland.

Stringer, C.B. 1989 Documenting the origin of modern humans. In *The emergence of modern humans.* (ed. E. Trinkaus), pp. 67–96. Cambridge University Press.

Stringer, C.B. 1990 The emergence of modern humans. *Scient. Am.* **263**, 98–104.

Stringer, C.B. & Andrews, P. 1988 Genetic and fossil evidence for the origin of modern humans. *Science, Wash.* **239**, 1263–1268.

Van Vark, G.N., Bilsborough, A. & Dijkema, J. 1989 A further study of the morphological affinities of the Border cave 1 cranium, with special reference to the origin of modern man. *Anthrop. Préhistoire* **100**, 43–56.

Vogel, J. & Beaumont, P. 1972 Revised radiocarbon chronology for the Stone Age in South Africa. *Nature, Lond.* **237**, 50–51.

Wendorf, F., Laury, R.L., Albritton, C.C., Schild, R., Haynes, C.V., Damon, P.E., Shafigullah, M. & Scarborough, R. 1975 Dates for the Middle Stone Age of East Africa. *Science, Wash.* **187**, 740–742.

Wolpoff, M.H. 1989 Multiregional evolution: the fossil alternative to Eden. In *The human revolution.* (ed. P. Mellars & C. B. Stringer), pp. 62–108. Edinburgh University Press.

Wolpoff, M.H. 1992 Theories of modern human origins. In *Continuity or replacement: controversies in Homo sapiens evolution.* (ed. G. Bräuer & F. H. Smith), pp. 25–63. Rotterdam: Balkema.

Wolpoff, M.H., Xinzhi, Wu & Thorne, A.G. 1984 Modern *Homo sapiens* origins: A general theory of hominid evolution involving the fossil evidence from east Asia. In *The origins of modern humans: a world survey of the fossil evidence* (ed. F. H. Smith & F. Spencer), pp. 411–483. New York: Alan Liss.

Wu, Xinzhi & Wu, Maolin 1985 Early *Homo Sapiens* in China. In *Paleoanthropology and palaeolithic archaeology in the People's Republic of China.* (ed. Wu Rukang and J. W. Olsen), pp. 91–106. New York: Academic Press.